EDUCATIONAL FINANCE AND RESOURCES

EDUCATIONAL FINANCE AND RESOURCES

W.F. DENNISON

CROOM HELM
London & Sydney

©1984 W.F. Dennison
Croom Helm Ltd, Provident House, Burrell Row,
Beckenham, Kent BR3 1AT

Croom Helm Australia Pty Ltd, First Floor, 139 King Street,
Sydney, NSW 2001, Australia

British Library Cataloguing in Publication Data

Dennison, W.F.
   Educational finance and resources.
   1. Education – Great Britain – Finance
   I. Title
   379.1'21'0941   LB2826.6.G7

ISBN 0-7099-0842-3

Printed and bound in Great Britain
by Billing & Sons Limited, Worcester.

CONTENTS

List of Tables and Figures
Acknowledgements

1. THE COSTS OF EDUCATION   1

   Purpose process and Practice   1
   Costs and Definitions   6

2. EDUCATION and the ECONOMY   13

   Changing Circumstances   13
   Educational and Economic Inter-depend-
       encies   19
   Economic Contributions   26
   The Future of Work and Education   31
   Education, Training - Investment,
       Consumption ....

3. DISTRIBUTING RESOURCES   61

   Four Territories of Decision   61
   Central Government   65
   Local Authority   82
   Local Education Authority   94
   Institutions   103

4. RESOURCES and the CURRICULUM   109

   A Dynamic Curriculum   109
   The Dominance of the Ratios   113
   Managing the Curriculum with PTR and SSR.   124
   SSR and the College Curriculum   128
   PTR and the School Curriculum   144
   Inflating and Protecting the Curriculum .   156
   The Curriculum and other Resources   163

CONTENTS

	The Educational Resource Interaction ...	170
5.	TEACHERS as a RESOURCE	177
	Matching Staff to the Curriculum	177
	Selecting, Training and Developing staff	184
	Using the Resource	191
	Paying for Teachers	195
6.	RESOURCES, PLANNING and the INSTITUTIONS	207
	Characteristic Features	207
	Flexibility	209
	Planning	220
	Management Control	228
	'Value for Money' considerations	241
7.	CONTRACTION, PRIVATISATION and other CHOICES	250
	Political Choices	250
	Costs and Benefits of Privatisation	253
	Prisoners of decision-making	257
	The Expansion of Education	263
INDEX		267

TABLES AND FIGURES

Tables

1.1	Resource utilisation profile for random selection of 19 LEA's	11
2.1	Technology Trade Balance in Selected Countries (in millions of dollars) .	35
2.2	Research and Development Commitments in Selected Countries	37
2.3	Participation rates of 16-18 year olds in Western Europe	46
2.4	Number of unemployed by age-range and duration (in thousands)	51
3.1	Expenditure profile by authority	83
4.1	PTR's within Schools of English LEA's .	117
4.2	PTR in ILEA by Division (September 1979)	118
4.3	Recommended distribution of Lecturer Posts in Further Education	136
4.4	National distributions of SSR, ASH, ALH and ACS (1981-82)	140
4.5	Staffing needs and deployment in a secondary school	159
5.1	Unit-Totals, Points, Scores for Schools, other than Special	197
5.2	Actual and estimated age-profile of teaching force	199
6.1	Institutional expenditure profiles	210
6.2	Projection of spending patterns (School A - Tables 6.3 and 6.4) by programme	227
6.3	Expenditure per pupil in ten schools of LEA district	230
6.4	Pupils studying at 'A' level (First-Year) in ten schools of LEA district	245
7.1	Allocations from Capped Advanced Further Education Pool to Polytechnics	261

Figures

2.1	Qualifications and Course Levels	41
2.2	Example of training families (possible progression over 1 or 2 years)	49
3.1	LEA budget document for 1983-84	95) 96)
4.1	Development costs over time	133
4.2	Calculation of fe staffing needs by 'Burnham' methodology	142
6.1	Expenditure per period (School A - Tables 6.3 and 6.4)	235
6.2	Faculty and Departmental expenditure by programme	237) 238)
6.3	Estimated Expenditure by Year (School A - Tables 6.3 and 6.4)	240

ACKNOWLEDGEMENTS

Any writer who tries to consider the practical aspects of public policy making (such as I have attempted to do in this book) cannot be failed to be impressed by the large number of personnel (both professional and elected) who are prepared to exchange views, information, knowledge and ideas. That they are so often very busy people does not seem to inhibit their willingness to participate. On this occasion I am particularly indebted to John Delany of the DES, Gordon Campbell of Newcastle Polytechnic, and Roy Jobson and Steven Corbett of Gateshead LEA. I am also grateful to various officers in the ILEA, and Cambridgeshire and Solihull LEA's for supplying me with the details of their various schools' spending arrangements.

On this occasion I am particularly indebted to Mrs. Pat Ramshaw (ably supported by Mrs. Maureen Purvis and Mrs. Lillian Keeling) for the especially arduous task of typing the finished work, and all the previous drafts. My thanks also to Jennifer Cheetham for her help in tracing numerous references, books and articles.

Chapter One

THE COSTS OF EDUCATION

PURPOSE, PROCESS AND PRACTICE

In recent years, interest in the organization of educational institutions has risen considerably both from a theoretical standpoint and in relation to the actual practice of managing schools and colleges. Most recently, there has been the example of a DES initiative to improve the in-service training (and by implication the management performance) of senior staff in schools.[1] It is often misleading in such situations to create the impression that before a particular intervention nothing was happening or, in this case, there were no previous efforts to prepare staff for managerial responsibilities. LEAs, colleges etc. have organized courses, introduced workshops etc: less obviously, but probably much more significantly, the attitude of many senior staff has become more inclined towards a management orientation (a clear perspective about organizational objectives and how these are best achieved) through a process of individually motivated self-development - that is, relying upon the most effective mechanism for adult learning. Yet, paradoxically, through all of this increased activity, the fact that a shortage of resources was probably the main catalyst has not stimulated much increased interest in the resource component of educational management. Much less so in FE than in schools, the main thrust of concerns have been towards the curriculum and timetabling, the development of staff, decision-making, inter-personal skills, education law etc. with resource issues as a peripheral, but not central, theme. To some extent this orientation is understandable. The scope for obvious financial decision-making in schools, for example, is small compared to total institutional expenditure.

The Costs of Education

Similarly, the opportunities for financial entrepreneurialship, in the sense of raising money or attracting activities which will produce funds through fee-income are limited and, although less true for college principals, the fact is that the main managerial foci tend to occur elsewhere.

In practice, many education managers work, according to their own perceptions, in non-costed situations. That does not mean they function without financial constraints, but for what in other contexts might be regarded as their main expenditure responsibilities, bills are paid (salaries, heating, building maintenance etc.) by the local authority. Often these managers have little knowledge of the detail of the arrangements. In addition, when they compete for resources the process occurs in non-cost terms - so many teachers to be employed, so much floor space to be used, a specific item of building maintenance to be performed and so on. Occasionally they may not appreciate the nature of the competition in which they are involved. Therefore, the constraints that are applied, and the arbitrations that occur, although made in financial terms elsewhere, translate into volume factors within institutions. However, because they rarely have to consider the financial elements in such issues, educationists can fail to understand their broader resource management responsibilities. Yet, every decision which is made in a school or college carries resource implications, both affecting the alternative use to which resources could have been put and being affected by their availability. Numerous examples are available. A decision in a secondary school to organize eight first-year classes instead of seven will be taken for educational or social reaons, but such a choice (if the school determines it has sufficient teachers to sanction such a change) must impinge upon teacher availability elsewhere in the school, the teaching loads of individual staff and possibly the level of staff performance. If the school uses the desirability of this change to argue for extra staff, only at LEA level will its impact be converted into financial parameters. Resource factors also permeate course development, the training, selection and utilization of all staff, the use of buildings, the organization of institutions: in other words they are central in the whole range of processes which constitute publically provided education. Particularly, in schools, many staff do not realize this component of their work. They are aware, usually only too well, of the adverse effects, as they would see it, of too few resources, but not of the total impingement of resource-based items on the organization and functioning of their institution. The most direct outcome of these situations concerns their ability to exploit resource acquisition and deployment flexibilities which become available. In general terms then, the resource management function within educational management is underdeveloped, and has received too little attention. The main purpose of this book is to correct that particular imbalance by considering the interactions between resource parameters and the practices of educational management, not as peripheral effects, but as central issues in determining educational outcomes.

The remainder of this chapter considers the main problems in defining and assessing resource issues in English education.[2] Chapter Two develops some aspects of the relationship between education and the economy: chief of which being the slow rate of economic growth and, relatedly, government attempts to decrease public expenditure in general, and educational spending in particular. The impact of the changes that have resulted for the attitudes of educational managers towards resource issues cannot be minimised: they have been forced into a series of coping tactics, with insufficient consideration of the strategies that have to evolve in circumstances of long-term decline. The Chapter attempts to place such developments in the wider context of societal change, particularly in relation to the futures of education and work, in order to highlight potential components in the evolution of appropriate strategies. In Chapter 3 the processes by which resources reach the institutions from government and local authorities are analyzed in relation to the circumstances in which decision-making occurs. Particularly in recent years, the main parameters impinging upon decision-making have been provided by the conditions of retrenchment, and these become especially important in relation to the main processes of the schools and colleges, the provision of curricular, as considered in Chapter 4. The enormous range of concerns that have been generated about the deleterious effects of contraction on courses and activities, and likely reductions in their quality, would appear to contradict the criticism that educationists have paid too little attention to resource management. What events since the mid-1970s have demonstrated is the absolute centrality of resource availability to the education

3

service, particularly when developments or changed practices are sought. An awareness which was much less important during expansion. Therefore, while Chapter Two, Three and Four contrast the effects of contraction and growth, they do not attempt to describe in detail the conflicts over spending decisions occurring in so many locations - central government, local authorities and institutions. That would be an impossible task, but more important fails to appreciate the relationships between choices at these levels, and the inherent tensions between those who supply resources and those who provide curricular. It is in relation to these factors that the management function remains deficient. That theme continues in Chapter Five, when factors associated with the utilization of the main resource, the teaching staff, is considered. In Chapter Six resource management at the institutional level provides the focus, while the final Chapter looks at the problem of sustaining education development with static or declining resources.

Essentially, then, this is a study of the formulation and implementation of public policy, as affected by the main parameters of resource acquisition and deployment during a period of rapid change. Yet, even in circumstances such as these, policy is still modified by a series of gradual adjustments. Additional activities are introduced, or alternative approaches developed, within existing organizations. Simultaneously, new institutions might be established. Whichever route provides the change mechanism, the practices that evolve will, most likely, not be too much different from those that existed previously. Therefore, to take the examples of major educational initiatives, the comprehensive schools reflected many of the processes found in the grammar and secondary schools they replaced: similarly, the new institutions of higher education that emerged from the late 1960s onwards performed many of the tasks, in similar ways, to the colleges they subsumed. The transfer of personnel, bringing with them skills and experiences already learned, guaranteed a certain level of continuity for the new organizations. Even when forced to attract a total staff complement, there are few alternatives to recruiting teachers and lecturers with similar experiences elsewhere. Clearly, advantages accrue from such continuity, more so in schools and colleges where clients can remain for several years. A swift change may well work to their disadvantage. More generally, however a process of incremental modification is potentially beneficial because it can represent a useful learning situation for the organization or system. It already has experience of particular processes and arrangements, and as circumstances vary (through changes in knowledge, methodology, environmental factors or staff) it responds, learning from previous arrangements, to arrive at new practices.

Obviously there are disadvantages in such gradualism. For example, often an organization relied on increases in the scope of its activities, through acquiring more resources, to achieve changes in working arrangements. As a result it tried to satisfy evolving needs by establishing new sections and attracting extra staff without altering the main emphasis of other activities. As soon as total resources stop rising then new methods of organizational learning have to be devised in which it adjusts to different, and new demands, by slowly modifying the interests of existing staff and re-organizing the use of facilities. The real danger to public organizations such as schools and colleges (not subject to the immediate pressures of reduced profits or possible liquidation) exists when they do not react with sufficient rapidity to changes in client needs irrespective of their own perception of resource availability. To a certain extent they can disguise the fact of inadequate adjustment, because of the lack of tangible outcomes. Their staff are also advantaged when they are not proved wrong, for they can argue that modifications in practices have been made to reform with changes in demand, when in fact they are no more than corrections for previous errors. Most particularly though, gradualism is flawed by a lack of clarity over priorities. Because all change is no more than a series of modifications, priorities may vary over time, through minor adjustments, but never receive a full review.

Yet in any study of public policy, irrespective of the benefits or disadvantages of incrementalism, the dominant issue must remain the achievement of outcomes, as perceived by those in a position to sanction the activities. In a democratic society of course, this should include everyone, ultimately through the ballot-box, more directly by election to committees or whatever, and for all who work in the institutions, but there are certain groups and individuals who carry differential influence. They assess, through their impingement on the decision-making arrangements, the extent to which a policy is being successfully pursued, and express their views most effectively through the next set of decisions. The intention, here, is to consider the whole series of processes of policy formulation and implementation, both to provide a broader perspective for participants, even if their role is highly peripheral, and a framework for those who wish to monitor the processes more rigorously.

COSTS AND DEFINITIONS

Even a question as deceptively simple as the present rate of educational expenditure has to be considered with caution. The problems are numerous. In fact, the notion of a rate is misleading: total expenditure over a period of time creates most interest. Yet, as a result, expenditure figures must either consist of estimates made before, and during, the year in question: or actuals, recorded some time after the end of the year, so as to allow opportunity to reconcile all the necessary detail. This may take two years or more.[3] Other factors must also be taken into consideration when studying expenditure. The difference between current and capital, for example. Basically, the distinction should be clear: current (or revenue) expenditures are made on items such as salaries, heating, lighting, rents etc. In contrast, capital expenditure produces resources lasting for a period longer than twelve months.[4] This raises potential difficulties, however, as local authorities make expenditures which can be classified as capital, such as the purchase of books or equipment, providing resources for long-term use (and also contributing a realisable asset, another definition of capital expenditure[5]) but bought through revenue expenditure. The divide between capital and current expenditure therefore relies more on physical than technical features: capital refers to the financing of physical projects (new buildings, extending or modifying premises) and some improvements through minor works: all financed, in the main, by loans with principal and interest sums repaid from subsequent revenue expenditure. In comparison, the differentiation between net and gross expenditure raises fewer problems, but still requires attention. During 1983-84, for example, it is estimated that LEAs in England and Wales, will spend an estimated £3.97 bn. gross on secondary schooling, net £3.86 bn.[6] The difference just over £100m., is small, compared to total expenditure because of the limitations upon generating income, from fees and sales. Much of the difference (£87.5m.) being contributed by inter-authority payments through educating each others children. In AFE,[7] by contrast, the estimated expenditure of the 30 polytechnics during the same year was £506m., reduced to £394m. in net terms: again, however, the bulk of the difference was made up of tuition fee income, paid by other local authorities.

These examples, because of the inter-government payment situations they reveal, raise the more general issue of defining public educational expenditure. In this book it refers to all expenditure by LEAs, and that part of spending sanctioned by the DES specifically directed towards education institutions (that is excluding spending on science through the research councils). As a result of this restriction a whole range of educational activities have been excluded - all of private education, except when places there are used by LEAs, and all of the training and education activities sponsored by firms and organizations, unless they utilize places in further education. Also outside the scope of this study are considerations of university financing, not because it is insignificant, either in total or in relation to comparisons with AFE spending, but the methods adopted by the Treasury and DES to finance 40 plus independent institutions, through the UGC, and the arrangements utilized by the institutions themselves, are quite separate from the mainflow of educational resources. The universities are excluded because their financing does not impinge directly upon the work of LEAs and their institutions: the same cannot be said for the rapid evolution of MSC activities during the late 1970s and 1980s. Many of these, directed towards education and training targets, have considerable implications for the traditional work of FE and secondary schools, and therefore demand attention, although the different source of their funding makes an integrative consideration of expenditure more difficult. Two additional problems arise in studying educational expenditure. The first, and less difficult in terms of analyzing the system, although it may create numerous problems in practice, is the non-coincidence of financial and academic years: the former beginning in April, the latter in September. Therefore the expenditure figures quoted, cover two separate academic years. Second, and much more difficult in both theory and practice, are the issues associated with relative price movements. If all prices changed at the same rate it would be easy

The Costs of Education

to convert every expenditure, wherever made, to a base year - say prices in January 1981. However, relative price changes, as the name implies, are never as simple as that, and differential allowances have to be calculated. For example, to convert an expenditure in 1978-79 on teacher salaries in primary and secondary schools to a November 1981 equivalent a multiplication factor of 1.6007 applies: for other costs in primary and secondary schools the factor reduces to 1.5414. Similar figures for nursery schools, FE etc., are available, and all of them, were greater accuracy sought, can be re-calculated to represent changes in smaller expenditure constituencies.[8] There may well have been, for instance, relative changes in salary levels between junior and senior teachers, so that the promotional profile of staff may effect outcomes.

The definition of expenditure also requires attention. Here, the terms expenditures and spending are used synonymously, in the sense that they both refer to outlays - the actual sum of money transferred from payer to payee, at out-turn prices. In other words, no attempt is made to calculate full economic costs.[9] The opportunities foregone, when an individual becomes a full-time student rather than taking a job, for example, or the alternative uses to which resources taken by educational institutions could be put, do not receive attention quantitatively, but their role as influential factors in decision-making cannot be ignored. In general terms, therefore, educational spending as defined, for 1983-84 is estimated at an aggregate of £10.26 bn. for current and £362m. for capital expenditure as compared to a planned total of public expenditure of £120 bn.[10] Within revenue spending the main educational categories being:

Primary schools	£2,371 m.
Secondary schools	£3,625 m.
Special schools	£ 368 m.
Advanced further education	£ 560 m.
Non-advanced further education	£ 877 m.

From a slightly different perspective (including university spending) the overall distributional pattern is more visible, relative to gross expenditure.[11]

Primary schools	23.2%
Secondary schools	29.8%
Special schools	3.7%
Nursery schools	0.3%

The Costs of Education

School meals and milk	5.3%
Central administration services	4.1%
Youth services	1.1%
Further Education (AFE and NAFE)	13.2%
Universities	9.3%
Student support (maintenance grants etc.)	10.0%

A further way to look at these global figures concentrates upon a different classification, using objects of expenditure with four principal categories identified, both in relation to aggregate expenditure and, in parenthesis, for secondary education.[12]

Teacher salaries	49.0%	(67%)
Non-teaching salaries	13.1%	(10%)
Premises and fixed plant	10.2%	(13%)
Books and equipment	3.3%	(4%)

Figures such as these, representing a single year cannot, of course, display the inherent dynamism as spending priorities vary among sectors, and between education and other activities. In general terms, education spending relative, to GDP at something under 5%, is well below the peak level of 6.3% in 1975-76, reflecting a decline in the prominence of educational expenditure. This has been most marked for capital spending, as in other public sector activities, but has also resulted in a reduction in current spending for all components of public education. Possible reasons for this decline, within a framework of public expenditure retrenchment, and its affect on resource distribution and deployment, are considered later in the book. With regard to pursuing the management function, though, aggregate levels of expenditure, particularly national figures, are much less significant than inter-unit comparisons of spending. The basic reason for this is that the exercise of managerial responsibilities occurs, in the main, in local authorities. For current educational expenditure, as defined, no more than 3-4% of annual spending emanates directly from the centre - payments towards some support services, the cost of the central administration of the service, and the maintenance of a small number of voluntary establishments, but nothing more. For the remainder of the service, LEAs retain the responsibility of paymasters, by employing the staff, maintaining the premises, buying the equipment, and so on. The fact

9

that to do so they rely on grants from central government to supplement the rates and (to a lesser extent) income they derive from their own sources does not alter the circumstances in which most managerial tasks are performed in LEAs, and by delegation, in the institutions. It is at these levels that comparative measures of resource utilization and availability are of most interest and value: whether it is relative to per student expenditure or per pupil availability of teaching time. Both as a result of exercising their responsibilities, and because of the different environmental framework in which they function, considerable variations in LEA spending patterns emerge. Table 1.1 demonstrates some of the disparities in a range of inter-authority expenditure and resource-based measures, which constitute a resource utilization pattern of the randomly selected LEAs. Such figures provide a profile: within each there are less visible, but equally important, variations in spending patterns and resource deployment as assessed at institutional level. These items constitute the starting point: a successful conclusion might discover why these differences occur, but much more significantly it would concentrate on their effects relative to the processes they finance and the outcomes they are supposed to facilitate.

NOTES AND REFERENCES

1. DES Circular 3/83, The In-Service Teacher Training Grants Scheme, 1983.
2. Although restricted to England, because of the Secretary of State for Wales responsibility for Welsh Schools, all expenditure figures, unless otherwise stated, refer to England and Wales.
3. For example CIPFA (Chartered Institute of Public Finance and Accountancy) actual expenditure figures for 1980-81 appeared in May 1982, those for the following year had still not been published towards the end of 1983. Usually DES finance publications are even more delayed.
4. CIPFA, Evidence to the committee of inquiry into local government finance (London 1975)p.34
5. N.P. Hepworth, The Finance of Local Government, (George Allen and Unwin, London, 1970), p.43.
6. CIPFA, Education Statistics 1983-84 Estimates, London 1983.
7. Throughout the book the term FE describes the general range of activities (Education Act, 1944, s41-47) being divided into non-advanced

TABLE 1.1

Resource utilization profile for random selection of 19 LEAs

	Costs per pupil £ Primary					Costs per pupil £ Secondary					TCR	(1)	(2)
	Net total	Teach. staff	Other staff	Prem- ises	Books Equip.	Net total	Teach. staff	Other staff	Prem- ises	Books Equip.			
Bromley	668	454	69	106	23	972	657	100	134	37	0.82	0	46.0
Harrow	722	488	100	101	23	1,163	776	134	159	49	0.78	0.08	53.0
Merton	703	478	109	82	18	869	626	87	101	26	0.79	0.51	40.2
Waltham Fst.	741	489	92	104	30	1,149	771	110	173	50	0.78	1.27	38.3
Oldham	594	408	68	92	18	808	556	72	121	31	0.81	1.12	30.5
Wigan	606	436	63	81	15	885	633	86	103	31	0.77	0.57	38.3
Wirral	583	410	63	86	16	841	595	75	107	23	0.80	0.44	46.9
Sheffield	724	485	93	101	27	947	634	88	149	33	0.79	0.98	64.1
Sunderland	632	445	79	84	16	869	615	78	116	29	0.83	1.81	59.1
Wolverhampton	730	486	107	98	21	935	651	91	126	35	0.77	1.60	82.1
Wakefield	633	436	84	82	17	775	554	67	100	22	0.84	0.94	37.3
Cambs.	581	411	59	77	15	871	594	71	115	28	0.81	0.66	42.2
Cleveland	625	430	73	90	17	892	598	83	141	31	0.80	0.38	49.5
Derbys.	587	425	62	70	18	827	570	76	100	34	0.82	0.65	39.9
Essex	557	406	58	65	15	840	575	85	107	26	0.82	0.09	34.9
Humberside	662	462	72	93	18	863	593	76	125	32	0.81	0.58	39.7
Notts.	615	422	66	90	25	886	601	81	120	38	0.82	0.33	47.6
Suffolk	633	453	59	79	16	810	560	58	111	26	0.83	0.13	33.9
Wiltshire	576	413	53	71	19	838	565	80	107	30	0.82	0	40.8

Source: From CIPFA Actuals 1981-82, and quoted in The Times Educational Supplement, 16/9/83, p.8.
Key: Nursery expenditure (1) and Net fe expenditure (2) per head population.

further education courses (AFE) at above 'A' level standard, occasionally described as higher education in this book.
8. CIPFA, <u>Education Statistics 1980-81 Actuals</u>, (London 1982).
9. F. Edding, Methods of Analyzing Educational Outlays, (Unesco, Paris, 1968).
10. CMND 8789, <u>The governments expenditure plans</u>, 1983-84 to 1985-86, 1983.
11. DES, <u>Statistics of Education, 1979, Volume 5., Finance and Awards</u>, (HMSO, London,1982), p.vii.
12. DES, <u>Statistics of Education 1979, Volume 5.</u> p.vi, and CIPFA, <u>Education Statistics 1980-81 Actuals</u>, p.3.

Chapter Two

EDUCATION AND THE ECONOMY

CHANGING CIRCUMSTANCES

Were education not publically provided there would still be need to consider numerous interactions with the economy. Teacher supply might be more subject to market forces, student participation rates could be more influenced by economic activity levels, but many components in the relationship would continue unaltered. The dominant question concerns the willingness and the ability of the economy to support an education service, and relatedly the effects on the intentions and functions of the service of economic factors. Clearly, the inverse question has also to be posed, about the economic contribution of education - the benefits sought and achieved by the provision of the service.

As regards each of these issues the three decades of the 1960s, 1970s and 1980s provide quite different perspectives. The 1960s were a period of unprecedented growth, following the expansions achieved since 1945. All sectors of education benefitted, with substantial growth in real terms and relative to most other measures. In brief, the education service expanded more rapidly than the public economy as a whole, which itself took a rising proportion of GDP.[1] The educational components, if not the economic costs, of such a policy were accepted without equivocation. When concerns were expressed, on political grounds or whatever, it was the methodologies or the priorities within the policy which were questioned, not its main thrust. The intention of more education for a greater number of clients seemed wholly acceptable. As a result, schools and FE increased enrolments, more children stayed beyond minimum leaving-age, new colleges and polytechnics were established and provision for

13

youth services and the handicapped was raised. Yet across this whole range of increased expenditure few overt attempts were made to differentiate consumption from investment components. Clearly, the introduction of a polytechnic was biased towards investment, because of the anticipated economic returns from college graduates, as compared to the development of a special school, but a discrete separation was neither intended nor sought. More practically, a major effect of expansion was an increased education work-force: not only in relation to teacher and lecturer numbers, but also in the evolution of a large supportive infra-structure, from education psychologists to domestic and cleaning staff.

The 1970s started similarly, with continuous growth and an expectation of its continuance. The Education White Paper (1972) envisaged a 53% rise in recurrent school expenditure over the next ten years (63% for higher education).[2] Significantly, the main theme was consolidation and improvement, to supplement previous expansions, as well as concentrating on activities which had up to then, received little attention. Recurrent expenditure on nursery education, for example, was projected to increase almost three-fold but these plans remained unfulfilled, for by the end of the decade the general situation had altered totally. In terms of expansion, instead of education occupying a premier position within a public expenditure sector advantaged relative to GDP, spending on education was forecast to decline more rapidly than any other comparable major programme within a government spending programme itself projected to shrink.[3] The actual turn-round was swift, given the cumbersome nature of the decision-making machinery (Chapter 3) taking no more than three years (1973-76): starting with capital expenditure, as this presents fewer problems, educational spending was rapidly transformed from expansion, through a short period of staticity to shallow decline. As for growth, no sector or activity was exempt. Naturally, this rapid transition, after such a lengthy period of sustained growth, provoked a view that the change was no more than a temporary abnormality, to be replaced at some stage by expansionism. Towards the end of the decade there were indications that these perceptions might prove correct, with some limited expansion in 1978 and 1979 (although without altering the relative position of education in public expenditure programmes)[4] but, in retrospect, these gains represented more a correction for previous underspendings and a pre-election boost than a prediction of what was to follow.

It is highly probable that by the end of the 1980s educational expenditure as conventionally defined - that is setting aside, for the time being, any measures associated with the MSC - will be several percentage points lower than the levels existing at the start of the decade: possibly (for reasons to be considered later) the decline may be much greater. The more detailed projections for the mid-1980s continue the pattern first established almost ten years previously of steady decline more or less evenly spread across the main sectors of education. Between 1983-84 and 1985-86 educational spending should rise by 6% in cash terms but, with the accommodation of pay and price increases the volume of educational activity seems certain to continue its decline. While education's share of public expenditure should decrease only marginally from 12.22% to 12.15%, this is within a total where restriction is a main objective of government economic policy. 5 The effects of these changing circumstances are less marked in relation to the actual conditions under which schools and colleges function, as compared to the changes in attitudes and practices that accompanied and followed the transition. Someone returning towards the mid-1980s, after an absence of 25 years, should not meet enormous classes with underpaid staff in out-dated buildings: although they would discover shortages of equipment, books and specialist staff. Depending, of course, on individual situations it would be difficult to find schools and colleges which, in terms of real inputs per head did not receive considerably more in 1983-84 than 1958-59.

However, this contrast, relative to attitudes, is much less important than the year by year situation. A rate of growth of 3%, say, does not seem too much different to a 1% contraction (after all 99% of the original resources are still available) but the implications for attitudes and priorities are considerable, particularly if these respective rates are sustained: attitudes, because of the advantages perceived by staff of working in an environment where additional resources are continuously being generated: priorities, as difficult decisions about what activities are no longer viable need never be made during growth. For example, views about resource shortages may be related more to funding levels than might have been anticipated

Education and the Economy

without contraction than to absolute assessments of deprivation. Additionally, expansion itself initiated arrangements and practices which made conversion more difficult, particularly by introducing inflexibilities if spending ever had to be reduced. The large numbers of staff, for instance, recruited as the service grew, joined on the assumption that they had a job until they chose otherwise, and that reasonable aspirational levels would be satisfied. Indeed, job-security may have been a factor which attracted them to the work in the first place. Obviously, they react adversely to possible job-losses, and to a related decline in promotional opportunities: even to the extent of resisting practices more appropriate to the new circumstances, particularly if they can convince themselves that these circumstances are only temporary. The whole situation being exacerbated by an age-profile, in which teachers recruited in their twenties, during the expansionist era of the 1960s and early 1970s, dominate.

Two factors directly related to the system go some way towards explaining this movement from growth to contraction. The first, more tangible and less contentious, results from pupil-shortage in schools, following birth-rate decline. The rate was high from the late 1950s onwards, peaking in 1964, falling slowly to 1971 and then more substantially. As a result primary school rolls began to drop from the mid-1970s, with a small up-turn anticipated in the mid and late-1980s, because of a birth-rate rise, centred around 1980. For secondary education, numbers in compulsory schooling did not begin to fall until the early 1980s, but the trend will continue for at least ten years with only a limited expansion likely in the mid-1990s.[6] Therefore, it was much more than coincidence that the transition from growth to shrinkage occurred simultaneously with the first real appreciation of the likely effects of birth-rate decline. Since 1945 much of the expansion had been to cope with additional pupils: by the mid-1970s total numbers were soon to fall - eventually by almost 35%. In other words, the most effective and persuasive lobby for extra resources was about to evaporate. Since then arguments that unless new schools are built, and additional staff employed, statutory obligations cannot be fulfilled, has largely ceased for most LEAs and is unlikely to be re-established, at least this century. Even the anticipated increases in numbers already mentioned, will be relatively small, raising the respective primary and secondary school population to well below the peaks of the 1970s and early 1980s.

It is more difficult accumulating evidence to substantiate the secondary explanatory factor, as it involves assessments of the public standing of the education service. Most directly, there has been a reduction in confidence in relation both to the processes and outcomes, and a resultant decline in public esteem, reflected in the translation from top to bottom placing in public sector resource distribution. Of course, an empiricist is entitled to ask questions about this erosion of public confidence (its level and extent, the time-scales involved, the previous standing of the service, the differential effect on sectors etc.) and whether, in fact, it has occurred at all. Without a sophisticated approach based on market survey techniques and already established before the transition, answers to these questions cannot be elucidated. However, it does not follow that the main statement has no substance. There is sufficient qualitative evidence to confirm the point, not indisputably of course, but to the extent that the education service should be concerned. It would be inappropriate, and highly complacent, for educationists to dismiss the "Great Debate" of 1977, for example, as an irrelevant exercise.[7] There were reactive elements sponsored by the DES. Criticisms particularly from employers, about the quality of school-leavers had to be considered, if not answered.[8] A forum offered that opportunity: more cynically, it diverted attention from more important issues, and the actual decision-making machinery. However, proactive factors also surfaced, in that DES, by launching the initiative, announced its attention towards more interventionism in those school processes it had traditionally left to professional staff. Similarly, the establishment of the APU during the mid and late-1970s, had both reactive and proactive components. Those, such as 'Black Paper' writers, who claimed that standards were falling, had to be assuaged by demonstrating that, at least, these standards were to be more systematically monitored than previously.[9] On the interventionist side, by being seen to be highly supportive of such an arrangement, DES registered growing concern for processes and outcomes to LEAs and school staff. More recently, the emergence of YTS for school leavers, in effect an additional year of education and training, but not school-based, can be viewed as an expression of government dissatisfaction with the outcomes when the leaving age was raised in 1972. On this occasion, by dominating resource determination and using high youth unemployment, it has sponsored alternative institutional arrangements.

The greater interventionism, illustrated by these examples, is best viewed as part of the evolution of a corporatist policy-making strategy, in which the DES (and government) organizes co-operation. In the case of YTS by ensuring that its own organization (MSC) has sufficient resources, and control of their use, government offered colleges, staff LEAs and firms no feasible alternative but to work with it.[10] Perhaps, the most striking example of the ability to organize co-operation was the local authority response to the government, TVEI (1983). The intention being to provide a four-year curricular for low-achieving 14-18 year olds (that is a wider brief than the YTS arrangements) containing general, technical and vocational education including work experience, with the aim of developing a range of occupational skills and competencies.[11] Many LEAs were opposed, both politically and ideologically, to the idea of separate arrangements and more particularly direction towards low-grade employment for a minority of 14-18 year olds, even as a pilot scheme as it impinged directly on their responsibilities, yet over two-thirds were willing to participate. Such was the response that the initial scheme was soon extended to cover more projects.[12] With this process of corporatism the pluralist strategy employed previously, whereby a neutral government adjudicated, when necessary, between participants who themselves were generating much of the policy becomes defunct. In this context, with pluralism, it was the professional staff (assisted by the LEA) and the examination boards which represented the main interests at institutional level: while nationally the local authority associations, the teacher unions and (to a limited extent) the DES were dominant.

Quite possibly this change of strategy would have occurred irrespective of other events. It was not restricted to education: major alterations in the government's relationships with other activities - manufacturing industry, local government services in general, nationalised industries, the health service - occurred almost simultaneously. Of course it can be argued that DES sponsored the erosion in public confidence to justify the new approach.

There is, perhaps. no better way to further lessen esteem for a service, than by publicising a 'debate' in which reasons for reductions in this esteem receive scrutiny. However, to pursue this argument overlooks a crucial issue. As the accusations of lack of control of process, lower quality of outcomes, and reduced standards proliferated, they were not countered successfully, either because they could not (that is, by implication, they were true) or as they were thought irrelevant and unimportant (because the system was too introspective). Whatever the reason, DES could change strategy largely unimpeded and, more significantly, a positive lobby, to prevent or dilute the government initiated change in the resource situation, never became established.

EDUCATIONAL AND ECONOMIC INTER-DEPENDENCIES

Much of the previous reasoning is based upon an underlying, but unstated, model of rational analysis and decision-making. According to this, the DES (for its part) overviews the total situation, formulates objectives, organizes co-operation, and then acts in a logical and ordered manner. [13] Similarly, LEA or school staff likely to be affected by DES activities, consider the available alternatives and then, having analysed the merits and disadvantages of each, make a clear choice. The reality is invariably different. Organizations of all types, often appear to behave quite irrationally: decisions are made which seem not to be based on logical analysis. Two education examples are not untypical. The first being the resistance some NAFE colleges have shown towards MSC financed courses for 16-19 year olds when this may be their most effective route towards long-term growth. The second, the tendency of certain schools to continue with options which cannot attract sufficient pupils, when the associated resources could be diverted elsewhere in the school.

The key issue concerns the inevitable politicisation of every organization, whether it is a school, college or DES. All consist of individuals working alone and in groups. As individuals they have views, interests and values which become modified as they interact with those of other group members. As a result, the group develops an identity, which it then transmits as its contribution to the organizational identity: but without totally subsuming the characteristics of individual members, particularly the most influential and powerful.

Therefore, while it may be convenient to speak of a DES view (about curricular intervention, for example) this disguises the range of interests that have dominated, or compromised, to produce this view. In this situation Teachers Branch, Financial Services and HMI might all have been involved, each represented by individuals arguing on the basis of their own perspectives within a sectional and organizational setting. If they, or the interests they represent, perceive an unsatisfactory outcome they will press to change the view. There can be no certainty of continuity in a political environment, or agreement over interpretation. Therefore, two members of the same organization (the DES in this case) may describe the official position somewhat differently, both because of interpretative uncertainty and in an effort to influence the reformulation of the position.

Within this frame of reference it would clearly be unwise to explain the growth to contraction transition of the mid-1970s as a rational piece of decision-making based on the likelihood of falling numbers and previously unrealised expectations. Even the logic of linking fewer pupils to lower expenditure could be disputed, because of the problems inherent in dealing with declining roll situations. Similarly, there is no irrefutable rationality in reducing provision following shortfalls in achievement. It could be argued, quite reasonably, that a lack of resources was contributing to this underachievement in the first place, and to reduce levels further would only exacerbate the situation. However, so far in this discussion one factor has been deliberately excluded: that is the rapid change in the status of public expenditure. Had it been introduced earlier to explain the changed circumstances of education it could have been both seen as the result of rational decision-making (which is debatable) and dominating the other two factors, which in education (compared to other public activities) are particularly significant. Undoubtedly the growth in education was facilitated by a buoyant public economy: not surprisingly as this began to falter towards the mid-1970s, education spending followed. However, even as the change began, total public spending, as a proportion of GDP, still grew from 38 to 46% between 1971-72 and 1975-76: an increase exaggerated by limited growth in the economy and almost stagnant industrial production. During this time, for example, annual expansion rates were little more

Education and the Economy

than 1%, in contrast to public expenditure levels in excess of 5%.[14] Clearly, differentials of this order were not permanently sustainable. Yet up to that time public spending increasing its share of national income was not an unusual feature of economic life in either the U.K. or elsewhere.[15]

Two further pieces of information exemplify the growth in public expenditure. In the twenty years from 1955 to 1975 the proportion of the working population (including part-timers) employed by local authorities rose from 6.3% to 11.3%: certainly, towards the end of this time, reducing an underlying increase in unemployment. More significantly, in terms of causal relationships, while the cost of public policy increased by 201% between 1950 and 1974 the average rise in take-home pay of 75% was much less substantial (a pattern repeated in other developed countries).[16] Therefore, to explain public expenditure growth simply, in terms of increased affluence enabling individual and group generosity towards public services requires some qualification. Perhaps it was a conscious decision to acquiesce to (or elect) governments and authorities more committed to collectively preferred, rather than individually selected, benefits - an acceptance of a higher social wage through increased public spending on education, as well as housing, social services etc. More generally the rate of social and economic change after World War II was higher than ever before,and governments found themselves (usually willingly, often as a component of policy) involved in activities which previously were either non-existent or performed by charitable and private organizations, as part of a more general process of converting from informal to formal support. In education, a good example of this evolution was the development of services for children with learning and other disabilities. Those invvolved, and the interests they represented (parents, teachers, counsellors and so on) generated a lobby for further spending. Practically, a special education pressure group was only one among many, ranging from some parents, pressing for new school buildings or an additional teacher, through to the national campaigns which usually preceded, and invariably followed, the major educational reports - Plowden on Primary Education, Robbins on Higher Education etc.[17]

It is difficult, if not impossible, to ascertain with certainty, using subsequent expenditure figures, the specific effects of particular lobbies.

21

Invariably the relevant decision-processes are so diffuse (see Chapter 3) while the appropriate time-scales are only rarely definable with sufficient accuracy. Occasionally, with the expansion of higher education after Robbins, for example definitive evidence to link an explicit decision with a resultant impact does exist, but such a case tends to be exceptional. In contrast, the more pervasive orthodoxy (in education and elsewhere) was an expectation of growth, supported both by a general view that this had intrinsic merit and arguments to favour certain priorities. A successful lobby for a particular item (more expenditure on youth work or a new school) was guaranteed to evoke an additional pressure group for better provision or improved facilities elsewhere. The vital issue of the rationality of the choices, or the criteria used in decision-making, received less attention than the creation of high aspirational levels in virtually every activity, and their sustenance by the successful acquisition of still more resources within a competitive environment. Cyclically, the satisfaction of a particular set of needs regularly produced still more wants: therefore the establishment of secondary education in the 1950s, with the elimination of all-age schools, was a substantial factor in generating increased demands for non-compulsory schooling and resultant expansions in further and higher education during the 1960s.

What began to emerge in the late 1960s, more strikingly in the U.K. than other developed countries (because of traditionally low levels of economic growth) was the coincidence of inflation and unsatisfactory increases in industrial output - shortly to be followed by rising unemployment - and the associated notion that public expenditure growth was a contributory factor in this inflation. Later the circle of culpability was complete with the argument that high levels of public expenditure, both by taking employees from productive work and utilizing too great a proportion of national income, was a course of static industrial output. [18] Up till the late 1960s, however, disparities between levels of public sector growth and economic expansion had been discounted, largely because of optimistic assumptions about government's role in managing the economy, particularly from a demand perspective, and its ability to promote growth. According to such a view any discrepancies were temporary and correctable. Events continued to disprove this idea, as the economy refused to grow at anything approaching actual or forecast rates for public expenditure, inevitably prompting questions about the size of the public sector relative to the total economy and, more particularly, likely future situations if existing trends were to continue. This debate, especially about the size of welfare services that the productive sector could (or should) support, was further intensified by the onset of world recession after the oil price rises of 1973 - further minimising economic growth - and the heightened influences of monetarist economists. Probably the most striking example of changed attitudes was in relation to the methodologies associated with the PESC projections by programme of future government expenditures. Originally, in the 1960s, these had been little more than a statement of aspirational levels and, as a result, a promotion of these levels, with some attempt to identify and order priorities. With the new environment a drive towards control purposes began to evolve.

The first element in control was the attempt to ensure that programmes remained within projected limits, which in effect became targets. Volume terms, in which the actual level of services is considered - so many teachers employed etc. - became less dominant: actual money expenditure assumed greater importance, particularly after the introduction of cash limits in 1974. Increasingly, both central and local government programmes had to finance expenditure changes occuring during the financial year caused by wage rises etc. from a sum specified at the start of the spending period. [19] With cash limits the accusation can be deflected that increases in government spending, automatically sanctioned, are themselves principal contributors to the inflationary effects they are supposed to alleviate. By 1983 all projections occurred in cash rather than volume terms. [20] The second element in this control, with implications well beyond the narrow boundaries of PESC methodology, concerns the attitudinal and procedural effects of stabilizing and reducing public expenditure. So long as aspirational levels relating to expansion are being met, at least partially, the discussion and the competition is about additional resources. The current state of affairs, the activities which have already been financed in previous years, receive far less scrutiny. There is an expectation they will continue with few changes, and given the scarcity of attention orthodoxy pervading all organizations - only limited time can be awarded to any problem - this skewed perspective becomes more understandable, if not defensible. In contrast, without expansion, new interests and different perspectives evolve, for in the context of resource allocation, scarcity of attention never produces nil attention, as the outcomes are so pervasive and important. Existing patterns of resource usage, previously accepted without question become subject to scrutiny, even in a no-growth situation, because the school or LEA invariably finds itself committed to a number of expansion items (a new course or project) and therefore reductions have to be found somewhere. Obviously, when an overall contraction is sought the numbers and scope of reductions has to rise, with several items and activities needing to shrink or stop. Quite naturally, the many interests threatened try to ensure that the totality of the expenditure scheme receives detailed attention.

A main factor in this greater scrutiny concerns the effectiveness with which resources are utilized. Up to the late 1960s, there were few objectives and systematic attempts to evaluate the performance of public services.[21] In general terms if there were insufficient adverse comments about a school, local authority or whatever, it was assumed, on this basis alone, to be successful. [22] That perspective accurately reflected circumstances in which public expenditure growth was anticipated and achieved. For when aspirational levels are satisfied, the demand for evaluation is minimal both from users concentrating on the competition for extra resources, and external critics, where attention diverts to the distribution and spending of these additional funds. In contrast reductions are planned and any activity which can demonstrate its effectiveness with resources already received is advantaged. It would be quite misleading to suggest a surge of evaluatory procedures accompanying the pursuit of less public spending. For example, the recommendation of 1972 on the management of the new local authorities,[23] that they should each have a performance review sub-committee, has only been formally adopted by a minority of authorities.[24] More generally though, as public spending moved away from growth expectancy the stridency of calls to demonstrate what is being sought and achieved with resources, and the need of activities to answer these calls, has increased. The fact that the underlying motive of many criticisms was to reduce spending is, in the changed circumstances of public expenditure, less important than their existence. As a more evaluatory conscious environment develops it seems highly probable that education will be disadvantaged compared to most other public services. Regularly the participants are in dispute about aims and objectives, the time-scales are long, usually the outcomes are diffuse and intangible, and it is rare for the processes themselves to be well understood. To take one simple example, if a school uses public funds to produce mature adults (as a defined aim) then what definition of maturity is accepted, when should it be assessed, by which method, and how have the committed resources contributed to any achievement? Clearly, evaluatory situations of this type, and they abound in education, are exacerbative factors in any attempt to dispel accusations of reduced standards and concerns for erosion in public confidence.

In more general terms, however, education has followed the pattern of public expenditure in moving from expansion to retrenchment over a period of a few years in the mid-1970s. Only in terms of the size of the move, from the most rapid expander within a growth environment to shrinkage within overall contraction, is education any different to other major public activities. Priorities have changed with time. In retrospect education grew most quickly from the late 1950s as spending on personal social services displaced that on defence. In the late 1970s defence again began to achieve a higher priority, along with law and order but increasingly, following high unemployment and low output, spending directed towards industrial regeneration received more support. For education the likelihood of a marked change in priority, as compared to the other main programmes, during the mid and late 1980s appears improbable. Unlike social services, for example, which in terms of spending requirements benefits from an ageing population,[25] it must cope with a continuing reduction in the numbers of its main clients - schoolchildren. For all programmes the critical item in assessing expenditure prospects remains the rate of economic growth. If relatively high levels can be achieved - perhaps 3 or 4% annually - then all programmes, including educational spending, will benefit. By comparison with negligible growth, the economic, political and social motivations to minimize and further curtail expenditure will be undeniable: placing education, disadvantaged by demographic factors, lacking in public confidence, and without acceptable methodologies to demonstrate effectiveness in a still less favoured situation.

ECONOMIC CONTRIBUTIONS

What the last fifteen years has made clear is the reliance of educational spending on economic growth, and the impact on schools and colleges of policies which follow shortfalls in this growth. However, the interaction and the interdependency of education and economy is two way: the place of education in economic development cannot be overlooked. Two issues dominate the partnership: the first being the primacy of economic matters over education, the second, as an explanation of the first, differences in time scale. When education effects economic development invariably it takes many years and numerous factors intervene. Indisputable evidence that a specific educational activity has produced a determinable economic effect does not exist: although, less directly, studies in developed countries have tried to discover (with some success) an educational contribution to economic growth.[26] There is, for example, evidence about the greater economic contribution of graduates over non-graduates (in terms of life-time earnings) but the key item of the role of the higher education course in generating these differences becomes less assessable with career progression because of the potential influences of other variables. Also in many occupations the actual differentials in earnings may be less important than the leadership a graduate provides to raise the salary levels of other staff through enhanced skills, knowledge and confidence accruing from the time spent in education. However, any study to elucidate this type of information requires a minimum time-scale of 20 years: in contrast a decision made on economic criteria to reduce educational spending can have an immediate effect. Of course, it does not follow that without direct evidence of success educational institutions have no interest in the contribution they can make towards economic development. In fact, with retrenchment these interests have increased: most specifically from colleges who perceive advantages in becoming more involved with vocationally oriented activities, for example: more generally but less tangibly, by facilitating economic growth as a vehicle for greater educational spending.

In some activities economic dependence on the work of educational institutions is well established and beyond dispute. Most obviously when the objective of producing workers with particular expertise and skills, and in numbers that the economy is likely to support, dominates. AFE, for example, is involved in a whole range of vocational training for specific occupations: lawyers, teachers, architects, planners, social workers and so on, attend courses in which the examinations are recognised by professional associations and employers: with them, government or local authorities (where appropriate) setting or influencing recruitment levels. In contrast, many activities have no vocational elements: most arts and social science programmes, for instance. The design of modern language courses, and their recruitment figures, are not determined in any way by the demands, or particular needs, of translators and export salesmen. Somewhere between these two extremes are many science and engineering courses, where some of the knowledge and skills to be acquired by students is directed towards their potential work situations. In sandwich-courses for example, employers participate in course design and (possibly) limited teaching. This employer involvement becomes even more pronounced in FE colleges. Before the erosion of the job market for young people in the mid-1970s, the bulk of NAFE work was 'off the job' training for students released and supported on block, day or evening release schemes by their employers. The network of courses and awards that evolved - to some extent national, but often local, in character - reflected commercial, industrial and professional needs (as interpreted by students, college staff, employers and professional associations) for the education and training of labour.[27] Even with high levels of youth unemployment changing the balance of college interests, activities associated with job performance still constitute a vital institutional task. Of course to claim that arrangements in every activity function effectively would be misleading. Mismatches between college courses and employers definitions of wants are inevitable, given the limited knowledge of each other's circumstances and possible conflict in motivations and intentions. Nevertheless, the main issue about the significance of the direct contributions of higher and further education to economic development, through a dominance in the institutionalized training of groups of workers, seems beyond doubt.

With regard to direct economic contributions, the attitude of schools is more ambivalent. Many staff, perhaps the great majority, would claim that their main responsibility is to provide a balanced and liberal education to equip the future adult for many situations, one of which happens to be work. In other words the general requirements of the labour market should only have a peripheral influence on school activities, while specific needs should be completely ignored. However, with the disappearance of employment opportunities for many leavers, schools are faced with a dilemma. With fewer vacancies and more competition, it is not surprising when parents, children, governors, local councillors etc. persuade staff to introduce more programmes focussed on job-preparation into the school curriculum, and imply that extra attention should be paid to the perceived needs of employers in relation to the skills and attitudes they seek in young workers. In these circumstances schools can react by arranging work-experience schemes, attempting to improve children's interview techniques, and strengthening their careers guidance procedures: while simultaneously attempting to match curricular objectives for older pupils to the learning methodologies and task performance required of young people at work. The dilemma is presented by an alternative perspective in which a combination of the practical problems involved in developing vocational preparation schemes, within a framework dominated by examination requirements, and because work is so scarce, makes any exercise to assist job-finding not only valueless to the majority but, by raising unsatisfiable aspirations, can easily prove counter-productive. However, to proceed from this perspective to a view that schools should distance themselves from external events, such as high unemployment, fails to appreciate the position of education in a developed society.

In primary schools the likely effects on the labour market of curriculum design, would seem to be a non-issue. The children are a minimum of five years from employment and whatever the behavioural objectives and curriculum content (other than as a base for secondary education) the assessable impact on the children's ability to find jobs, and the skills and attitudes they will take to any work, cannot be other than minimal. Even were a school to adopt a highly utilitarian view of the curriculum, emphasising English Language, Mathematics and computer work,while dispensing with creative subjects, it would be difficult to prove that because of this curriculum the children were more

employable several years later. If they obtained
additional 'O' levels their job prospects might
be improved, but still the issue of disentangling
primary and secondary school factors from other
effects remains. This example, simple in itself,
is highly significant in demonstrating the multi-
plicity of factors, long time-scales, lack of focus
and ambivalences of those involved, in any assessment of the potential contributions of much educational activity to economic growth.

Indirectness is the dominant factor. As a
result, in organizing and implementing the curriculum teachers are most unlikely to have any economic intentions even in the most general terms.
Their aim is the provision of a broad education.
If, because of what happens in school, children make
a greater economic contribution through higher remuneration or are more encouraged to start their own
businesses, say, this would be an unsought and (in
view of some staff) an unattractive outcome. In
the same way a history degree course will not specify the production of potential business executives
as a goal. If graduates are appointed, it will be
on the strength of course completion and the assumption that some of the skills and attitudes acquired - the ability to collate information, to write
succinct reports, to search for evidence, and to
organize their own learning - should transfer to the
work situation. Some employers will have experience
with previous graduates that this does occur, others
will be attracted by the credentials of recruits
(and a trust that the appropriate transfers are
available and achievable) while for many education
is providing no more than a filter. That is ident-
ifying a group of personnel with above average
intelligence, adaptability, commitment, ability to
work under pressure. Particularly with job-short-
ages a crude selection utilizing the education system facilitates a firm's recruitment procedures.
More generally, an organization such as the Civil
Service, demands five 'O' levels, not because it is
interested in course content, but on account of the
filter this supplies.[28]

This intangibility of many economic contributions has two main organizational effects. The
first concerns the attitudes of teachers and lecturers. They can argue, often with a great deal of
justification, that their relationship with economic
and financial issues is one way. Resource parameters dominate the conditions in which teaching
occurs: inversely, so diffuse are the processes, so

long the time-scale, so ubiquitous the other factors that the demonstrable impact their work can have on economic growth is so negligible it should be totally ignored. A view which could be shared even by staff working in activities which attempt a direct contribution to economic development. An engineering department, for example, would not necessarily accept that its most important goal is economic, by enabling ex-students to design marketable products improve production etc., in whatever organization they were employed: and this view could still be related, in all probability, to college courses specifically organized for firms to familiarise their staff with new products or techniques. In any educational situation the economic goal is one of several. Additionally, most of the evaluatory difficulties continue unresolved even when a course is specifically directed towards the needs of a homogeneous population. For the individual teacher the problem is relating institutional activities to the totality of economic development. On size factors alone, what a person or college does can only be minimally significant. Resultingly, within a hierarchy of objectives, the economic dimension tends to be downgraded. More generally, the economic and educational systems are easily perceived as functioning independently, apart from the item of resourcing. While many staff might find this notion appealing (possibly on political or ideological grounds, as they do not accept the aims of the economic system and think that schools and colleges should never be seen to support them) it represents a gross over-simplification of complex and dynamic processes.

The second effect involves external critics. Because the time-scales are long and the effects defy determination by traditional and objective assessment methodologies, it is very easy for critics to argue that the education system is making an inadequate contribution to economic development. Then, either developing this theme alone, or as part of more general comments on the efficacy of the system, the case for fewer resources can be made. Two interesting, but significant, issues emerge. First, the absence of evidence: it is as logical to propound that inadequate effectiveness follows from too few, rather than too many resources. Second, critics have few facts to demonstrate that education gives insufficient support to economic development: instead they can use the lack of positive evidence to support their negative case by exerting whatever influences they can on resource decisions. From an educational perspective, the potential relationship between the two effects is disadvantageous as the more that professional staff accept the notion of economic and educational separatism, the easier to argue a lack of impact by education on a rapidly changing economic and work environment thereby further eroding public confidence. Education based, but conventional counter-arguments, even using empirical studies such as rate of return analysis, are insufficient both as times involved are so long (and policy-making demands much shorter horizons) and because results emerging in the 1980s will reflect the conditions of the 1950s and 1960s, with expansion and full employment. The real case for a return to educational growth - not necessarily based on the institutional mix and practices that have evolved - is its potential impact and essential role in a society increasingly effected by technologically induced change. If economic growth is to be re-established on anything approaching a permanent basis, appropriate educational arrangements are an unavoidable pre-requisite. The main thrust of the argument, therefore, is not that economic expansion will assist educational spending, but that without educational development sustained levels of economic growth are impossible, in the likely circumstances of the 1980s and onwards.

THE FUTURE OF WORK AND EDUCATION

A main effect of rapid technological change is the natural links it produces between the futures of work and education. At both local and national level they become inextricably connected: first as rate of change generates its own further requirements for yet more technological developments and refinements. If these are to be satisfied, educational needs and practices have to be included. Second, change, by eliminating jobs necessitates a re-consideration of many assumptions inherent in educational planning and provision in relation to work. The changing relationship between work and education has a number of complex features, made more so by the speed of evolution and the necessity of a global perspective, but in this context four distinct components can be defined. The first three occur directly from the work-education interaction: the fourth would only appear to impinge upon education but must also influence the others: a) the inter-relationship between the rate and direction of technological development, and education: b) the effect of these developments on the expertise and skills required in the workforce: c) the implications for education and training of changes in these requirements, and the associated reduction in the availability of work: d) the potential effect of technological change on the educational processes themselves.

a) It would be quite misleading to view technological development as a new phenomenon to which education, having helped create by producing engineers, scientists etc. and facilities for research and development, must now adapt. The introduction of new products (using previously unknown materials) and the evolution of innovative processes (involving more effective and faster communication modes) has occurred since the Industrial Revolution, but with quickening speed this century. Workers in the plastics and television industries exemplify situations which did not exist 50 years ago. There seems no reason to doubt that all the 1970s, and now the 1980s, are witnessing is an acceleration in developmental rates, assessed both in terms of the emergence of new products and processes and the time-lag between discovery and practical application.[29] Equally, there appears few factors which might slow, or even decelerate these trends: especially with current rates of advancement in computers, semi-conductors, instrumentation technology, microprocessors, robotics, fibre-optics etc.[30] The scope of these 'high technology' developments, and the actual and potential range of their impacts on productive processes and service activities, can create the impression that a totally new situation has arisen through some non-specified 'quantum leap' in technology. In fact, the reducing prominence of large scale manufacturing industry as a user of labour, in vehicle-building, textiles, ship building etc. following assimilation of new processes, has been a well established feature in a developed country such as the UK for many years. The emergence of a post-industrial society does not necessarily involve the abandonment of these traditional activities, but it does mean the production of more, new and different goods with fewer staff, using evolving techniques and components as they are researched, developed and applied.[31] Simultaneously, whole new industries entirely based on high technology - in telecommunications, microcomputing etc. - become established. Perhaps, the key element in these change processes is gradualism,

Education and the Economy

but at a continuously increasing rate.

The other factor, important everywhere, but particularly so in the UK, which seems to make the current situation somehow different is the effect of recession. The erosion of large scale and high employment manufacturing has been exaggerated by low demand, reduced profitability and inadequate investment. The direction of causality in this sequence, from a historical perspective, is less significant than the cyclic element, in that less technological development in a competitive environment further reduces demand and limits innovative opportunities. However, change has still taken place as new and revamped processes have been introduced. Indeed, it can be argued that the extent of recession has been heightened by investment in new techniques which do no more than refine processes in industries which are out-dated in the context of a developed country, when such investment could have been more effectively focussed on 'high technology' activities.[32] Yet such a divide into traditional and high technology industries is artificial and quite unnecessary. A modern glass manufacturer will utilize many recently discovered and technologically sophisticated processes. It would not be categorized as a high technology unit, compared to say, a computer soft-ware firm or a producer of advanced instrumentation, but in relation to the interaction with education such a separation is irrelevant. It also implies two discrete entities, when a spectral range from some craft occupations hardly affected by current developmental trends, through to newly emerging jobs in high technology activities provides a more realistic description. Nevertheless, whether it is a traditional manufacturer remodelling old processes or a firm at the forefront of technological innovation, the role of education both as a facilitator of development and a supplier of skilled manpower, becomes increasingly self-evident as the rapidity and scale of change expands.

The most direct way of describing these processes is in terms of a growing dominance of knowledge-based activities. In terms of time-scales again, this is not a new phenomenon that emerged in the 1970s. However, relative to the scope and rate of technological development that decade may well be viewed as a watershed. As far as the direct impact of educational institutions on these change processes is concerned, the actual generation of new ideas and the evolutionary rate for innovative products and processes from inception to viability, provide useful monitors. They depend upon a complex range of factors: among them the mix of pure and applied research, and the industrial-commercial infrastructure, but work within educational institutions can make a direct contribution. What new organizations associated with high technology have discovered (and longer established ones were already aware of this) is that the findings of academic research, even those with commercial possibilities, do not readily translate into an alternative environment without supportive arrangements. Higher education institutions, and the academic community generally, have differences in priorities, attitudes to secrecy, and views about the free exchange of ideas, as compared to a commercial enterprise. The objectives of the two types of organization are so disparate, in relation to timings or the need for returning an investment, for example, that to anticipate non-problematic transfer of inventions, discoveries, patents etc. into commercially viable projects would be naive. By experience the most effective mechanism in the current situation is for academic staff to move from technical consultancy, through the establishment of testing and design services, to eventual product manufacture when wishing to market their research findings.[33] Of course, educational institutions (and any spin-off organization) comprise one component, and in financial terms a small part, of the total research and development activities which also involves firms, research councils, the military and so on. It should become increasingly important, however, as a generator of ideas and techniques first because of the increasing rate and sophistication of technological change and second as the time lapse, on a global scale, between research and commercial application reduce.

From a national perspective the relative importance of pure, applied and developmental research is highly significant. As Japan has demonstrated, a country with little basic research can achieve and sustain high growth levels in technologically advanced activities by relying on the import of innovatory ideas and techniques (Table 2.1).[34] The basic research element has been historically low, and in some activities almost non-existent, but compensation came from a strong applied base, and an even more powerful developmental thrust, facilitated by the large number of engineers produced by the Japanese education system.[35]

TABLE 2.1

Technology Trade Balance in Selected Countries (in millions of dollars)

	Japan			USA			France			W. Germany			UK		
	Recd.	Paym.	R/P	Recd.	Paym.	R/P	Recd.	Paym.	R/P	Recd.	Paym.	R/P	Recd.	Paym.	R/P
1965	17	166	0.10	1534	135	11.4	169	215	0.79	75	166	0.45	138	131	1.06
1966	19	192	0.10	1515	140	10.8	181	244	0.74	73	175	0.42	168	143	1.18
1967	27	239	0.11	1747	166	10.5	195	231	0.85	90	193	0.47	183	174	1.05
1968	34	314	0.11	1867	186	10.0	270	282	0.96	99	219	0.45	211	195	1.08
1969	46	363	0.13	2019	221	9.1	336	332	1.01	98	256	0.38	218	223	0.98
1970	59	433	0.14	2331	225	10.4	344	357	0.96	119	306	0.39	273	255	1.07
1971	60	488	0.12	2545	241	10.6	398	467	0.85	149	377	0.39	288	270	1.07
1972	74	572	0.13	2770	294	9.4	585	587	1.00	201	433	0.46	339	307	1.10
1973	88	715	0.12	3225	385	8.4	844	741	1.14	216	539	0.40	410	350	1.17
1974	113	718	0.16	3821	346	11.0	989	823	1.20	262	582	0.45	465	413	1.12
1975	161	712	0.23	4300	473	9.1	1332	1035	1.29	308	729	0.42	493	484	1.02
1976	173	846	0.20	4353	482	9.0	1461	1180	1.24	289	692	0.42	-	-	-
1977	233	1027	0.23	4725	447	10.6	-	-	-	335	816	0.41	-	-	-

Source: Calculated from Kagakugijutsucho (Science and Technology Agency), Kagakugijutsu hakusho (White Paper on Science and Technology) 1978.

35

More recently, there have been attempts to establish more balance among the three functions for reasons of self-sufficiency and because of the increasing reluctance from countries (particularly the USA) to continue as technology exporters if it may lead to their eventual disadvantage. In contrast, bias in UK has been towards basic research, complemented by relatively low level production of qualified engineers. Quite deliberately Finniston[36] was part of an effort to redress this particular imbalance, but the time-scale from acceptance that a problem exists to amelioration, in this context, may take decades. However, it would be wrong to infer that concentration on basic research is reflected by a positive technology trade balance.
While import and export levels are roughly equivalent, compared to net importers such as West Germany and particularly Japan, the contrast with France, in recent years, is more instructive. Especially in terms of a per capita comparison the UK's performance as a source of technological innovation falls well below that of other countries. In terms of gross estimates of research and development commitment the UK might appear satisfactory but only in relation to national income: as this latter figure is so low, actual expenditure (and that is the most important criteria) is well below that of other major developed countries. (Table 2.2).

The paradox, and the causalities, which link the 1980s circumstances of low growth in the world economy with high and accelerating rates of technological advancement, are difficult to explain satisfactorily. However, one clear issue does emerge: so complex and numerous are the international associations, through the exchange of goods, technology, services and personnel, that a country such as the UK has no feasible option but to pursue a policy intended to maximise technological development through effective transfer from research to application on the assumption that this provides the only means for a re-establishment of economic growth. Part of that policy has to be support for, and appropriate priorities among, basic, applied and developmental research activities, and the co-ordination of the organizational base (including many education organizations) in which they should occur. Another component concerns the supply of trained manpower. There are, of course, other investment priorities, assistance to newly-established firms, industrial location and relations to social policy for example - but it is the first two

TABLE 2.2   Research and Development Commitments in Selected Countries

	Japan	USA	France	W.Germany	UK
R & D Expenditure (billion $)	8.8	34.6	6.1	10.1	4.8
R & D Personnel (thousands)	255.0	533.0	62.0	94.0	78.0
R & D/National Income	2.1	2.5	2.0	2.7	2.3
R & D Personnel/ Thousand Population	2.3	2.5	1.2	1.5	1.4
Per Capita R & D ($)	80.0	162.0	115.0	163.0	85.0
Growth Rate of R & D Expenditure 1966-1975 (Annual Rate)	20.1	5.6	10.2	12.2	-

Source: Kagakugijutsucho (Science and Technology Agency) Kagakugijutsu hakusho(White Paper on Science and Technology) 1978.

elements which directly influence, and are affected by, the work of the education system.
b) Undoubtedly, the impact of recession has made it more difficult to estimate the extent of structural unemployment generated by technologically induced change. Numerous examples of job-loss can be quoted, but it is often impossible to differentiate structural and recessional forces. Numerically controlled machines in an engineering works doing in five minutes a task which originally (and recently) took a skilled man several days, automated arrangements in clearing banks which eliminate much of the mechanical handling of cheques, computer aided design in drawing offices, word processors performing routine clerical duties, provide a collection of typical examples. The general pattern consists of redundancy for some jobs and skills, with the simultaneous creation of needs for new expertise and knowledge. However, the overall effect on the totality of working hours seems certain to be negative. Some caution is essential: absolute definitiveness would be foolish when so many factors can effect the outcome. In some situations a new process, even though technologically further advanced than the old, will require extra staff because the product is more marketable: elsewhere a previously non-existent product will be made. In each of the four examples already mentioned, the innovative product (or process) had first to be researched, and then developed and maintained, providing some jobs to compensate for those that disappear with its use. An extra uncertainty in prediction concerns the many personnel whose jobs will only be marginally influenced by such change. Retailing provides a good example, and also highlights the problems of precise forecasting. The number of counter staff in shops will be strongly affected by circumstances which in turn will be influenced by consumer preference. In some situations, a small outlet for example, the job will hardly alter. Elsewhere with computer stock-control and point of sale re-ordering of goods, new elements will be introduced. Therefore size of firm, its personnel policy and attitude towards innovation will determine job-content as well as staffing requirements: but, over and above these factors is the potential effect of shop-customer interactive communication systems. If made available by a firm, and sufficient consumers find them preferable to normal shopping, counter-work itself would be threatened.

Education and the Economy

The trend towards less work is therefore much more significant, in the context of education effects, than the exactitude of projections about numbers unemployed - dependant as they have to be on estimates of economic growth, international comparisons of competitiveness, consumer preferences, inter-industry allowances, the levels of recessional unemployment etc. However, for the UK any claim that a 3 x 48 work pattern (48 hours for 48 weeks for 48 years) can be re-established for the whole of the potential working population seems implausible. There is little likelihood of a major decline in this population, unless artificially induced by lowering the retirement age (improbable because of the effects on the social security programme, already the government's main spending commitment) and no possibility of a reduction in the size of the young work-force (16-25 year olds) until the early 1990s. Compared to other major developed countries low levels of investment in all types of industry, both currently and historically, present particular difficulties. In traditional activities such as shipbuilding, textiles, and garment manufacture, vulnerability is raised by the increasing availability of products from third world countries, with cheaper labour costs and more flexible working arrangements. In 'knowledge based' industries competition comes from developed countries, in the first place, although that situation might change with developments in intermediate countries, such as Taiwan and South Korea, but inadequate investment in these industries may prove even more disadvantageous: significantly investment is required not only in plant and equipment, but also in the education and training of the work-force. For while technological development means few workers it also demands a different collection of skills and knowledge. Take the example of a computer controlled engineering machine-shop replacing a traditional workshop. As a result much of the expertise associated with a whole range of jobs - millwright, fitter, turner etc. - is no longer needed. However, the change like so many others, is unavoidable, for even were the firm to trade domestically it has no option other than to make the necessary capital investment to sustain long-term viability. Perhaps a stringent policy of import controls ruthlessly implemented would avoid this necessity by isolating the UK from global technological development, but such a step seems improbable on economic, political and social grounds. More practically, the firm will have workers it must deskill- essentially setting and monitoring machines now doing their jobs - while others (even in higher output situations) will have to be made redundant, unless they can be retrained for the jobs in programming and maintenance which the new arrangements require.

In relation to a profile of employee requirements this engineering example is not untypical of many manufacturing and service industries adjusting to changing circumstances. Compared to before, and after, gradually, many traditionally skilled, semi-skilled and unskilled staff will be needed with some finding deskilled work in routine maintenance and machine tending - that is processes which on technical or cost grounds, cannot be automated: in contrast, additional staff will have to be found to invent, refine, initiate and implement the myriad of elements which sustain and constitute technological development. For the UK this last item is potentially the most disadvantageous aspect of the evolving situation. A combination of low investment, research and development expenditure, and growth undoubtedly hinders the countries ability to generate, or be used as a base for 'knowledge based' activity. In the case of the engineering firm, the new machines and the supportive computer facilities, can be selected in a competitive market. If they have to be imported (as often occurs) traditional jobs not only are disappearing from the engineering works, but those that might be viewed as compensatory employment in high technology have to be established in other countries.

As this example is by no means unique the most likely outcome, after recession, would be low-level skill jobs servicing imported technology (insufficient in number to abate the real rise in unemployment) with an inadequate supply of new jobs in knowledge-based situations, as more and more advanced expertise and processes have either to be imported or ignored. The fact that West German and Japanese industries thrived on technological imports until quite recently reflects their ability to convert discoveries and innovations into commercial products. As a potential solution to the UKs problems this route has two disadvantages. First this conversion process has often lacked dynamism in many UK industries: second, with the increasing rate and sophistication of change, the package of basic, applied and developmental activities has to be more cohesive. For example, a firm may import some new telecommunications equipment. It does not, however, import the technology for the next advance, as this utilizes knowledge and funds generated by the refinement and marketing of the previous generation of machines. Still more disturbing for the UK is the potential circularity in prevailing circumstances, in that insufficient commitment to 'knowledge-based' activity will further reduce growth and investment, which in turn must again lower this commitment, and onwards and downwards.

There seems to be only one strategy away from this 'cycle of decline' and this relates to the skills and knowledge (and therefore to a large extent, the education and training) of the work-force. Even if an alternative starting point were chosen - a huge investment of capital into high-technology industries for example - the issue of recruiting adequately educated staff, and their in-service training, would still be central items. In other words, unless the staff have the appropriate skills and knowledge, or were trainable within the necessary time-scales and financial parameters, much of the investment would be wasted. An alternative strategy, involving the import of skilled workers for a temporary period, is simply not feasible. Therefore, the case for an expanding system of education and training for a developed country, if it wishes to retain that status in conditions of rapid technological advance, is unanswerable. This does not, of course, imply that growth in current patterns of provision provides the most appropriate arrangements to support technological change or that all additional activities should occur in formal settings. In fact, quite the reverse, as this provision was established in very different circumstances and for educational institutions has mainly evolved in terms of self-determined criteria. Concentrating on the institutions, however, in general terms the requirement is for higher level qualifications (interpreting Figure 2.1 as a hierarchy).

FIGURE 2.1   Qualifications and Course Levels

Occupational Group	Occupational Skills	Judgement Expected	Entry Educational Performance	Examples of Course Types
Professional Technological	Mental	New ideas innovation policy	2 or 3 levels A	Degrees Professional Quals

FIGURE 2.1 (cont'd)

Occupational Group	Occupational Skills	Judgement Expected	Entry Educational Performance	Examples of Course Types
Higher Technical	Mental	Complex diagnostic appraisals	4 O levels 1 A level	HTC/D Dip HE HND
Technical	Mental and Manual	Some diagnosis and appraisal	2/3 O levels or CSE Grade 1	TC/D OND
Craft	Multi-manual	Decisions limited to job	2/3 CSEs Grade 3 Foundation	CGLI occupation specific. Integrated
Operator (Unskilled semi-skilled)	Single Manual	Set conditions Common Sense	Little expected	CGLI UVP occupation specific

Source: Central Policy Review Staff, Education, Training and Industrial Performance (HMSO, London, 1980).

The emphasis should not be on the qualifications for their own sake, this would only further exaggerate the importance of credentials, but because of the greater premium the courses leading to them place on mental abilities, and the enhanced opportunities they provide for a worker to achieve a wide range of skills, allowing them to boost their expertise, knowledge and, ultimately, confidence.

With the increasing dominance of knowledge-based industries, more emphasis on mental abilities requires no further explanation. The desirability of a diverse collection of skills (mental and, where appropriate, manual) follows directly from the accelerating rate of technological change. Looking forward, and returning to the example of personnel in television and plastics (working in situations which did not exist fifty years ago) it is impossible to specify dominant products and processes twenty five years (or even ten years) ahead. Many staff will have to familiarise themselves with materials yet to be developed, utilizing methodologies still requiring invention. Therefore, a training programme which may be perfectly adequate in introducing personnel to a specific technique, has little long-term value, unless it provides a base of knowledge and skills which can be transferred to novel, and currently unknown situations, as well as promoting a flexibility of attitudes to facilitate such transfers, and an alertness as to when they are appropriate and necessary. Because it rarely includes such elements, the traditional apprenticeship, as a preparation for working life in many occupations, is becoming increasingly inappropriate. Indeed, the pursuit of a limited range of skills, by downgrading generalisability and adaptability even if unintentional, and by seeming to offer the security of training for a well-defined job, is potentially counter-productive. First, because the specificity of the thrust is towards jobs with no certainty of continuing: second the earlier training by failing to prepare for subsequent change, risks antagonism towards it. For while personnel increasingly require training for current positions, that activity is not an end in itself, but an asset to be utilized for retraining in newly-emergent job situations. In other words, the thrust, whether in schools, colleges or any training situation, should be assisting individuals to a position where they take a large measure of responsibility for their own learning. In a competitive job-market adults are undoubtedly advantaged if they have this general competence, and the confidence to exploit their abilities.

c) With technological advance more and more dominant in international competitiveness the provision of a cohesive (and comprehensive) education and training programme, in relation to industrial and commercial, becomes an increasingly key issue.

In the UK, until quite recently, two themes were allowed to dominate this provision. The first involved schools and those parts of higher education not specifically vocational. They aimed to offer a liberal education uninfluenced (quite deliberately) by any specific needs likely to be required in the work situation. The second placed upon employers the main responsibility for providing job-related training.[37] Naturally many employers utilized other agencies often through the formal education system (with the satisfaction of those requirements being an important feature in the growth of further education during the 1950s and 1960s) but the separation into the two discrete activities of education and training follows inexorably, and practically from the two themes. Even the terminology can be used to sustain a dichotomy - education, an open-ended process of knowledge acquisition in which the

43

individual defines the limits of his/her ignorance and proceeds from there: training, the mastery of specified skills, attitudes and knowledge within a clearly defined framework - and an implication that training is the inferior activity.[38] According to this definition, training by being so specific will be of limited value to participants, because of new demands generated by changing employment prospects. Significantly, governments have in the past exaggerated separateness, if not the hierarchy, by divorcing the two activites administratively, for example, with the Industrial Training Act, 1964.

Yet, the introduction with this legislation of Industrial Training Boards (to promote and monitor training on an industry by industry basis) was indicative of concern for training provision. Even then economic and fiscal measures to correct low levels of economic growth (by international standards) were being nullified, to some extent, by skill shortages among the work force. In addition there was gradual acceptance of problems endemic to any arrangements with employer dominance, although the intention of this legislation (unlike that which followed in 1973) was mainly to assist firms in meeting, and increasing their commitments, rather than introducing additional state intervention. Overall, the aim was both to ensure an adequate supply of trained labour, and improve the quality of that training. This latter factor, when left to individual organizations, can vary enormously.[39] Small firms have particular problems. Although there is no simple relationship between size and the standard of training, a large organization, which can support its own training department, should be able to sustain more effective programmes than a small firm with half-a-dozen employees. The expansion of the small business sector, and the complementary decrease in personnel employed by large organizations may well produce a decline in the quality and quantity of employer sponsored training. Then, there is the tendency of organizations perhaps understandably in a commercial environment, to concentrate on short-term issues, to the detriment of the wider training needs of employees, if not to the disadvantage of the firms longer-term training requirements. An organization must always face a dilemma in determining the specificity of any programme for employees, of matching training to profit maximisation objectives. For example, when it introduces a new process, or makes a capital investment its main short-run concern is sufficient staff with the requisite skills and knowledge to maximise the benefits: future training needs, local, national or within the firm itself, and the wider needs of employee training, impose less rigid priorities.[40]

Given these potential deficiencies in employer centred methods it still seems highly improbable that government concern for training provision would have achieved so high a priority in recent years had it not been for the effects of world recession. Perhaps some reform of the training structure might have occurred. The case was powerful, with continuing decline in the UKs competitive position, long-standing inflexibilities and inefficiencies in the use of manpower, no apparent solution to the problem of skill shortages, and considerable doubts about the overall quality and efficacy of training, all pointing to the need for fundamental reassessment. A partial response to these criticisms appeared with the Employment and Training Act, 1973, including increased availability of government resources to assist the individual activities of firms and Industrial Training Boards. In retrospect though the most significant factor was the establishment of MSC - a quango to focus on employment and training policies at national level.

However, it is doubtful whether its increasingly interventionist role in post-school activities, co-ordinated by the Training Services Division (TSD) would have achieved such prominence without rising levels of unemployment. In effect, the political pressures were so great that had it wished otherwise government had no alternative but to become more involved in the sponsorship of training. Yet, to take one example, the need for more comprehensive facilities for school leavers predates the most dramatic rise in youth unemployment during the early 1980s. Comparative figures in other Western European countries highlight the deficiencies in provision, with the UK having the highest proportion of young people not in either full-time education or training: that is, either in work (perhaps, but not necessarily, receiving some form of training) or unemployed, even in 1977. (Table 2.3). Obviously the inadequacies inherent in these figures were set to be exaggerated both by more unemployment and the impact of recession on the training programmes of many firms. For employer dependant training is highly vulnerable to economic activity rates: if these decline, as during the early 1980s, so does the actual volume of training (less people are in employment and fewer new workers

TABLE 2.3   Participation rates of 16-18 year olds in Western Europe

Country	Full-time Education & Training	Part-time Education & Training	No Education or Training
Belgium	78 (64)	3 (6)	19 (30)
Denmark	43 (29)	20 (13)	32 (58)
West Germany	50 (33)	35 (45)	15 (21)
France	75 (54)	10 (8)	15 (40)
Ireland	60 (29)	9 (4)	31 (67)
Italy	55 (40)	11 (9)	34 (51)
Luxembourg	60 (37)	29 (19)	21 (49)
Netherlands	84 (64)	8 (13)	10 (23)
UK	60 (32)	7 (12)	33 (56)

The figures represent percentage participation rates for each country at age 16-17 (for 17-18 year olds in brackets).

Source: Compiled by CEDEFOP - European Centre for the Development of Vocational Training - as reproduced in Bacie Journal, March, 1982, p.100.

recruited) with a likelihood, through reduced profits, of a greater bias towards short-term training needs.

Any substantial shift in government policy, even directed towards long-standing problems, must include a number of short-term palliatives if it is to sustain support. More directly, the policy has to be seen to be working. In this context perhaps the best example is MSC efforts to supplement apprenticeship schemes from which employers have withdrawn. However, in more general terms it is important to realize that the strategic change in government attitudes towards training was catalyzed by concerns for unemployment (particularly among the young). A desire to provide a totality of education and training for a work-force increasingly affected by technological change might be the main intention in the sponsorship of new activities, but the immediate political pressures which influence their design cannot be overlooked. Therefore, while the MSC New Training Initiative[41] identified three main objectives: a) the development of skill training as a basis for progression through further learning, b) the provision of education and training facilities for all under age 18, c) the facilitation of adult training and re-training through opportunities for skills and knowledge updates, the Youth Training Scheme (YTS) in pursuit of b) received the highest priority.[42] Since September 1983 under 18s (leaving full-time education) have been entitled to an integrated 52 week programme of work experience (maximum 39 weeks) and off-the-job training (minimum 13 weeks) during which they are paid a wage. Essentially two main stated aims relate to the individual - that the scheme should act as a foundation for subsequent employment, training and education: and that it should equip them with a range of skills and experiences in relation not to a specific job but a group of occupations - while a further collective aim, about the creation of a more versatile and adaptable work force also exists.

Yet, with the potential to convert these into subsidiary aims, is that associated with the reality of the situation in many local authorities where without this measure (or something equivalent) over 90% of school-leavers would be unemployed. Although this figure ignores the effects on employers of a scheme such as YTS which, either because they perceive it reduces their obligations to provide school-leaver opportunities, or as they are participating in the scheme reduce the permanent employment they would otherwise offer, it still remains a situation which cannot be ignored on social, educational, humanitarian, training or whatever grounds. The dominant aim is, therefore, short-term - the minimization of the adverse effects of youth unemployment by whatever means. As a result the main practical problem (if long-term benefits are to be realized) relates to the attitudes that pursuit of this aim can sustain, and the need to isolate these from views more conducive to the fulfillment of the stated aims. How, for example, to convince participants that the exercise is the first part of a training programme which should extend throughout their working-life, rather than something to keep them of the streets: and how the skills, attitudes and learnings of this experience can provide a foundation for future activities?

Two subsequent questions demand consideration. The first involves the likely effectiveness of YTS in its own right. There are many potential advantages in some of the suggested practices. The utilization of the concept of occupational training families, in which individuals acquire a common core of skills which they then try to extend within a broad job category (Figure 2.2): and attempts to systematically integrate experience and formal training, are particularly attractive. However, previous MSC experiences with YOP (Youth Opportunities Programme an earlier, although less ambitious initiative to alleviate school-leaver unemployment) suggests caution. When the labour market was more buoyant many YOP graduates found permanent employment. As job opportunities reduced many had to return to unemployment register with the completion of their scheme: at best having extended their potential employability.[43] Not unexpectedly the quality of the individual experience proved to be uneven, but also a vital factor in the accretion of benefit. Undoubtedly, considerable variation in experience and benefit will be a feature of YTS, as many organizations (public, private and newly established for that purpose) take on the role of Managing Agent. Disparateness in both provision and standard being an outstanding characteristic of any programme which attempts such rapid expansion with potentially conflicting aims. There is always a risk that Agents will interpret their role in vocational preparation from a limited perspective, training young people for jobs which even if they exist have low expectation of continuing. Increasingly, in an environment of change, the task of vocational

FIGURE 2.2 Example of training families (possible progression over 1 or 2 years)

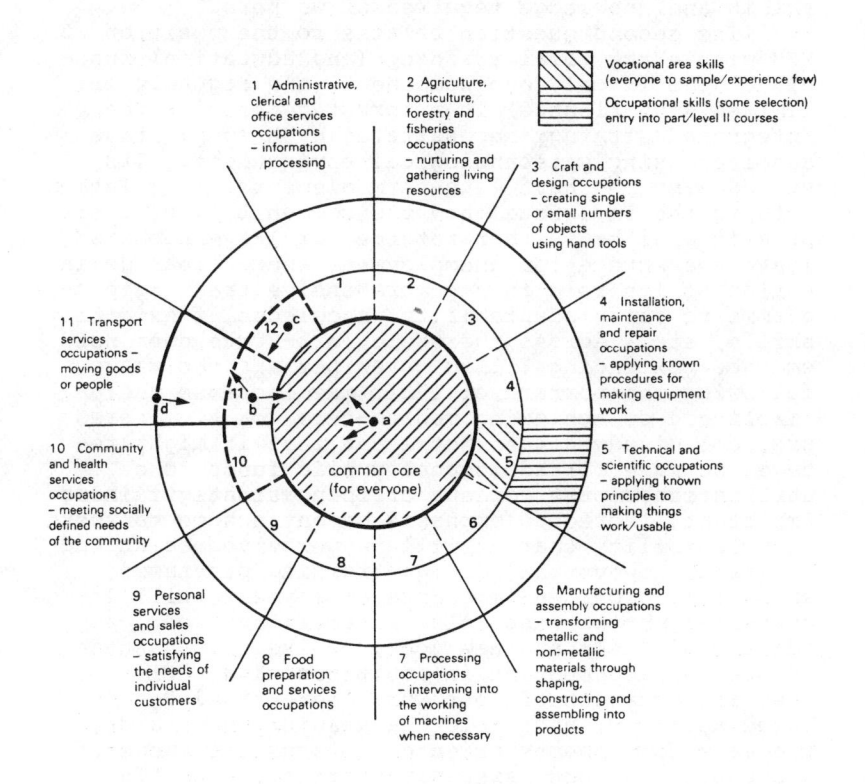

Diagram showing concentric circles divided into 11 occupational sectors around a "common core (for everyone)" centre. Legend indicates: Vocational area skills (everyone to sample/experience few); Occupational skills (some selection) entry into part/level II courses.

Sectors:
1. Administrative, clerical and office services occupations – information processing
2. Agriculture, horticulture, forestry and fisheries occupations – nurturing and gathering living resources
3. Craft and design occupations – creating single or small numbers of objects using hand tools
4. Installation, maintenance and repair occupations – applying known procedures for making equipment work
5. Technical and scientific occupations – applying known principles to making things work/usable
6. Manufacturing and assembly occupations – transforming metallic and non-metallic materials through shaping, constructing and assembling into products
7. Processing occupations – intervening into the working of machines when necessary
8. Food preparation and services occupations
9. Personal services and sales occupations – satisfying the needs of individual customers
10. Community and health services occupations – meeting socially defined needs of the community
11. Transport services occupations – moving goods or people

Illustrative points:

point a: a teaching/learning approach dealing initially with essential core skills;
point b: an approach based upon experience in practical situations;
point c: an approach based upon experience in another occupational area (e.g. because of change in local employment pattern);
point d: an approach based on significant expertise (e.g. considerable work experience).

Source: Further Education Curriculum Review and Development Unit, <u>Basic Skills</u>, (November 1982).

49

preparation becomes more difficult both because of the shortage of work and the uncertainty about skills and knowledge required of workers.

The second question relates to the position of YTS within the total training (and education) function. YTS is only one component (and arguably of limited significance) in a thrust to provide the integrated strategy necessitated by a competitive and increasingly technological environment. Its stated aims may have long-term elements, in relation both to the individual and the community, but their pursuit will be further retarded if large numbers leave the scheme for unemployment and a clear delineation of its role in a comprehensive training programme to raise adaptability, knowledge, flexibility skills, etc., across the whole work-force does not emerge. Extending YTS to cover perhaps two years, following the pattern of TVEI, may increase the likelihood of achieving medium-term goals. There are some disadvantages:not least that it might reduce the case for additional public funds to be used in other parts of any training strategy. More important, increased emphasis on any scheme raises the possibility that it will be perceived as an end in itself.However,an initial training programme, even if it provides immediate employment, will increasingly be of less value later in a career, as additional tasks and new jobs, evolve. It has to be seen as a component in adult training. Given the circumstances of less work, more knowledge-based activity, and rapid changes in job-demands, the case for schemes oriented towards the needs of all adults is more persuasive than that for YTS: although a cynic might add that only if unemployment rates among over-25s rose to the levels of those beneath (Table 2.4) would parity between initial and in-service training priorities be established. In fact the age-unemployment profile is highly significant. It shows clearly the level of under employment as employers recruit fewer new staff (to the obvious disadvantage of young people not already in post) and, with the numbers of 16 year olds not declining substantially to the late 1980s the size of the cadre of young, long-term unemployed which is being created.[44] With a relative boom they may be unable to find work, even with extensive training, as their lack of experience other than in training schemes, will make them unprepared for the demands of jobs provided by expansion. It could be argued that with less work a group who might never hold jobs is to be expected

TABLE 2.4

Number of unemployed by age-range and duration (in thousands)

Length of time unemployed	Up to 26 weeks	Under 25's Over 26 and less than 52 weeks	Over 52 weeks	Up to 26 weeks	25 - 54 Over 26 and less than 52 weeks	Over 52 weeks
(a) Totals						
1981	770	246	155	618	340	321
1982	761	257	279	561	316	567
1983	603	273	321	549	297	618
(b) As percentage of total in each category						
1981	50.0	35.8	24.7	40.1	49.4	51.2
1982	52.7	38.0	26.1	38.9	46.7	52.9
1983	46.7	41.9	29.1	43.4	45.6	56.1

Source: Figures for United Kingdom in July of each year: from Department of Employment, Employment Gazette, Vol. 91, No. 10 (October 1983), p.533.

in any circumstances. The potential divisiveness in such a situation is inestimable. More likely, many people will move in and out of regular work, providing an over-large reservoir of labour. The main issue, therefore, remains and is strengthened. The need is for a strategy to cover all workers and, more important still, those between jobs, for a country's ability to participate in sustained expansion in the 1990s (or whenever) is greatly reduced if it does not possess a training system capable of producing a work-force with a reservoir of talents and a flexibility of attitudes and a diversity of skills. Obviously many issues (both tactical and strategic) are raised relative to the arrangements that might satisfy this need - the co-ordination of the activities of employers, other providing agencies, and the enormous volume of training activity generated by individuals.[45] This last factor, in particular, cautions against the imposition of some rigid framework which tries to include all potential training situations. However, experience has already shown that to leave development to the chance of firms, individuals and some government sponsorship is highly unsatisfactory.[46] The methodologies for determining employer, employee and unemployed requirements in relation to local, regional and national dimensions have to be reassessed: as have the arrangements for the delivery of training packages, and the evaluation of changes in job-content, job-requirements, etc.

However, in focussing on any new training package in the UK context, the most important strategic issue of all is too easily overlooked - the formal separation of education and training. While the full potential of relationships between adult training and educational institutions is never easily realized because of lack of awareness of shared objectives, non-matching priorities, bureaucratically erected barriers, and indifference. Yet, whatever definition is selected, agreement exists that both education and training are concerned fundamentally with the same aim - the enhancement of student learning. The divide is more administrative (influencing attitudes) than pedagogical. It would, for example, be impossible to devise an adult training strategy without regarding as integral the potential contribution of further and higher education colleges. Many are directly involved in a range of activities from vocationally oriented degrees to specialist short courses for firms or professional associations: but, taking the last example, administratively and financially, it is invariably more attractive to concentrate on traditional award-bearing courses. For staff, as well, there are potential career and status disadvantages in spending too long on what must be regarded as peripheral work. In other words, there is an organizational inflexibility (exaggerated by local authority and government arrangements - Chapter 3) thrusting colleges towards what might be regarded as educational rather than training activities.

Similarly, as YTS is sited and staffed separately from the secondary schools its participants have left, some natural links will be less easily exploited. What happens in schools might still be regarded exclusively as education, with YTS viewed as a narrow training exercise: in other words, two different and non-related processes, when they should be no more than two components of one activity in pursuit of the same overall aims. In this case, on practical grounds, some aspects of the divisiveness can be defended. Many YTS entrants will have been low-attainers at school, some will have rejected it completely, and therefore a change of venue, staff, methods and attitudes offers certain attractions. Yet, such thinking reflects badly on both elements: secondary schools, as they have been unable to devise programmes which satisfy a large number of clients: YTS because, if it is perceived as a consolation prize, both its own effectiveness and its claim to be a foundation for later career training will be impaired. The obvious routes towards eliminating this divide of either making YTS an additional year at secondary school or extending YTS throughout the secondary age-range miss the main issue. It is the more general separateness of organization and attitudes between education and training which has to be overcome. More directly, in the context of less work, and demands increasingly made by technological change for additional skills and knowledge within the work-force, the aims of compulsory schooling require a new perspective. Not that they should attempt to predict future needs, but the provision of programmes which prepare individuals for the uncertainties of a world where work will be in short supply, and will demand of them a capability to respond to training and further education, must be the main priority.
d) It would be entirely inappropriate to consider the changing interaction of education and work,

without appreciating that technological progress which so influences the relationship can also powerfully influence educational processes. For years the dominant organizational parameter has been the class or cohort: a group studying the same topic, at more or less the same pace, in one venue, with overall teacher control. There are obvious disadvantages in this arrangement, centred around the individuality of human learning: but without alternatives it remains the most effective method of organizing education on a large scale. Increasingly however, with developments in computer and communication systems, alternative learning modes become available. Almost as important as the technology itself, are the changes in attitude which the availability promotes. It would be quite misleading however, to move on from these developments and depict a situation (not too far distant) in which every child or student has a personal computer terminal interacting with a mainframe machine storing all required programmes. The teacher would be redundant: replaced by programmer, electronics engineer and systems analyst. From a pedagogical standpoint in many activities that may eventually prove to be the most effective method of organizing individual human learning, but the orthodox teaching class and the tutor-student interaction serve many other purposes. For example motivationally, by enabling the tutor to encourage individual students often utilizing group norms: socially, by entitling students to group membership: educationally by facilitating peer-tutoring: and even custodially, by keeping students from less desirable activities.

Neverthelss, a technology is gradually emerging which eventually will enable most routine instructional activity to be performed by machine, particularly in topics with a dominant cognitive element. Progress is (and must) remain slow, because the instructional learning processes are so complex, involving a myriad of variables. Even when the technology proves adequate, this does not necessitate immediate usage in the class or lecture room. Implementation depends upon other variables-the availability of capital, attitudes of trade unions and individuals to the substitution of capital for labour, the role of staff in the pursuit of non-cognitive objectives and the establishment of new relationships between pedagogical and other objectives. Yet, long before these issues will need full-scale resolution lesser flexibilities offered by technological development can be exploited. To a limited extent this has been happening with the National Extension College and the Open University: significantly both concentrate on adult education. Because they deal with cohorts, schools and colleges must impose certain rigidities over timing and attendance. Courses are of pre-determined length (most conveniently coinciding with term-time) demanding specific attendances. Many potential students, unable to meet these requirements and resentful of other formalities characteristic of institutions, prefer to make their own learning arrangements when available.

What Open Tech (another initiative of TSD) has already shown is that alternative delivery systems, more efficient than conventional arrangements, largely because of their increased flexibility, can be sustained. One firm, for example, introducing open learning techniques has reduced the time requirement of one programme by 35% with minimal disturbance of other working practices.[47] The key element in such arrangements is to enable individuals to learn at a time, place and speed most suited to their needs. In an industrial situation this may happen in the factory (as above) but a training centre, college, library or home can be appropriate venues, dependant upon individual circumstances. Such flexibility introduces an additional dimension into potential learning patterns, and can be combined with systems based on discrete modules and the utilization of new technology to facilitate the availability of adaptable delivery systems. The intention being to sponsor a wide-range of activities from courses leading to qualifications through to short 'up-date' programmes. The initial aim relating to the education and training of adults at supervisory and technician levels being readily extendable to other individuals and groups whether in, or temporarily out, of the labour market. What is being sought includes a widening of access to current provision, while initiating and developing new provision, and simultaneously extending the use of computer assisted learning, individually focussed audio and visual materials, and programmed learning facilities alongside more conventional teaching arrangements. Quite clearly, traditionally organized activities, institutionally based, conventional teaching and instructional techniques, will not be able to generate the momentum, and promote the changes demanded by a technological environment.[48]

Education and the Economy

EDUCATION, TRAINING - INVESTMENT, CONSUMPTION

The theme of this chapter has been simple, if contentious. Educational expansion up till the early 1970s was permitted by economic growth which when not present, was thought imminently achievable. That permission relied both on an investment (education was a contributor to that growth) and a consumption element (individual benefits made more readily available). As this growth disappeared, along with future likelihoods of re-establishment, so did certainty about the educational contribution. Simultaneously, the competitive standing of education in resource allocation was eroded: a situation exacerbated by recession. Yet this deterioration in the position of education in relation to resource allocation relied on a false premise - that the inter-relationship between it and the economy could be set aside. In fact the effects of technological change on the labour market demonstrate that education and the economy are increasingly and inextricably linked. If the UK wishes to participate in world-wide growth, whenever this occurs, then a number of conditions have to be satisfied but one of these, undoubtedly, is the provision of a flexible work-force with the requisite skills and knowledge.

It is contentious for two main reasons. First, it places education more directly as a production function within the economy. Many will totally reject this view. They would argue that with less work the main thrust should be towards the needs of more leisure (and increased unemployment): while preparing individuals for jobs which do not exist (and may never do so) is immoral, as well as educationally unsound. This reasoning however, is flawed. It ignores the probability that a comprehensive and continuing system of adult training, although job-orientated, can offer experiences, transferable to the non-work situation. It also fails to learn from retrenchment experiences, in that a lobby for educational expenditure based on mainly consumption values carries little weight: those intentions are best achieved in a growing system demonstrating its investment priorities. Second, there is no attempt to distinguish between education and training: all activities are part of the learning process. However, this last statement is at variance with current developments. Although many TSD initiatives are perceived as solely training, they can still be viewed as a threat to the activities of schools and colleges. This occurs because an either-or mentality is easily stimulated, in which funds either come from TSD or along traditional LEA routes: with contraction, according to this view, accelerated growth of the former must necessarily induce an even greater retrenchment in the latter. This view is over-simplified: as Chapter 3 shows the processes of resource allocation to be more complex (and convoluted) than demanded by such a closed equation. One aspect of the threat, if it is to be viewed as such, arises from new activities in which schools and colleges might have expected to be dominant participants. YTS offers an additional year of education, but not in secondary schools: similarly, TVEI pilot schemes include a longer programme, but away from schools. Plausible explanations are available: for example, that central government can more effectively target expenditure with its own agency (MSC) rather than having to utilize the cumbersome mechanisms of local authorities, and, relatedly, how through bypassing LEAs, it can react more quickly to changing situations. However, a defence of increased separateness between education and training, whatever the organizational validity, is far less important than the potential disadvantages. MSC officials criticise the schooling system for providing an inadequate base for the satisfaction of their training responsibilities: conversely college staff accuse MSC (and an over-extended bureaucracy) of wishing to dominate, rather than co-ordinate, any new strategy for adult retraining. Some competitiveness between the institutions and MSC is potentially beneficial: particularly for longer standing institutions forced to reassess many basic assumptions. However, both parties constitute the publically provided education function: as such the need for shared objectives, methodologies, attitudes, personnel and organization should prevail. The real threat in the long run is to the total function, not the separate elements: it has to demonstrate its ability to respond to changing circumstances and, in some activities, create that change.

A main difficulty in interpreting public responses to the challenges of technological development are the ambivalencies, and occasional contradictions in government policy towards education and training. Understandably, the traditional education system with fewer clients, and some erosion of public confidence fared badly in resource distribution from the mid-1970s. Arguably, the main thrust of this policy was to reduce government expenditure and education presented some relatively easy targets. That certainly would explain why all sectors suffered cutbacks more or less equally, even though AFE up to the early 1980s might have anticipated more generous consideration on demographic grounds. However, if this explanation has validity why were some public sector activities (defence, law and order) favoured during a time of overall retrenchment? Possibly the activities of TSD provide an analogy of growth surrounded by contraction, and government commitment to promote the training function, but if that is so, why withdraw the framework and finance to encourage organizational activity by withdrawing many Industrial Training Boards. Most important of all though in these contradictions the different attitudes and procedures towards traditional education activities and the public initiatives in training require clarification. Their end-on, and overlapping, structural arrangements, and the fact that they are inter-supportive components of the same function, have to be established as clear policy before they become acceptable by the participants.

49

NOTES AND REFERENCES

1. W.F. Dennison, Education in Jeopardy, (Basil Blackwell,Oxford,1981), pp.6-22.
2. CMND 5174, Education:A Framework for Expansion, (1972), pp.48-49.
3. CMND 8789, The governments expenditure plans 1983-84 to 1985-86, (1983)
4. CMND 7439, The governments expenditure plans 1979-80 to 1982-83, (1979).
5. CMND 8789, (1983).
6. DES Report on Education, Pupils and school leavers: future numbers, (Number 97, May 1982).
7. The comments in the education presss at the time (Times Education Supplement and Education for example) are highly significant. Also see CMND 6869 Education in Schools: A consultative Document, (1977).
8. For example Times Education Supplement, 23.1.76, p.2.
9. C.B. Cox and R. Boyson, (eds.) Black Paper 1975: the first for education: (Dent, London, 1975)
10. D.E. Ashford, Policy and Politics in Britain: The Limits of Consensus,(Basil Blackwell, Oxford, 1981).

11. Bacie Journal, May/June 1983, p.81.
12. Bacie Journal, September/October 1983, p.147.
13. G.T. Allison, Essence of decision: explaining the Cuban missile crisis, (Little Brown, Boston, 1971).
14. M. Wright (ed.), Public spending decisions, (George Allen and Unwin, London, 1980).
15. R.E. Wagner, The Public Economy, (Markham Publishing, Chicago, 1973).
16. M. Wright (ed.), Public spending decisions.
17. Central Advisory Council for Education (England), Children and their primary schools: a report, (HMSO, London, 1967), and CMND 2154 Committee on Higher Education: Report (1963)
18. R. Bacon and W.A. Eltis, Britain's economic problems, (Macmillan, London, 1978, second edition).
19. Department of the Environment Circular 129/75 (DES Circular 15/75), Rate Support Grant Settlement 1976-77, (1975).
20. CMND 8789, (1963).
21. W.D. Hawley and D. Rodgers (eds.), Improving the Quality of Urban Management, (Sage Publications, London, 1974), p. 39.
22. D. Keeling, Management in Government, George Allen and Unwin, London, 1972), p.116.
23. The New Local Authorities: Management and Structure, (HMSO, London, 1972).
24. A. Norton and F. Wedgewood-Oppenheim, 'The Concept of Corporate Planning in English Local Government - Learning from its History', Local Government Studies Vol. 7, No. 5 (1981) pp.55-71.
25. Central Statistical Office, Social Trends, No.13 1983 Edition, (HMSO, London, 1982), pp. 11-22.
26. M. Blaug, An Introduction to the Economics of Education, (Penguin, Harmondsworth, 1972).
27. L.M. Carter and I.O. Roberts, Further Education Today, (Routledge and Kegan Paul, London, 1979).
28. P. Wiles, 'The Correlation Between Education and Earnings: The External-Test-Not-Content Hypothesis', Higher Education, Vol.3 (1974), pp. 43-58.
29. D. Bell, Coming of Post-Industrial Society: A Venture in Social Forecasting, (Basic Books, New York, 1976).
30. J. Botkin, D. Dimancescu and R.Stata, Global Stakes: The Future of High Technology in America, (Ballinger, Cambridge, Massachusetts, 1982).

31. D. Bell, Coming of Post-Industrial Society: A Venture in Social Forecasting.
32. J. Botkin et al., Global Stakes
33. Academic Enterprises, Industrial Innovation and the Development of High Technology Financing in the United States, (Brand Brothers, London, 1983).
34. M. J. Peck and A. Goto, 'Technology and Economic Growth: The Case of Japan', Research Policy, Vol.10 (1981).
35. M. Morishima, Why Has Japan Succeeded? Western Technology and the Japanese Ethos, (Cambridge University Press, Cambridge, 1982), pp.174-183.
36. CMND 7794, Committee of Inquiry into the Engineering Profession, (1980).
37. P.J.C. Perry, The Evolution of British Manpower Policy, (P.J.C. Perry, London, 1976).
38. R.W. West, 'Purpose and values in science education', School Science Review, Vol. 64, No. 228 (1983) pp. 407-417.
39. K. Drake, Financing Adult Education and Training, (Manchester Monographs, No.21, 1983).
40. MSC, Outlook on Training: Review of the Employment and Training Act, 1973.
41. MSC, A New Training Initiative: a consultative document, (1981).
42. MSC, Draft Corporate Plan 1983-87, (1982).
43. ee Education, 25.3.83 for report on public lecture by T. Blackstone.
44. MSC Labour Market Quarterly Report (Feb.1983) and MSC, Manpower Paper No. 5 (1982).
45. K. Drake, Financing Adult Education and Training.
46. MSC, Towards an Adult Training Strategy,(1983)
47. MSC, Open Tech. Programme News, No. 2 (1983)
48. Bacie Journal, Nov/Dec. 1982, pp. 325 & 327.
49. Employment and Training Act, 1981.

Chapter Three

DISTRIBUTING RESOURCES

FOUR TERRITORIES OF DECISION

Ask most teachers or lecturers how their institution acquires resources and the response will normally be vague. Most likely, something will be known about the respective duties of LEA (the employer) and DES: while the reliance on the rates for local revenue, and the need for government support through the RSG, will probably also be appreciated. If knowledge levels have risen in recent years - the lecturer in AFE aware of the 'pool' and capping arrangements, for example - it is probably more due to the impingement of adverse financial factors than an inherent desire for additional knowledge. In fact, the implicit assumption that staff ought to be better informed deserves clarification. It could be argued that if they have adequate resources to do their job effectively, irrespective of the mechanisms by which they are supplied, that is sufficient. Yet a statement like this raises a series of questions. What does adequate mean in the context of resources? How is job effectiveness, a resource issue in its own right, to be assessed and what are the influences upon it of other resources? As staff constitute the main resource, how many should be employed for adequacy? Most significant of all, what are the distributive mechanisms, according to which criteria do they function, what freedoms are available, who selects the criteria, what intentions are sought, who specifies them, and who monitors their achievement? Obtaining answers may not be easy but staff, wishing to extend their professionality, ought to want to know

The lack of knowledge is easily explained. The resource supply mechanisms to institutions are cumbersome, if not complex, and subject to frequent

61

modification. A detailed understanding would therefore take time to acquire, and need regular updating. This, however, assumes that the process of acquisition is straightforward. More so in recent years, the education press has taken an increasing interest in resource matters. A LEA to reduce its budget, a college likely to make staff redundant, and so on: but the main thrust is to highlight some particular aspect of resource allocation rather than provide deeper insights into the totality of the processes or the intentions of the participants. In contrast articles and books on educational finance are comparatively scarce, and face the continuing problem of keeping pace with changing events and procedures.[1] Similarly initial and in-service training courses, even those in educational management, have paid scant attention to finance and resources, except as a component in some studies of policy formulation. From a utilitarian perspective, of course, the argument about additional awareness among institutional managers lacks some credence. The hierarchy of decision-making, involving the Treasury, Department of Environment (DoE), DES, local authorities, LEAs through to school or college would continue and arrive at many unchanged outcomes, irrespective of what staff know about the relevant processes. According to this restricted view, the real challenge to education managers is the allocation, and subsequent monitoring in the use of resources in the school or college.

This view, however, is challengeable because of a dual restrictiveness. First, the issue of resource control by institutional managers requires qualification. They may be able to allocate resources (teachers to classes, scaled posts to teachers etc.) but only if what decided agrees with parameters imposed by the previous stages in the allocative hierarchy. Also the process of deciding can never rely on definite unchallengeable criteria. There can be no absolute certainty about a decision to award more resources to one faculty rather than another: such a choice may obey established rules but these in turn are contestable by those who perceive a legitimate right to be involved in resource decision-making. So the college principal might be criticized by a group of lecturers when the academic board determines faculty allowances using standard college procedures. Their intention of modifying the decision may be thwarted by the principal's use of positional power, but there is no objective and ultimate test of correctness on

Distributing Resources

which to rely. Second, as the lack of objective
criteria, and the related debate about constituency
membership to determine criteria, pervades all aspects of resource allocation, attention must be directed outside the institution. The perspective
needs to be much broader than the headteacher or the
college principal taking decisions affecting one
place. In the process of resources reaching schools,
colleges etc., decisions are made in many places
and subject to innumerable influences. The participants (both with specific responsibilities and
those less directly involved, such as the group of
lecturers mentioned before) meet and interact. The
teacher - headteacher- governor - education committee members, and education officer - committee
chairman - civil servant - minister, types of link
provide formal and informal communication networks.
In these circumstances arguments for more knowledge
among staff about the range of processes in which
they are participating, and greater awareness of the
influences on decision-making, become much more
sustainable.

The thrust, therefore, in this chapter is not
in search of some direct return, based on a naive
view that if staff know about resource allocation
this will advantage them, and benefit the whole of
the education service, in the competitive processes
of acquiring resources. Instead, the intention is
tc enable the establishment of a broad base of
knowledge through considering the key issues of
where decisions are made, by whom, using which
criteria and under what influences, in the flow of
resources to the delivery systems of schools and
colleges. A number of objectives emerge: to extend
influences within the choice processes, to facilitate a better informed debate, to increase the awareness of staff with direct decision-making responsibilities about the influences on them and the effects of what they decide: but most important of all,
to provide a framework for considering how resource
availability interacts with class - or lecture
room - activities. It may seem utterly banal to
state it as simply as this, but the purpose of resource allocative mechanisms is to sustain the
education processes of schools, colleges and elsewhere. It is easy to overlook the fact when discussing the complexities of the RSG or LEA arrangements for inter-school distribution of funds, but
these activities are entirely supportive not means
in themselves. It is the use of resources to pursue educational objectives which should dominate

Distributing Resources

the debate about educational finance, but discussion will be stunted, as well as the professionality of staff restricted, unless a grasp of the key issues in resource distribution exists.

To the first question of where decisions are made the answer is, literally, thousands of places, from the cabinet room through to innumerable faculty departmental offices etc. In categorizing these locations, four discrete territories can be described, although it would be an over-simplification to think of each as a single decision-centre.

1. Central government - Although government, through the DES, is only responsible for a small fraction of the actual expenditure on education (Chapter 1) its dominance of the RSG settlement with local authorities and their reliance upon it (and, increasingly, government dominance over authorities total financial situation) means that a centrally determined package of expenditure decisions constitute the natural starting point in studying the flow of resources.

2. Local authority - The fundamental requirement upon each authority is to acquire sufficient resources (from rates, grants and charges) in any year to at least fulfil its statutory duties. It can also, if it chooses, spend additionally in those activities where it has powers. The collection of decisions which are made involving a range of activities and services, one of which happens to be education, clearly represents a distinct territory.

3. LEA - For locally provided education services the previous two territories represent the acquisitive stage. The LEA allocates these total resources to the activities and processes which then constitute the local education service.

4. Institutional level - The final allocative stage occurs in schools, colleges and services (psychological, advisory, school playing fields etc.) with the distribution of resources to the sub-sectors of faculties, departments etc.

Essentially the territorial discreteness arises from location, with a set of decisions in central government (Treasury, DoE, DES): local authority (Policy and Resources Committee, main Council, political groups, chief officers meeting): LEA (education committee, sub-committees, officers meetings), and institutions. Looking at each territory separately is neither an attempt to reduce the significance of interactions between the stages nor an effort to ignore the overlaps that do occur. For example, when unavoidable decisions within a LEA resulting from statutory requirements, impinge upon the previous stage of distributions effecting the whole authority. Irrespective of these considerations, the main perspective consists of a flow of resources down a hierarchy, with one territory unable to make firm choices until a set of decisions has been handed on to it by the territory above.

CENTRAL GOVERNMENT

The fact that DES is only directly responsible for a small proportion of educational spending does not stop the Secretary of State from making specific projections for expenditure. In December 1981, for example, total spending of £12.2 bn. was forecast during 1982-83, with some detail of what this target figure might allow. Including, for example, a national PTR of 18.6:1, involving 13,000 fewer teachers, an estimated additional £20m. to restore book and equipment allowances to 1978-79 levels, in schools: an anticipated £840m. expenditure on NAFE, including a tightening in SSRs: all within a total budget 3½% higher, in cash terms, than that planned twelve months previously.[2] Yet, significantly, DES does not determine the number of teachers and lecturers to be employed, or the priority to be given to book and equipment purchases. These are local responsibilities, although increasingly exercised within the parameters of totals and targets centrally determined. Nevertheless, DES projects expenditures as part of the government's strategy to control public spending and as guidance to local authorities on how they might apportion their resources in pursuit of policy objectives. From a procedural perspective there are two interactive elements. The first, involves the actual projections, including situations unlike education, in which government itself has executive responsibility for spending: the second concerns the particular circumstances of local authorities, unable to raise sufficient of their own resources, and therefore reliant on a mix of central and their own resources for task performance.

During the last 25 years interest in expenditure forecasting by government has risen considerably. Up to the late 1950s, except for capital spending, discussion was limited to the year ahead, with the disadvantage of 'piecemeal' decisions, under-developed relationships to general policy issues, and inadequate attention to future commitments relative to prospective resources. The suggestion of the Plowden Committee that regular surveys of public expenditure covering a few years was attempted occasionally during the 1960s, but was regularised as an annual event in 1969.[3] At first these White Papers were published towards the end of the calendar year to cover the next four financial years: more recently they have appeared around 'Budget Day' (facilitating the links with the traditional twelve month expenditure specification) and concentrated on a shorter time span. In terms of a different orientation to the exercise these changes are important. Up to the mid-1970s it was no more than a planning activity reflecting the growth aspirations of the time with differential expansion rates nominated for each programme. That for education was invariably advantaged, even among other programmes anticipating expansion. By the mid-1970s, however, alterations were stimulated by the changing economic situation, the increased assertiveness of opinions critical towards public expenditure growth, and an increasing realization that the planning machinery as it had then evolved, was of minimal value in a control capacity.

By the time of the 1977 PESC White Paper, three important modifications had been made to the procedures for managing public expenditure.[4] The first involved a switch in orientation from planning to control. Previously, figures which represented definite expenditure commitments had not been separated from those that expressed little more than tentative intentions to spend. Now only those for one year ahead are viewed as firm decisions. However, new machinery was needed to monitor discrepancies between these decisions and actual spending. The second was to pay more attention to the financing of programmes, rather than the considerations in volume terms which, till then, had dominated. Before, a planned 4% rise in expenditure on teachers (say) implied a 4% increase in the number employed: the cash requirements in paying the salaries, dependant on relative price movements, received scant coverage. As a result, it was difficult to relate the planned volume of activity to 'out-turn' expenditures which ensued. The intention was simple, in that a more disciplined approach to spending would occur, for example, if a decision to spend £10m. on lecturer salaries displaced a commitment to employ 10,000 lecturers, irrespective of cost. By 1982-83 all planning in PESC White Papers used cash terms.[5] The third modification, a derivative of the second, was the increasing prominence of cash limits. Introduced in 1974, they soon covered over half public expenditures, including education, and had the most immediate impact of all the mid-1970s changes. The difficulties induced when working in volume terms by relative price movements have already been mentioned. Price changes over time, and across programmes, cannot be accurately foreseen, therefore inhibiting the accuracy of the planning process: much more though, they provide mechanisms which might reduce the potential inflationary effects of public spending.

With the specification for each programme of a cash limit to meet unforeseen price changes the purpose is to both force a review within the programme as circumstances alter and, by reducing expenditure relative to national income, lower aggregate demand in the economy (to which public expenditure contributes) and lessen inflationary pressures.[6] More directly, through using limits, government can pursue an objective of lower price rises by only buying goods and services when they are below certain levels. Possibly, these intentions might be more readily satisfied if inflationary levels are understated, reflecting aspirations rather than expectations. Also, with cash limits pitched low, they can act as an incentive to increased efficiency or, more controversially, be a subtle means of achieving a lower volume of activity. From a local authority perspective, the immediacy of the impact resulted from effects when nominated limits were not revealed until during the financial year. Some of the unstructured expenditure decisions described later in this Chapter produced lower spending on certain items, only because they were available for reduction. They were not the result of policy-related deliberations: the imposition of stringent cash limits made that impossible.

It was no coincidence that new procedures emerged in the mid-1970s. By then the ability of government to promote adequate economic growth to sustain an expanding public sector was becoming increasingly less evident. It was also a time of high inflation. With hindsight, of course, it is easy to suggest that new machinery to control public expenditure would have been more effectively developed during a period of expansion. Indeed, it could be argued that had such controls evolved then, some of the later difficulties would not have occurred.

Throughout this period, though, the fundamental problem arose from low-level economic performance. From the mid-1970s to 1979 the prevailing goal was, at worst, to hold increases in public spending at about the same level as those expected for the economy as a whole: with the election of a Conservative administration that year a new goal of maximum feasible contraction in aggregate expenditure became established, to support the view that an over-high level was itself a prime contributor to unsatisfactory economic performance. What the period since has demonstrated are the practical difficulties in achieving such an objective. It was made difficult by a continuing commitment to major increases in two areas (defence, and law and order and protective services) meaning a proportionately larger reduction among remaining programmes. Also a separation between 'planned' and 'unplannable' activities became obvious. In some programmes, Roads and Transport are a good example, government can specify expenditures and introduce detailed monitoring. There may have to be some small allowance for contingencies, but spending can be accurately projected and control exercised. In practice, underspend can often result. By contrast, in the unplannable sector, legislative provision or irrevocable commitments can produce high levels of unanticipated increase in spending, on the social security programme for example, following a rise in the number of unemployed, or on items such as debt repayments and loans to nationalized industries. On occasion unplanned overspend can more than counteract reductions achieved in other programmes: one effect was that in the years following 1979 government was less successful in staying within its planned aggregate expenditure than in preceding years.

In broad terms two areas of activity have fared disproportionately badly under both administrations. The first, capital expenditure was to be expected. When reductions have to be made it invariably presents the soft targets, and provides choices which will create least dissension. A decision not to proceed with a project rarely causes job loss among those in post, or produces additional deprivation. Of course the factors ignored in this context, when pursuing easy targets, are the long-term disadvantages being established by low levels of capital spending. The second area, involving local government spending, requires more careful consideration. There are obvious explanations.

Distributing Resources

Local government does not have direct responsibility for either of the main favoured programmes. Almost all local spending is contained in the planned sector, and a major spending area, education, has been subject to particular restraints because of demographic and other factors. Between 1978-79 and 1981-82, for example, while central government expenditure rose 7% in volume terms that by local authorities decreased 10%[7] However, the visibility of these explanations disguises a more substantial change in central-local financial relationships. If the only concern of government was the aggregate level of public expenditure then all it need do would be to set spending limits for outside bodies, such as local authorities, and allow them to determine their own priorities. The complexities and history of the situation do not allow such simplicity. Local authorities consist of several services: the more important being characterised by a particular relationship with a central government department, which in turn has its own views of policy and priorities. The nature of the DES-LEA relationship may be unique, but cannot be separated from the total central-local arrangement, so is subject both to government efforts to curb public expenditure by reducing local spending and DES views of what levels of activity should still be achieved. In global terms education spending has fallen markedly since the mid 1970s in real terms, and is projected to continue doing so:[8] more specifically, within this decreasing total, DES specifies, often surprisingly precisely, how, according to its priorities, allocations should occur. In 1982, for example, it was expected that spending in real terms during 1982-83 on primary and under-fives would be 7% lower than the previous year (a cash increase from £2,514m. to £2,563m. was forecast but without an inflationary allowance) assisted by a planned reduction in under-fives participation rates from 40.2% in 1980-81 to 33.2% in 1984-85. The equivalent spending projection for secondary schools was a rise from £3,318m. to £3,488m. in cash terms between 1981-82 and 1982-83: while an increase in 50,000 full-time 16-19 year olds in NAFE was envisaged, as well as the additional £20m. allowance for books and equipment already mentioned, extra to a 2% annual growth in those items already planned.[9]

The figures both in aggregate and detail are exact. A casual observer could easily be misled into thinking that an additional £20m. was to be spent on books and equipment to take one example:

that the sum had somehow been set aside, or that
there is some mechanism which guarantees changes in
participation rates at nursery or NAFE levels.
They would be wrong. What such figures require
(apart from no unforeseen circumstances) if they
are to be proven correct, is that all local authorities have a total expenditure, an allocation
pattern to services, and a LEA spending scheme, as
centrally projected. Of course, correctness may
occur by chance with misallocations and overspends
(according to plan) balancing underspends elsewhere,
but this only highlights the extent to which decisions are made locally. Those responsible will be
aware of the general tenor of central policy (particularly of the constraints imposable on aggregate
expenditure) and probably some of the detail, especially when used by groups to lobby for specific
items, but not of the detailed requirements demanded in their spending decisions, if the total expenditure distribution, and the inherent policy objectives, are to satisfy centrally determined criteria. However, an assumption that they would wish
to accept these priorities before their own goes to
the very nub of central-local relationships. For
with that acceptance, even if tacit, the case for
locally elected councillors, and the rationale of
local authority arrangements, loses much credibility.

The characteristics of the relationship are too
complex to dismiss either as a partnership (government and local authority working together as equals)
or a principal-agent, central control model (a
hierarchy with government handing down instructions,
rules etc. to local authorities).[10] The more useful
perspective is of a mix of dependencies and local
independencies. Local authorities exist and derive
their duties and powers from Statutes passed by
Parliament: often these confer on government ministers the duty of monitoring the exercise of local
authority powers. Education ministers, for example,
oversee LEA primary and secondary school provision
in some detail, with regard to facilities, teacher
qualifications etc.[11] In addition, through performing these tasks, local authorities must rely on
government for grants to cover about half their
spending. As the sums involved come from general
taxation, ministers remain accountable to parliament for their distribution and use. Taken together, these elements present a formidable dependancy, and a perception of local authorities implementing national policy, with some interpretation,

according to local needs, under the supervision of ministers and civil servants. Such a view, however, overlooks the independent stance local authorities are able to take because of their status as locally elected councils accountable not to the centre, or particular government departments, but to local electorates. The two main inter-related components of this accountability being, first, a knowledge of local needs, beyond that available centrally, and how best these might be satisfied: and, second, a responsibility for raising and spending the rates (an independent taxing power) in pursuit of these needs.

So far this discussion of local dependency has implicitly assumed a single centre and a typical local authority. In practice the relationship consists of a series of government departments communicating with appropriate local authority agencies (DES with LEA, DHSS with Social Services etc.). Each of these links has certain features. In the mid-1960s, for example, the DES was seen as the most promotional of government departments in relation to LEAs:[12] now it would be categorised as more interventionist. That, however, describes the general situation, but as secondary school re-organization has demonstrated, the alacrity with which individual LEAs accept DES policy leads and interventions, even when supported by legislative provision, varies enormously. More generally, numerous relationships and associations have evolved, covering the full range of authorities, services and government departments. The local authority assocation provide a unity when representing all authorities, for example in grant negotiations, and add a new dimension to the total relationship, but do little to hide inter-authority and inter-service differences in approach to central government. As a result of the uniqueness in the link between central and individual local departments, not to mention that involving local department within their own authority setting, it is more profitable to view the relationship as a web of interaction between ministers, civil servants, councillors and officers. Implicit in this network are a series of dependencies, without them the network would not exist, but the main characteristics of the relationship are consultation, negotiation and bargaining between separate organizations, each functioning in its own political environment. For every local authority is itself a political system with parties and factions representing various ideologies and pursuing certain

Distributing Resources

objectives, usually at variance, and sometimes clashing, with those nominated centrally. Conflict must, therefore, be added to the other characteristics.[13]

The extent to which that conflict is realizable has been clearly shown during retrenchment since the mid-1970s. Although there is a powerful element of interdependency, the reliance of local authorities on a central grant introduces a significant bias. Sufficient evidence has appeared over time to confirm that government would not change that situation. For example, the Royal Commission on Local Government (1969) considering structure and functions had finance excluded from its terms of reference,[14] even though a preceding White Paper (1966) on local government finance reported that there was no prospect of reform within existing arrangements, while the desirability of change was given by government as an additional reason for the Royal Commission.[15] More specifically, much of the interest in modifying financial arrangements has centred, in recent years, on supplementing local authorities solitary tax source - the rates. In this respect, British local authorities are exceptional by international standards, and while the Layfield Report (1976) suggested Local Income Tax (LIT) as the only feasible addition or alternative to rates,[16] progress towards offering local authorities a broader tax base lacks impetus. The idea of LIT is not new, but has always been opposed by central government, particularly if involving local autonomy in fixing tax levels.[17] In fact the impression, increasingly in recent years, has been of government reluctance to accept local freedom in determining rate poundages. Autonomy remains, but has in effect been gradually constrained by elimination of the right to raise a supplementary rate, the various penalty clauses (to be described later), and the probability of legislation to limit rate rises. The whole notion of rates as a form of taxation has, simultaneously, been criticized, because of unfairness in its imposition and impugned unpopularity. The idea that rates, on account of their lack of buoyancy (a slow rate of growth, unaffected by inflationary boosts, as compared to income tax or VAT) provide an unsatisfactory tax base, and the advantages of the rating system (local in character, cheap to administer) have received much less attention.[18] In the foreseeable future, therefore, a rating system modified so as to reduce local freedom - will continue exaggerating central resistance to any measures which might reduce local authority financial dependence. By giving local authorities statutory responsibilities without the complementary financial infrastructure, government implies that local authority reliance on grants for a main share of resources is a desirable and necessary component in consulation, negotiation, bargaining and conflict.

Although central grants to local authorities have a long history, it was with the introduction of RSG in 1967 that much of the detail in the current arrangements emerged. A block grant (a sum paid to each authority which then determines its distribution) supplemented by specific allowances (grants paid for nominated activities) it contains two main equalization elements, as well as a domestic rate relief component to reduce the rate-bills of local residents. The intention with the resource equalization element is to reach a situation in which each local authority can raise the same revenue with identical rate-poundages. For example, a 1p. rate in Sutton would raise £297,000, while a similar rate in South Tyneside, with a similar population, would only raise £154,700.[19] In other words, to achieve the same revenue South Tyneside would have to impose a rate in the pound almost double that of Sutton. Needs equalization, in contrast, attempts to eliminate the differences which arise because expenditure requirements across authorities are not consistent. The necessary fiscal equity happens when each local authority spends the same proportion of resources on a service to achieve equal levels of performance: in practice assessed relative to input costs. In simple terms, an authority with a high proportion of children will need to spend highly per capita on education. From 1967/68 to 1980/81, therefore, RSG included three separate elements. Domestic (constituting around 9% of total grant): resources (about 30%), with grant paid to each authority which fell below a 'standard' rateable value per head set by government, although without a compensatory attempt to reduce those authorities above to this average level: and needs (approximately 60%) in which the grant payable to each authority every year was the result of complex calculations based on local parameters, with the particular choice of variables being determined annually by government, based after 1974/75 mainly on past levels of expenditure.

A number of factors explain the modification to RSG introduced in 1981/82, following the Local

Distributing Resources

Government, Planning and Land Act, 1980. The calculation of the needs element, in particular, was becoming increasingly complex and readily subject to political whim. Up to 1974 the detail of the calculation was specified in regulations, but the Local Government Act (1974) gave the Secretary of State for the Environment much more flexibility in nominating variables and determining the allocation. Therefore, on an annual basis, adjustments could be made to favour inner cities, rural areas, or London authorities, depending upon the current priorities of the government. However, the main defect, as perceived by the Conservative administration of 1979 was that the method of implementing RSG frustrated their attempts to control public expenditure. In particular, the needs element, by concentrating on previous expenditures as a determinant of need, favoured high spending authorities and offered few inducements to lower expenditure. The new RSG that emerged consisted of two elements. Domestic rate relief grant replaced the domestic element but was otherwise unchanged: while a new block grant, directed towards the simultaneous pursuit of resource and need equalization was substituted for the separate resources and needs element.

As might be expected, the two main components of the grant still reflect need and resource considerations. An assessment of the Grant Related Expenditure (GRE) of each authority has first to be made.[20] Equivalent to the needs element, the intention is that by estimating the expenditure requirements of an authority, dependant upon its characteristics (population, number of children requiring education, recreational facilities, miles of road etc.) weighted by an evaluation of the unit cost of each service it provides, rate poundages can be equalized across authorities for the same standard of provision. More directly, GREs are supposed to supply an objective assessment of what authorities ought to spend on each service. It cannot, though, be a simple calculation, because of the numerous variables involved, and any claim that the mechanism for calculating GRE is more comprehensible than that for needs elements remains unproven. In fact, GRE now includes a much higher number of factors, as a result of having to assess the size of the client group, and the unit cost of each group, while simultaneously making allowance for particular features in a local area (the number of non-white children, say) which influence expenditure. In education for example, actual size of group (number of children or students) is used in nursery education and NAFE: but for schools an additional factor appears to allow for the age-distribution of pupils. In this respect education seems comparatively straightforward because the client group is relatively well defined. In social services or planning that is not the case: more obviously with parks, for example, the need to spend depends upon levels of provision previously determined, and for all of these services past expenditures enter the calculation. However, once the size of the client-group or its equivalent has been determined, its product, and the cost of supplying one unit, represents the GRE for that service. The outcomes of a GRE for each service (including education) aggregates to give a GRE for the authority. When the new arrangements were introduced, opposition to the notion of publishing service GREs emerged, mainly because the resultant grant was not sub-divided. Significantly, DES led the way to the publication of education GREs with figures for each service in all authorities readily available, although they do not appear until after rates have been fixed so as to minimise their potential influence on decision-making. [21]

In terms of one of its objectives, the elimination of rewards to high spending authorities, GRE offers more potential than the needs element. By concentrating upon the size of the client group, and the costs of supplying each service in relation to a direct payment to each providing authority, government has clarified the link between grant acquisition and service provision while minimising the financial incentive to retain high expenditure. In fact, authorities which reduce spending on some discretionary services can be relatively advantaged by the calculation. With those modifications, however, the criticisms of complexity and influences of political whim levelled at the needs element remain. The rationale may be clearer but, intentionally, by adding so many additional factors to the calculation understanding has not been assisted. In addition, by adjusting variables and dominating the whole process of calculation, government retains control and is enabled to pursue its political objectives. Indeed, that was a powerful motivation when initiating the change. Perhaps this is most clearly demonstrated with discretionary services. Authorities have both statutory duties and discretionary powers but in the latter, for example with

Distributing Resources

social services, a number of authorities (particularly those Labour controlled in metropolitan areas) have established a high level of commitment. GRE calculations, however, because they tend to use average costs, and on occasion overlook the actual number of clients receiving services, penalise those authorities. Yet, some authorities have built up what they would regard as irrevocable commitments, such as social workers in employment, as well as heightened aspiration levels among recipients. When potential client numbers (possibly the whole population) replace actuals the benefits of this GRE component effectively transfer from authorities which offer services widely to those with few actual participants. In the limit, an authority can be credited with a GRE for a discretionary service it does not offer. Although, in expenditure terms, education organizes comparatively few discretionary activities, and would appear exempt from such effects, as the grant to each authority deriving from GRE is general, any deficiency, even arising from non-educational factors, can still have considerable implications for resource availability.

More fundamentally, however, GRE introduces an additional dimension into central-local grants. For the first time some form of itemisation of what ought to be spent, authority by authority, service by service, is made. Of course, an authority does not have to comply with the specified figures, but their existence is potentially significant at both levels. Centrally, they provide a framework for much tighter control, if required: locally, they can be used as nominated national norms by particular groups in the authority to argue for preferred spending patterns. However, GRE is only one element in the calculation of grant and its combination with the second main component, Grant Related Poundage (GRP) must now be considered. As for the 'standard' rateable value per head of the resources element, the main intention involves equalization necessitated by the different tax bases of authorities: but on this occasion, by using GRP in conjunction with GRE, the aim is to satisfy both resource and needs requirements simultaneously. The initial step involves the calculation of a GRP for all authorities (134.42p. in the £ for 1981-82, 151.34p. in 1982-83). That is, were the country considered as a single authority, this figure would represent the rate levy to cover expenditure equal to GRE not met by the block grant. The national GRP has then to be disaggregated, in terms of the range of services an

Distributing Resources

authority has to provide, by use of an average GRE for different groups of authorities (metropolitan districts, non-metropolitan counties etc.) The outcome is a percentage allowance for each authority in the same area. In non-metropolitan areas, for example, during 1982/83, county level took 86.6% of GRP and district the remaining 13.4%: giving respective GRPs of 130.99p. in the £ and 20.35p. GRP and rateable value per head are then combined and deducted from GRE, in the equation which determines the size of the block grant payable to each local authority.

Block grant received = GRE - (GRPx rateable value per head)

In other words the higher the per capita rateable value (that is wealthy authorities) the more the grant received is below GRE

By telescoping needs and resource elements into one grant a full equalization of tax bases for all authorities is made possible. This did not occur previously as authorities with low tax-bases were only raised to a standard level, for to offer all authorities a base equal to that of the wealthiest authority would have proved too costly. Also, unless all authorities had been similarly placed to those with the lowest required expenditure per head, a complete needs equalization would have been impossible. In effect, with the new grant, tax rich authorities (high r.v. per head) with low expenditure needs (small GRE) are effectively penalised to the advantage of poor authorities with high spending requirements. Politically, this part of the change was acceptable because the great majority of authorities continued to receive some grant, while government had achieved inter-authority equalization at a relatively low level of grant. However, most appealing of all to a Conservative administration determined to reduce public expenditure by devising arrangements in which a standard rate levy across all authorities should lead to a uniform level of provision (in theory at least) a route towards increased central control over total spending had been arranged. This possibility was already foreseen with the inclusion in the 1980 Act of 'thresholds' and 'tapering multipliers'. The idea, basically, is to penalise those authorities which overspend in relation to their GRE. When expenditure goes above a threshold (for 1981/82 and 1982/2 10% above the GRE for the authority) a tapering

Distributing Resources

multiplier is introduced so that an increased proportion of the spending above the threshold has to be met by local ratepayers (a 25% rise in rate poundages to support excess expenditures was used during these years). In terms of the equation for calculating block grant, the GRP for an authority becomes dependant upon deviation of actual spending from GRE.

These developments proved inadequate, as far as government was concerned, in limiting increases in local spending. Apart from the difficulties it encountered with high expenditure authorities, more general problems arose from the transition to the new block grant, particularly the assessment of GRE associated with discretionary services. Owing to under-development of these activities some authorities were actually encouraged to increase expenditure and this, combined with the normal tendency to over-budget, produced anticipated spending nearly 6% above GRE. To some extent because of these factors even though they were probably transitional, government still found it necessary to introduce more long-term measures to further restrict what it would assess as overspending. As well as the elimination of local authority power to levy a supplementary rate (Local Government Finance Act, 1982) an additional threshold based on volume assessments was introduced during 1981-82, affecting those authorities which were more than 5.6% above their 1978-79 figures. By 1982-83 the volume and GRE thresholds were combined so that not only were overspending authorities subject to tapering of block grant, but they could actually lose part of their grant through abatement. When this notion was first introduced during 1981-82 government concern was directed towards a small number of authorities (invariably Labour controlled) who despite exceeding thresholds, and being subject to tapering, refused to lower planned expenditures to levels closer to GRE or volume targets. When threatened with abatement (or holdback) of some block grant most agreed to lower anticipated spending, but despite this government still introduced, for 1981/83 and later years, a complex system of target expenditure for each authority largely based on spending in the previous year.[22] Spending above the target allows government to abate grant by means of a penalty. With these developments the whole basis of the relationship is changed. Through determining targets, and the other items of thresholds, multipliers, GRE and GRP, as well as nominating the factors which in-

78

fluence their determination (such as predictions about the effects of price changes) government has not only introduced a new grant system, but also sponsored a major increase in central control over local decision-making.

Undoubtedly, any transition from needs and resource elements to a block grant would have introduced uncertainty for authorities. Had it occurred at a more favourable time economically, there would still have been need for 'safety nets' to protect some authorities from individually disadvantageous aspects of changeover: that is losing substantial grant through the different base for calculation. However, the pursuit by government of its own objectives of reduced local spending have introduced complexity far in excess of anything experienced with the original system. More confusing still, further modifications and details often emerged as government itself discovered by experience the intricacies of the arrangements it was initiating. Familiarity with the new arrangements will eliminate some uncertainty, but as the final assessment of actual expenditures, and their effects on tapering multipliers and penalties etc. will have to take place some time after the year in question, it seems that the processes of local resource management and planning will be hindered by a considerable time-lag before the exact total grant is known. It might be argued that some measure of uncertainty is intentional to assist a government imposing its own view of preferred spending. On this basis local authorities are more likely to comply with GRE figures, or not exceed thresholds, when not fully aware of the precise effects of doing otherwise. Yet within this framework of increasing centrality procedures for consultation remain largely undisturbed, particularly before the start of the year. The impression to an external observer can still be of two equal partners (local authority associations and government) considering spending requirements and tax.

Actual discussion for each year, involving authority officers and civil servants, begin up to twelve months before its start. A framework exists with PESC expenditure projections (which are not yet firm for the year in question) and the foci are both the expenditure plans of local authorities, and the arrangements for grant distribution. Negotiations about the actual grant system occur in the Grants Working Group, while expenditure groups (including one covering education) consider actual and

Distributing Resources

projected spending in each of the main service areas. Outcomes from the groups are used by an 'Officers Steering Group' feeding into the Consultative Council on Local Government Finance, a mix of politicians and officials - both central and local, representing all major interests and chaired by the Secretary of State for the Environment. To an outsider, therefore, it is easy to create an image of continuing negotiation and bargaining, even following the changes, with the same three pieces of main information emerging a few months before the start of the year: an estimate of relevant expenditure in the coming twelve months (£21.76 bn. for 1982-83), the proportion of this total to be met by a central government grant (57.1% in that year), and the actual distribution of the grant to individual local authorities.[23] Not all of the total sum transferred from central to local authorities (12.43 bn. in that year) is distributed as block grant: first specific grants, most prominently to urban aid and the police (nearly £1.7 bn. in 1982-83) and supplementary grants to transport and national parks (nearly £0.5 bn): and second, almost £0.7bn. to achieve the 18.5p. in the £ relief for domestic ratepayers, have to be subtracted. The remaining money (£8.7 bn. for 1982-83)is then allocated through the block grant mechanisms, although clearly, some authorities will receive more and others less than 57.1% of their relevant expenditure, depending upon individual circumstances.

Up to 1981-82 central efforts to reduce the aggregate level of local spending had two inter-supportive components. First, by dominating the negotiations with local authorities (both on account of the resource dependencies which the discussions were intended to satisfy, and the possession of a more sophisticated information base) government views about aggregate expenditure, and the percentage it would support, provided the framework within which local decision-making had to take place. In minimising increases in exchequer grant, for example, it forced many local authorities into simultaneously reducing services and increasing rate poundages: in effect it raised the visibility (and unpopularity) of their accountability to the local electorate. The most effective mechanism of achieving this minimisation was by lowering the percentage of total relevant expenditure government was willing to support from 66% in 1975-76, to 57.2% in 1982-83, and then to 52% in 1984-85. Second, government could try and persuade, or perhaps cajole, local government as a whole, and individual authorities, to restrain spending within centrally determined guidelines. However, to that time spending both in total and relative to priorities (provided all statutory objections were met) was solely a matter for local autonomy. In fact, given this dual approach, government efforts to restrict local authority expenditure had been remarkably successful, certainly in relation to government efforts to restrict its own spending. Between 1975 and 1981, for example, local government expenditure as a proportion of GNP fell from 16% to 14%, and as a proportion of total public expenditure from 32% to 28%: for central government the equivalent figures were increases from 33% to 35% and 68% to 72%.[24] Were the main component of unplannable central spending ignored, that associated with unemployment and social security payments, government was still less effective in containing its own expenditure than local authorities.

It is within a framework of increasing constraints since the mid-1970s that efforts from 1981-82 onwards to further reduce and control local authority expenditure must be judged. According to some central government perspectives, no reason exists why local spending should not be planned and controlled in detail and to effect both to restrain aggregate expenditure and facilitate the pursuit of policy objectives, but this will happen far more readily if most decisions are made centrally rather than within 400 or so local political systems. Extending this view, arrangements involving low level control through resource dependency, coupled with persuasion, proved inadequate not so much relative to an intention of lowering local authority spending, but more as a mechanism to contest with those authorities who either decided it was impossible to keep, or were determined to ignore, guidelines. Clearly, the introduction of the block grant encompassed a number of government objectives: an ability to be more specific in circumventing the expenditure plans of some authorities was one, but so were more effective control over aggregate expenditure, greater emphasis on centrally determined policy objectives, and the development of a fairer system of distributing grant. Naturally with retrenchment, and in a political environment, the emphasis in any consideration of the efficacy of the new system has been on the adverse effects of less grant, and the conflicts between government and a few authorities to which it is opposed politically. More generally

it seems improbable that, with hindsight, local
authorities would have accepted the Local Government
Planning and Land Act with so little concerted resistance.[25] Yet, following all the modifications
the situation still continues for the time being at
least, that a local authority is accountable to its
electorate for the total level of spending and the
decisions about priorities among its services.
Thresholds, tapering multipliers, targets and grant
abatements have not altered that fact, although they
make it certain, that spending well in excess of
target will force authorities to impose intolerable
rate-poundages. Some authorities may try to retain
previous freedoms by raising rate-levels, or even
continuing to spend when they have no balances, but
government will always retain ascendancy because
of the nature of the dependency and its ability to
introduce new legislation. In this case by limiting
the right of authorities to increase rate-pound
ages.[26] The risk of course, from a government perspective (on the assumption that it wishes local
authorities to continue) is that eventually the
notion of local autonomy will be reduced to a meaningless level. It has always been circumscribed and
its continued erosion must produce circumstances in
which those elected (and eventually the electorate)
will percieve that no choices remain open to them.
Undoubtedly, that would mean a major constitutional
change with no further place for local government,
as duties could be performed by central officials
working locally. In the case of education a
'national service locally administered', the government has views and policies, but has made little
attempt to translate these directly into financial
decisions in such a way as to affect the detail of
activities. Changes in the grant mechanism, and the
abolition of rate-raising autonomy could alter that
situation. If this were to result in few opportunities for the determination of local needs and limited decision-making about optimum means for their
satisfaction, the logical outcome would be a national service nationally administered.

LOCAL AUTHORITY

With a national service the second and third
territories in the hierarchy of resource flow would
be redundant. Obviously, there would be no need for
a local authority to allocate resources to its education service, as LEAs in their current form could
no longer exist. However, there is an interim

position, that has received publicity in recent years, involving a block grant to education, which would still continue in local control but separate (in financing arrangements) from other local authority services. In other words the second territory would cease to be local, replaced by a national approach, although the third area, involving LEA allocations to schools, colleges etc., would continue largely as before. While the introduction of a block grant to cover all educational spending seems improbable, arguments about it, and the fact that a powerful lobby could be mounted in its favour, are highly relevant to a consideration of the procedures by which local authorities distribute resources to their services.

A number of reasons can be mobilised to support a view that education is atypical among other local authority services. The idea of a national service is probably more significant, and has extra substance than for other local activities. To a teacher or lecturer, for example, the employing institution is of greater importance than the employer, because of the idiosyncracies of the former, and items such as national salary scales inter-institutional mobility and similarities in conditions of service reducing the influence of the latter. A teacher discovers more differences in changing school than changing authority. The LEA relationship with the DES, particularly its promotionality and versatility, as well as the guidelines and regulations issued by the centre, all confirm the notion of a service with national rather than local parameters. By international standards, also, there appears no special merit in having a locally organized education function. Advantages and disadvantages can be quoted for state, local, federal or regional arrangements. Education is insufficiently specifically local in character (as compared to road repairs or refuse collection) to argue powerfully against national arrangements. While this may strengthen the atypicality of education in a local context, the factor which above all others confirms it is the scale of activities and, as a result, the resources required. If situations in which an authority makes a direct charge for a service are omitted (these occur rarely in education) most authorities spend, on education, over 50% of total revenue (Table 3.1)

Distributing Resources

TABLE 3.1 Expenditure profile of authorities

(a) Aggregate expenditure (all authorities). (thousand £)

| Education[+] Gross | 10 10,724 | Net | 9,931 | } 50.25% |
| All services Gross | 26,216 | Net | 18,601* | |

(b) Aggregate expenditure (metropolitan districts only)

Education[+] 2,534 } 62.2%
Net expenditure all rate fund services 4,075*

(c) Aggregate expenditure (non-metropolitan counties only)

Education[+] 5,648 } 62.1%
Net expenditure all rate fund services 9,089*

* Including central government specific grants.

\+ Except meals and milk

Both metropolitan district councils and non-metropolitan county councils are LEAs.

Source: Department of the Environment; <u>Local Government Financial Statistics 1981-82</u>, (HMSO, London, 1983).

In other words the summation of the GREs for all other services is less than that for education. On this basis alone, if the gap between what authorities have to spend and the revenue acquirable through their own tax base becomes too large, with the effect of either raising the percentage of resources supplied by government or levels of rate-poundage, an obvious solution might be to transfer educational expenditure from local to central authorities. Were education nationally financed, for example, many authorities would not require 'needs' support, some could lower rate levies even without a central grant, and emphasis in the block grant would switch to resources equalization.

The argument for an education block grant, therefore, begins with the discrepancy between tasks to be performed and tax-base exacerbated by the adverse climate in which local authorities work. It continues by looking at some effects of reducing education expenditure (the reduction in option choices in some schools, the non-availability of certain facilities) and the increasing disparity, among LEAs, in level of provision, as noted by HMI (Chapter 7).[27] It is particularly concerned with the ability of local authorities to raise adequate

84

Distributing Resources

revenue through the rates or, more precisely, the
unpopularity that can arise through high rate-poundages, exaggerated by the effects of penalties. In
some respects such an argument constitutes a lobby:
reasoning that a separate block grant could provide
a mechanism for acquiring more educational resources. Essentially it is critical of two aspects of
current procedures: first, the dependance of local
authorities on central resources and, second, the
detail of block grant distribution: for clearly
some aspect of equalization must be flawed if inter-
authority disparities in provision are, in fact,
widening. Implicitly, however (and this is the type
of issue which specific lobbies tend to ignore) a
case for more educational spending, within existing
structures, must mean either an increase in total
expenditure or less spending by other services.
Yet, within an environment where the outstanding
characteristic is the thrust to less spending, and
the inter-service rivalries this induces, neither
outcome appears particularly likely.

The actual detail of any new block grant (for
example as suggested by the Society of Education
Officers) is also significant.[28] There are a number of potential variations but the main theme is
to increase the percentage contribution from central government to above the current 57% of RSG,
but only for education. Were the figure 75% then
that proportion of total educational GRE would be
centrally financed (ranging from 60% to 85% for
individual LEAs). Additionally, if compensatory
decreases in percentage grants to other services
did not occur a major change in burden from ratepayer to taxpayer would follow. In other words,
higher taxes but allowing local authorities to
offer the same level of provision at a lower rate
poundage. There are certain attractions in such
a move, even to central politicians, because of
the apparent unpopularity of rates as a form of
taxation, but before it could sanction a change of
this nature, government would require some certainty
of lower rate calls by agreement or through using
penalties. It is difficult to envisage a government intent on restricting public expenditure permitting a transition which could potentially boost
spending, with higher taxes and unchanged rate
bills. Recent experiences in central-local relationships suggest that even if most authorities did
obey demands for rate reductions in such circumstances, a few would defy in an attempt to create a
conflict situation. Far more likely therefore, if

the idea of an education block grant is to receive more favourable attention, would be 75% support, say for education, 25% for other services (a level which would allow inter-authority equalization) with no change in total rate calls or exchequer support, and arrangements for multipliers, targets and thresholds, to avoid individual overspending.

Such an arrangement would raise a number of technical, but practically important, issues: about the separate assessment of GRP for education and other services, the relationship between thresholds and tapering multipliers in the two areas (whether overspending in education should be more heavily penalised than that elsewhere, for example) and the possibility of compensating for overspend relative to GRE between the two sectors. However, from an educational perspective the most probable outcome of increased central finance would be both a definition of GRE for each LEA, and measures to ensure that actual spending coincides with this figure. It is easy to see why such an arrangement could appeal to DES. While still having to work within PESC projections and cash limits, it would be possible to specify the total expenditure for every LEA through minimising overspending (to appease the Treasury) and eliminating underspending among those authorities either reluctant to support their LEA or unwilling to achieve their GRE figures. In fact detailed analysis of actual spending in comparison to assessment of GREs shows a small number of authorities well in excess, but also several spending below the levels that might be anticipated. A standardisation of provision, nationally, might be possible, because a block grant with refinements can be turned into a sophisticated mechanism for achieving approved total expenditures. It would be misleading to imply that such a situation would necessarily yield overall expenditure that DES might wish, because of general public expenditure constraints, but it would perceive itself more in control of total spending and able to deal with inter-authority provision disparaties. From a LEA perspective such a block grant might be attractive, at least by lessening the need to compete within the local authority for resources, but much would depend upon the determination of educational GRE, particularly in relation to previous spending. If a LEA, under new arrangements, has no real alternative but to reduce spending to GRE, when previously a higher level of expenditure was effectively subsidised by spending below GRE in other services or high rate poundages, it would be disadvantaged: certainly relative to another LEA which must raise expenditure to GRE, possibly at the expense of activities elsewhere in the authority.

However, in broader terms, a block grant presents a potential dilemma to LEAs. The differences in provision which are to be ameliorated, result to a certain extent, and sometimes totally, from local autonomy. If an authority chooses to give less priority to its LEA, or a LEA thinks it can use its teaching staff more effectively by raising PTR, provided in both cases that statutory requirements can be satisfied, these are matters, which until present, have been locally determined. The DES can try to persuade the authority otherwise but without disturbing the main route of accountability to the local electorate. The process of achieving direct change through the ballot box may be very slow, but that alongside the micropolitics of lobbying, pressure-groups etc. remains the basis of local democracy. Therefore, if disparaties arise, they are the result of local preferences. Now, it can be argued that this is a gross over-simplification: that many authorities, particularly during retrenchment, cannot support the level of services they would choose even with grant equalization mechanisms, unless forced to impose unacceptable rate-poundages. In other words, the underspending which concerns DES is as much the result of a defective system of funding local authorities as the exercise of local preferences. Yet, if this case is followed through as a practical defence of continued local autonomy, it must be supported by the possibility of corrective outcomes. The steady refusal of the centre to consider widening local authority tax bases (in, for example, alternatives to the Domestic Rating System[29]) linked to adverse government opinions about local authority spending, in general, make these extremely unlikely. The issue must remain that as some part of spending differences emanate from local choices, a reduction in their availability will limit autonomy, while eliminating many local developments and initiatives often resulting from expenditure above GRE.

If, however, DES is also concerned about effective resource usage with a block grant system, as it would be, total expenditure by each LEA becomes less significant than its distribution and utilization. As experiences since 1981-82 have demonstrated, a block grant can become highly directional. There is no reason why, within a specified total expenditure, there should not be pre-determined priorities as between the main sectors of education (primary, secondary, special etc.), for compulsory as opposed to non-compulsory schooling, or schools as compared to NAFE, and among support services (school psychological, careers and so on). The grant could also define the boundaries of educational expenditure relative to recreation and leisure, for example, or youth training, while including spending specificity on (say) in-service training. The key items then become the control of goal definition, the allocation of resources, and the monitoring of their use. If block grant arrangements did pertain it would be surprising if such activities occurred locally. First, because of the high proportion of the grant which would have to be supplied by government, inducing demands for central control. Second, the inherent inflexibilities affecting allocative decision-making in education mean that comparatively minor restrictions usually produce major reductions in local freedoms. In such circumstances a LEA might be able to maintain a facade of local autonomy, but if total expenditure is in effect, determined nationally, as well as the main priorities, all that remains are a series of minor financial decisions. Additionally, from a management perspective, a separation of financial from other decision-making (personnel, staff duties and responsibilities, buildings etc.) has nothing to recommend it. In other words it is difficult to view a block grant arrangement as anything other than interim to a national system, nationally administered. Ironically, some impetus towards separate financial structures for education resulted from increasing central controls over local authorities in general, yet a block grant seems more likely to accelerate a reduction in autonomy rather than safeguard local freedom in educational decision making.

The fact that introduction of a block grant seems unlikely is less significant than attitudes about education within local government which arguments about it displayed. [30] A change in legislation to permit a small measure of specific educational grants, assisted by central-local allowances to facilitate accomplishment of a few DES policy objectives seems probable, but with the main components of the financial arrangements undisturbed. [31] What many supporters of a block grant appear to want is a financial disturbance but with all other factors continuing unchanged. However, they fail to appreciate the integrative nature of financial and other arrangements within the local authority setting. It would be impossible to change education's relationship with government, for example, were finance involved, without radically altering its position and interactions within that setting. The case for a block grant exaggerated the uneasy placement of education in local government, more so since the introduction of corporate management followed rapidly by contraction. For education, the introduction of block grant would represent a return to the organizational structures which existed up to the late 1960s. Until then, local government had evolved as a collection of separate services, brought together under a single authority largely as a matter of convenience. This separateness was maintained through a system of quasi-sovereign committees (one for each service) reporting directly to the main Council of the authority which usually accepted or occasionally rejected the recommendations from the service committees. On the officer side these arrangements were reflected in a series of largely independent departments, each responsible for a service, and headed by a professional officer, but without anyone holding responsibility across the whole authority. The Director of Education, therefore, was accountable through the Education Committee to the Council, but not to the County (or Town) Clerk who held seniority, but only by status.[32]

Arrangements such as these presented easy targets for criticism. Problems that arose which did not match the administrative structure, either had to be ignored, or somehow construed to fit. Advantages that might have accrued from co-ordination of activities were not exploited: in relation, for example, to the natural links between social services and education in work with very young or deprived children. More generally the complexity of the situation in which each local authority functioned, and the social, physical, economic and political components which sustained this complexity, could not be as effectively confronted by a collection of separate services than by a total authority approach directed towards the maximisation of human welfare. Clearly, such a goal could not be readily achieved with divisiveness among staff, resulting from each department being associated with a service having its own professional entry and training requirements, and no inter-service transfer of members. The common relationship linking the committees was that with the finance committee, but its main duties were limited to fixing the rate by approving (or disapproving) the separate budgets of each service. As a result policy matters were seen as a department, service-committee responsibility. Although there were isolated attempts to move away from rigid departmentalism before 1967 it can now be seen that the Maud Committee report had a catalytic effect. In particular it criticised the absence of a managing body of elected members (possibly analogous to the cabinet at central government level), the lack of unity in the work of authorities, the disadvantages of departmentalism, and the non-existence of a professional staff leader: and recommended a management board of between five and nine members, a smaller number of Committees and a Chief Officer. In fact, authorities were not prepared to implement the full range of suggestions, mainly because of resistance to the idea of a potentially over powerful management board, with reduced power and status for service committees. Yet, by the time local authorities were established in 1974, almost without exception, organizational arrangements had emerged which bore little relationship to the pre-Maud separateness. Most authorities followed the broad lines recommended by Bains on internal structures, with a relatively small Policy and Resources committee on the members side (perhaps 20 or so strong) taking over the traditional duties of the finance committee, and also responsibility for discussing, deciding and monitoring authority policy. While among professional staff, a Chief Executive was appointed to lead a team of Principal Chief Officers including (for authorities with LEA functions) the Director of Education.[33] Details and nomenclature may vary, but the general pattern is consistent and largely continues.[34]

The structural response of authorities to criticism, assisted by local government re-organization, was rapid and visible. Changes in the processes that were facilitated present more difficulty. The main thrust sought with new arrangements was the conversion from a collection of separate departments reacting within legislative provisions to situations that presented themselves, into a corporate organization trying to consider the full range of issues concerning the community and devising the most effective means of alleviating these concerns. In broad terms, therefore, the intention was that corporate management would enable authorities to

Distributing Resources

pro-act having identified gaps in provision or community needs, within a framework (say) of urban decay or high unemployment, in ways that it could not have achieved within the traditional boundaries of separate departments. The general intentions of corporate management seem beyond reproach. It does make more sense to have a unified and authority-wide approach to problem-solving, instead of a series of separate departments. What the years after 1974 demonstrated, with the increasing prominence of retrenchment, was that corporatism, in the local authority context, is essentially an expansionist concept. It need not be: but large organizations find it much easier to proact, or react to new situations, by setting up additional sections and employing extra staff, rather than through internal re-organization and diverting the work-loads of individuals to novel, or previously non-existent, situations. This facet of organizational functioning inclined most authorities, with contraction, towards their original role of fulfilling statutory obligations, as opposed to a wide exercise of discretionary powers which corporate management approaches would have demanded. Authorities, therefore in pursuing corporatism, within strict financial parameters, often tried to achieve objectives no more substantial than closer liaison between departments. In any discussion of corporate management, however, the accompanying nomenclature (teams of Senior Officer, Chief Executive etc.) has to be separated from the reality of processes and outcomes. To take one example, an authority could have regular meetings of Chief Officers, but this offers little by way of an integrative stance, or an alternative perspective on problems, if third and fourth tier officers have minimal involvement with the work of other departments. An educationist, planner and highway engineer may consider the location of a new school, as they have always had to do, but if in their normal work they continue to perform separate and independent tasks this does not constitute a corporatist approach.

    This specific example highlights the reliance upon expansion. Integration is facilitated by additional finance, and the consideration of projects, as new work patterns can be established. A number of authorities have been able to adopt multi-discliplinary approaches to problem situations, such as inner-city deprivation but only because of extra funds from government sponsored schemes such as IAP (Inner Area Partnership).[35] In these cases education officers have formed teams with leisure, recreation and social services staff, but in more typical circumstances loyalties and commitments to individual services have been little disturbed by the overall intentions of corporate management. From a solely educational perspective a few practices have been changed with corporatism. Teaching staff job applications considered by a Personnel Department (in the first instance, at least) of responsibilities for building maintenance transferred to an Establishments section being two examples. To an external observer such changes seem trivial, to an education officer they may appear to be a gross erosion of traditional, and essential, freedoms: leading in one case to the resignation of a Chief Education Officer because of the apparent intrusion of corporate effects on task performance and responsibilities.[36]

Attempts by authorities to develop corporate management emphasised the ambivalences with regard to education as a local activity. More specifically it raised the issue of whether a service, perceived in many ways as national, could (or should) be integrated with other services more easily given a clear local orientation. It was this factor, often displayed through minor complaints of educationists about the adverse effects of corporate management, which created so much antipathy. There were, of course, other issues. The size, in resource terms, of education as compared to other services, exacerbated the difficulties of inter-service approaches to problem-solving. A situation further exaggerated by the high proportion of professional staff in education working away from the civic centre, and with little commitment to it, and therefore separated from the main thrust of corporatist activities. Similarly, the background and previous experiences of education officers, unlike their senior colleagues in other departments, directs their interests and commitments to educational institutions rather than to the central activities of the authority. Almost without exception, education officers have worked in schools or colleges and enter administration as a result of an interest in education. Any loyalty they develop towards the authority as a whole is secondary, arising from the fact that education happens to be locally administered. Unsurprisingly, there are few examples of Chief Education Officers becoming Chief Executives of their authority.

However, from a resource perspective, the

Distributing Resources

fundamental question raised by structural changes in local authorities concerns funding. Most directly, have local education services been advantaged or disadvantaged by corporate approaches through the resources they receive? From an empirical perspective such questions are largely, if not totally, rhetorical. In the first place there are enormous methodological problems. The physical restructuring of local authorities in 1974 coincided with, and accelerated, internal reorganization. Then there are the problems of separating structural from process changes within education and other local authority services, and all the related issues of funding levels as compared to duties and responsibilities. Secondly, there is the potentially still more difficult issue that resource-based measures assess inputs: corporate management, if nothing else, should turn attention towards the satisfaction of needs. The fact that in an individual authority (say) it can be shown that education has suffered during corporatism represents one side of an equation: the other might come with different outcomes from an integrated approach to needs satisfaction. Yet, concentrating on one authority highlights the main issue in assessing the position of education in acquiring resources. As already described, the processes of resource distribution within an authority have become increasingly circumscribed by centrally determined parameters, but the major decisions of spending to be sanctioned service by service, as well as the total expenditure, are matters for local decision-making. Therefore, any consideration of the impingement of corporate management on education resources must be treated with caution. Basically, each authority receives a block grant (and some specific allowances), decides what it will spend on each service, and makes up the deficit by a mixture of charges (where appropriate) and fixing a rate in the pound. Clearly, each authority as a political entity, will have developed its own characteristic approach, influenced by tradition, the inter-relationship among services, government targets, and the interactions between officers and politicians: in other words, a mix of internal factors and external items as they impinge upon the authority. However, within this pattern of individuality, certain principles can be established, but it is impossible to consider these and their influences upon the outcomes of the second territory of decision-making, without first discussing the third territory, that within the LEA.

Distributing Resources

LOCAL EDUCATION AUTHORITY

The overlap between LEA and local authority decision-making although exaggerated by corporatism, has always existed. A discreteness and a hierarchy still pertain, of course: the local authority as a whole makes a series of inter-service decisions and fixes the rate, at the same time the LEA must distribute resources among schools etc. with both the distribution and the total expenditure subject to Council control. However, the authority cannot sanction education expenditure without a clear plan of what is to be spent. As a result, the production of a budget for education (and simultaneously in other services) constitutes an integral component of resource distribution. Probably the most effective way of considering the influence of the processes in budget construction on the disbursement of resources is through the outcome - a typical budget document (Figure 3.1). Essentially a spending plan, completed just before the start of the financial year, its formulation combines both technical detail with political and educational priorities. However, once an item appears in the final budget that represents permission to spend up to whatever level is specified. Therefore, the main thrust is towards the demands of fiscal accounting, which is well suited by the object of expense approach: so much to be spent on a whole series of items - teachers salaries, books and equipment, heating, lighting etc.[37] The requirements of fiscal accounting (that money should only be spent in categories, and up to levels, as agreed) are also demonstrated by the precision of the forecast expenditures. Clearly, it is impossible to estimate spending on salaries, for example, involving several million pounds, to the nearest hundred pounds, given the variations and unanticipated events likely to happen during the year. Instead, the specified figure for each item is best perceived as an expenditure target, which can be used to monitor the rate of spending during the year to strengthen the control element sought by the document. In the same way, categorization of planned expenditure facilitates fiscal accounting by enabling the separate scrutiny of spending on each item, although making virement procedures - the transfer of expenditure between sub-heads after the document has been confirmed - more difficult.

In such a document there are two outstanding, but potentially conflicting, features. The first, and more obvious, concerns the detail, implying that

FIGURE 3.1
LEA budget document for 1983-84

A. Estimated net cost of current levels of service*

	Employees Teachers	Employees Others	Running Expenses	Debt Charges	Total Expend.	Income +	Net Expend.
Admin. & Inspection	–	2,480,620	1,435,560	–	3,916,180	286,320	3,629,860
Nursery Education	36,890	56,270	28,220	–	121,380	–	121,380
Primary Education	17,560,320	3,072,660	5,172,600	1,872,640	27,678,220	278,980	27,399,240
Secondary Education	21,462,240	2,207,630	7,254,720	2,073,190	32,997,780	254,390	32,743,390
Special Education	2,576,310	867,320	1,974,460	250,740	5,668,830	490,320	5,178,510
FE: Colleges	5,024,810	1,032,680	1,674,980	258,960	7,991,430	2,587,260	5,404,170
Adult Education	100,760	2,750	16,720	–	120,230	86,790	34,440
In-service trng.	–	–	68,960	–	–	–	68,960
Teachers Centres	25,280	18,960	37,490	–	81,730	4,820	76,910
Community Education	56,110	112,720	190,190	96,390	455,410	59,780	395,630
School Meals	–	3,172,660	2,452,100	59,280	5,684,040	1,710,390	3,973,650
Youth Service	–	382,920	310,290	62,280	755,490	49,240	706,250
Outdoor Study Centres	112,920	149,610	225,740	6,280	494,500	280,620	213,930
Careers Advisory	–	690,780	170,120	20,220	881,120	292,480	588,640
AFE pooling	–	–	5,220,420	–	5,220,420	820,340	4,400,080
						Total	84,935,040

* For the sake of conciseness only the main categories have been included.
+ Including specific government grants.

FIGURE 3.1 (cont'd.)

B. Secondary education proposed gross spending 1983-84 (in cash terms)

	1983-84 Proposed	1982-83 Proposed	1982-83 Probable
Teachers salaries	21,462,240	20,876,520	21,004,760
Non-teaching salaries	572,280	528,690	532,280
Other salaries	1,635,350	1,592,740	1,608,710
Building maintenance	1,006,780	970,620	960,480
Building alterations	124,320	136,220	140,480
Grounds maintenance	637,690	620,110	630,470
Heating, lighting	1,976,450	1,896,720	1,884,630
Furniture and fittings	125,160	131,720	129,640
Rent and rates	2,176,430	2,080,340	2,146,720
Books and equipment	826,970	834,720	836,410
Printing, stationery & telephone	196,980	198,740	195,370
Insurance	58,720	61,220	59,470
Aid to pupils	125,220	110,590	108,160
Debt charges	2,073,190	2,001,420	1,964,110
	32,997,780	32,040,370	32,201,690

Distributing Resources

construction demands considerable technical expertise and knowledge about the system. Second, and less clearly, the document contains within that detail the most important statement of LEA policy. Priorities as between primary and secondary education, teaching and non-teaching staff etc. are established and pursued, not perhaps in ways which can be readily understood from the document. Nevertheless, by committing itself to certain expenditures, the LEA has specified its preferences. The budget, therefore, is not a neutral document, although the technicalities involved in its construction can sometimes make it appear as such, and all parties - politicians and officers particularly, other interest groups less directly - have a stake in production. Particularly during contraction it is relatively easy to depict the whole process as entirely incremental, in the sense that the current budget represents no more than an extension of the previous year. A view strengthened by the object of expense format which places previous and proposed expenditure on each item alongside, in a way that directs attention towards possible changes in spending. Essentially, each line appears as
        NAME OF ITEM   A   B   C
where A and B represent previous or current expenditures (during the year in which the document is being prepared,)and C the proposed spending on the item. Even during expansion, however, there is usually a powerful measure of sameness about an organization's budget over time. Two types of reasoning can be used to explain this situation. The first, and more negative, utilizes the limitations of all decision-makers. They are attempting to maximise needs satisfaction in circumstances of resource shortage, and although an infinite number of solutions exist, the constraints on time and limits of knowledge concentrate attention upon a few. As a result, when changes are possible during budget production, modifications to current arrangements dominate.[38] Second, this argument can be developed from a positive stance. In effect, the latest budget represents an investment by the organization in obtaining a resource allocation scheme which has been accepted as a compromise, in addition to providing a spending pattern already being used and as a result supplying experience in this use. In many sectors, quite possibly, circumstances hardly change from year to year, and therefore arguments for a comprehensive review of resource distributions gain little support.[39] More practically, the budget of

every organization consists of a base to which, because of shortages of time and knowledge and as existing distributions appear to be adequate, it is already committed before budget-making starts, and a series of increments. Obviously, it is to these that attention switches in decision-making, for they represent the allocative freedom available.

The notion that budget choices takes place entirely at the margins is not an over-simplification. It would be to imply that a clear divide exists, visible in the budget document, between those items which constitute the base, and those at the margins: or that all organizations of the same type functioning in similar circumstances perceive the same base-increment relationship.[40] To take two cases: one authority will, by having a 'no-redundancy' policy, erect a larger staff salary base than another willing to reduce teacher numbers, while a LEA deciding, irrespective of other factors, to maintain school capitation allowances in real terms sustains a high base for that item. What, however, these examples also illustrate is both the clarification necessary in the concept of incrementalism, especially with contracting or static conditions, and the impact of organizational factors. An increment is that part of the planned spending where decision-makers could induce a change if they wished. Clearly, with expansion this component of potential spending grows, although as a result the organization, as happened with schools and colleges, may increase the base by entering into new and irrevocable commitments. Conversely, during a time of retrenchment there may still be opportunity for incrementalism provided the planned spending, determined as the base, is less than the total expenditure allowed. Essentially, the problem faced by LEAs during contraction was to ensure that, with a high level of committed expenditure through organizational arrangements and statutory requirements, the base spending was below that likely to be permitted. Indeed, some LEAs argued that a base to total spending deficit, in their perception, was sufficient grounds to make a case for extra resources. In doing so, however, they overlooked two important issues. The size of a base can always be challenged as it is not an objective entity, and by accepting that no gap between base and spending exists, they risk turning budget making into a wholly technical exercise in which the previous document converts into the next budget.

There has, of course, to be a powerful

Distributing Resources

technical component in LEA decision-making. The complexity of the organization would not permit otherwise. A typical LEA is distributing tens of millions of pounds to several main sectors and hundreds of discrete items. The starting point for budget preparation, several months in time before the year, can only be the previous document. By any standard the base must be large, because of the labour intensity and the high level of fixed costs, and therefore the first task, performed by professional staff, is to extend last year's figures either into the potential cost of irrevocable commitments or, more likely, an estimate of spending if present patterns of provision were continued in the likely circumstances of the new year. That is attempting to make allowances in expenditure terms for changes in pupil and student numbers, increases in salaries and prices, and other foreseeable variables: essentially, a cash determination performed in volume terms. Although these procedures occur at officer level, the political dimension is provided by both national and local parameters. Central government as a whole, and DES in particular, publicise expenditure expectations on their part, but it is not until these are converted into individual RSG settlements (four months, or so, before the start of the year) that authorities know with any degree of certainty their potential financial situation. Up to that point, the assembly of the education budget, and those for other services, is influenced by no more than general guidelines from the main Council or Policy and Resources Committee, produced as a result of their interpretation of government policy and the likely circumstances of the next year. Perhaps a standstill budget is suggested, in real terms by the authority, or a 2% reduction or a 1% increase in level of services. Often, at this stage, these guidelines will be consistent across services, but it is with the receipt of a RSG figure that the authority begins to balance likely income (from rates, grants and charges) against expenditure it will permit. From an educational perspective, the spending estimates have then to be converted into a detailed plan. Practice varies among authorities, but in general terms this process is sanctioned by sub-committees and the main education committee. As they assemble the estimates, education officers are liaising with schools and with colleges (who will be producing their own budgets in most cases) and officers in the finance department, while working with more detailed contraction or growth parameters established by the authority, alternatively a total aggregate expenditure to be allowed might be specified. The separate outcomes for the various sectors of further education, schools etc., are then presented to the appropriate further education or schools sub-committee. After adjustment, perhaps, these separate components are used to prepare a full budget document for the Education Committee. Following approval it proceeds to the Policy and Resources Committee, and after agreement there, normally by 'rubber-stamping', to the main Council before becoming the spending plan.

It is, however, much more than a series of technical procedures, and the accompanying determination of local priorities, as expressed through the political processes of the authority, demand attention. In the first place the statement by the authority of growth rate guidelines to be used in early budget preparation represents local intentions relative to national priorities. Although enormously curtailed by targets and penalties, authorities still determine aggregate expenditures. Government may suggest a 'no-growth' situation from one year to next across all authorities, for example, but that does not prevent some aiming for a measure of expansion, either because they are willing to impose large rate increases or as some aspect of the grant calculation is working in their favour. Similarly, the specification by government of expenditure priorities between and within services, in PESC and other statements, does not prevent a LEA exercising its own and different prerogatives. A government view that the RSG settlements allows some increase in books and equipment expenditure, for example, does not commit a LEA to any extra spending. Such adjustments, at variance with government policy, can only occur with increasing difficulty, and at the margins of expenditure, but in an activity like education, with a high level of spending inflexibility, that is the area on which much budget decision-making centres. So that when a sub-committee is presented with draft estimates there are few major choices likely to be available. In the circumstances of a standstill budget, for example, some potential savings could be listed alongside the possible priorities that might be sought if total spending is to remain constant in real terms. As can be seen from Figure 3.2, the sums involved are miniscule as compared to total spending, but by deciding which expenditure reductions to sanction, and determining whether extra remedial teaching staff in employment should take priority over an increase in capitation allowances, for instance, the overt inclusion of political interests has been accommodated. More drastic changes, such as increase in PTR to generate more flexibility, is usually circumscribed by covert political pressures, as all of the processes, including the construction of the estimates, occurs within the local political environment. To take the example of a proposed rise in PTR, which almost certainly will create job-losses: the teacher unions, once alerted, must pressurise for alternative spending patterns, even if this involves spending reductions elsewhere with still less flexibility and fewer choices. As a proposal, therefore, it is unlikely to come before a sub-committee without prior discussion. For except in the case of apolitical authorities (of which there are very few) or those with no overall control, the ruling group will have arranged a majority throughout the committee structure so as to sustain a political consistency.

It is very easy to go on from this fact and portray budget decision-making in a local authority as a series of technical procedures performed by professional staff, within a framework established in private by the main political party, leaving a small number of relatively minor decisions to the public arena of education and other service committees. In some authorities this description will be close to reality, yet even in such circumstances there are several elements which require consideration because of their centrality to distributive outcomes. Clearly, if decisions about aggregate expenditures, and spending priorities among departments, occur within the controlling political group, the relationship between senior members of Policy and Resources, and Education Committees, most especially at chairman level, becomes of crucial importance to education spending. At any time, but particularly with contraction, inter-service competition for resources cannot be resolved other than by the exercise of political power. Without rational arguments to prove that one suggested expenditure is better than another, perceptions by committee chairmen about the potential benefits of rival spending proposals provide, in the limit, an arbitration. All that happens in these cases, as opposed to a discussion in full committee, is that bargains are struck beforehand, but in either case only incremental expenditures reach the agenda. At the same time, in such a political environment, the relationship between the education committee chairman and the chief education officer assumes considerable significance. Between them they are responsible for combining technical details with the interpretation of educational and political priorities for the establishment of the budget. Within this framework they co-ordinate the conversion of estimates into a final document as it moves through sub-committee to education committee and main Council. Also, as happens with contraction, when reductions are demanded by Policy and Resources they must organize opposition to ensure that the cutbacks are minimised and arrange that whatever retrenchment has to be made is accepted, however grudgingly, by the various lobbies within, and impinging upon, the sub-committee and committee structure.

The LEAs need to compete for resources with other services has been exaggerated, not only by contraction, but also through the provisions of the Local Government, Planning and Land Act, 1980 in relation to capital expenditure. Previous to that, central government permission to spend (essentially allowing the authority to raise a capital sum subsequently repaid through revenue expenditure) was strictly categorized between, and within, services. Under the changed arrangements each LEA, and the rest of the authority, present a case about the capital expenditure they would choose to make on major projects and minor works. separated into basic needs and improvements, and phased over more than one year, if necessary. The Department of the Environment, having received bids from each authority, then converts these into a series of maximum cash expenditures (again through a permission to raise capital) for every authority. The process of conversion, although obviously related to aggregate government spending intentions, is little understood at local level. Although categorized by service, and within education into nursery education, schools and further and higher education totals, authorities are allowed to vire expenditures.[41] Ultimately, the only restriction is on individual authority levels of total spending. Therefore, during contraction, and reduced need for buildings, not only is education's case diminished, but it cannot be sure of its capital spending allocations. Of course, sustained virement on a large-scale might prejudice authorities subsequent bids for spending permission: but the issue of enhanced inter-service competition remains. Whatever the causes - reduction in resource levels, modifications to the main thrust and

Distributing Resources

some of the detail of government policy, variations in demographic factors - the potential for rivalry between education and other services has risen, paradoxically during a time when many authorities have been pursuing corporate management approaches.

Some evidence that education has been disadvantaged by such changes exists, for example, since the first year of the new local authorities (1974-75) until 1981-82 the total of net local authority expenditure by the education service has declined from 51.9% to 50.3% (Table 3.1). In absolute terms this deficiency, had education remained at the higher figure, involves considerable and significant sums of money, particularly as they would have represented expenditures at the margins where decision-makers can exercise some autonomy. However, the circumstances of the two years are not exactly comparable. For example, the number of clients in education has declined while those in social services (another main spending department) have increased: central policy towards school meals and milk has reduced expenditure on these items, and overall government intentions during the intervening time has been to lower educational spending disproportionately to other expenditures. Unsurprisingly, education's percentage of total spending commitment has dropped, but the key yet unanswered question, from an objective perspective, concerns the rate of decline and its appropriateness. Whether there should be only decline is an issue which has been pre-empted by direct, but unsubstantiable political parameters. In the same sense, projections about the implications of the existence of items like GREs governing each service, target expenditures etc. for educational spending may suggest that these procedures will in themselves produce a further decline, but it will be extremely difficult, if not impossible, to prove the extent to which they are contributory factors. For example, a knowledge of GREs relative to decisions being sanctioned, even when there is an awareness of them,[42] may have little effect, because of the numerous other factors that impinge upon, and in fact constitute, the political processes in each local authority. These define the base and determine incremental expenditures in education and other services.

INSTITUTIONS

The fourth territory, that concerned about the distribution of resources within institutions, receives less space than the others, not so much because it is less important but, within a hierarchy of decision-making, many choices have already been foregone before schools and colleges can exert a direct influence. In addition, many issues in the resource decision-making of schools and colleges receive attention in the next three chapters. As far as receipt of resources from the LEA is concerned, two distinct approaches exist which condition institutional practice. In the first, involving most FE institutions, a budget is presented to the authority. Categorized into the main expenditure areas (teaching and non-teaching staff salaries, heating, lighting and cleaning services: building maintenance costs etc)[43] its preparation and eventual acceptance as a spending plan by the authority resembles in many ways the procedures for the main LEA budget. The formulation of estimates within local (and national) guidelines and subsequent negotiations involving sub-committees, Policy and Resources committee and so on, all occur. When finalised, though, most colleges are subject to strict local controls over freedom to vire between main expenditure heads, for example, and carry forward unspent balances into the next year. Limitations on autonomy, such as these, have exaggerated the problem of colleges adjusting rapidly to substantial changes in client (and sponsor) demands: most especially with MSC activities when they have employed additional staff and developed new facilities while integrating income from fees to conventional resource acquisition. More generally, though, the college-based preparation of budgets means that many of the main resource distributional issues, as between faculties and departments for example, occurs during assembly. Budget construction was a facility which emerged on a large scale in most colleges during the late 1960s, as a component in wider attempts to increase their independance from the local authority through the use of governing bodies, academic boards, and fewer controls in general.[44] Rather surprisingly it was not a change, in relation to budgetary procedures, reflected in, or sought by, schools, even in those situations where, with comprehensive reorganization, large secondary schools evolved. Paradoxically, responsibility for the preparation of school estimates is often mentioned in the articles of government.[45] As a result of this ommission, the second approach, applying to the majority of schools, involves the effective rationing of resources. In other words the compilation of the estimates of each school takes place in the education office, and school awareness of the final outcome, after the LEA budget has been approved, consists of a ration of so many teachers, non-teaching staff, alongside allowances for books and equipment with many other expenditures, heating, lighting etc. paid directly by the LEA (Chapter 6).

From a school perspective it might appear that distributional freedom relates to very few items. In fact, as the following Chapters attempt to demonstrate, such a view is an underestimate of the true position. In particular, schools have considerable autonomy, although decreasing, in their deployment of staff as inter-school variations in curricular and time-tabling detail make clear. The debate in schools about the curriculum, when associated with the staffing of subjects, class sizes etc., may not be thought of as such, but is resource distributional in content. However, in the perception of many school staffs, allocative freedom, in a direct sense, is restricted to book and equipment allowances, and staff promoted posts. In the former LEAs utilize a capitation principle, with some modifications, to distribute to schools. Usually, it is related to pupil-age, being higher for older pupils: occasionally smaller schools or for those with special difficulties can claim larger allowances: often, there are particular arrangements for the purchase of more expensive items of equipment. Basically, however, schools receive permission to spend up to an annual limit, which is mainly roll-size dependant, on books, equipment and consumable materials. The sums of money involved, even when running into thousands of pounds for larger schools, are rarely more than 5% of revenue expenditure. In terms of arrangements for the internal allocation of these funds procedures range from highly participative structures, in which sectional bids for resources are sanctioned by a committee of staff, through to situations where the headteacher alone decides, and has an overview, about the total distribution. The second area of freedom involves the allocation of promoted posts. The number involved depends upon school size and pupil age profile, as interpreted by the authority relative to Burnham arrangements, and the issue which makes this distribution so much more important is that a promoted position once offered to an individual can only be taken back with difficulty. Such a distribution is analagous to a capital allocation situation in that a single inappropriate decision may generate a whole range of further difficulties.

Interestingly, in comparing FE and schools, a small number of authorities through feasibility studies, are enabling schools to exercise a wider measure of distributional autonomy, often with powers over virement, for example, in excess of those available in colleges. One objective of such developments is that by demonstrating to staff the ubiquitousness of resource factors a vital, but under-considered, component of educational management, can be highlighted. The effect of resource availability, and its impingement on all aspects of work, has become increasingly obvious with contraction. What is perhaps not so clear, but becomes even more relevant in these circumstances, concerns the extent to which much decision-making appears to occur at the periphery of expenditure. The example of Scale posts within a school makes the point. A school may have twenty promoted staff, but at any one time the headteacher is only able to distribute one or two posts. Similarly, a LEA may plan to spend £40m., but in budget construction perhaps no more than 10% of that total is reckoned to be freely allocable. As a result, the importance of situations in which decision-making autonomy is perceived, increases. Simultaneously, numerous issues, relating to the utilization of the 90% of resources apparently already committed, are raised. Particularly, when the results that emanate from LEA and institutional decision-making procedures, extended over a period of time, demonstrate the difference that can emerge. The next chapter looks at this issue in relation to curricular processes.

NOTES AND REFERENCES

1. Books on educational organisation, for example K. Fenwick and P. McBride, The Government of Education, (Martin Robertson, Oxford, 1981) consider finance but not as a central issue.
2. Education, (1.1.82) p.5.
3. CMND 1432, 'Control of Public Expenditure, (1961): CMND 1434, Public Expenditure 1968-69 to 1973-74, (1969).
4. P.K. Else and G.P. Marshall, 'The Unplanning of Public Expanediture: Recent Problems in Expenditure Planning and the Consequences of Cash Limits', Public Administration, Vol. 59 (1981), pp. 253-278.
5. CMND 8494, The government's expenditure plans

1982-83 to 1984-85, (1982).
6. Else and Marshall, (1981), p. 271.
7. G.W. Jones and J. D. Stewart, 'The Treasury and Local Government', The Political Quarterly, Vol. 54 No. 1 (1983) pp. 5-15.
8. See CMND 8789, The government's expenditure plans 1983-84 to 1985-86, (1983).
9. Education, 1.1.82, p.5.
10. O.A. Hartley, 'The Relationship between Central and Local Authorities", Public Administration, Vol. 49, (1971), pp. 439-456.
11. Mainly through regulations see, for example, SI 1086/1981, The Education (Schools and Further Education) Regulations, 1981.
12. J.A.G. Griffith, Central Departments and Local Authorities,(George Allen and Unwin, London, 1966), p.522.
13. Jones and Stewart, (1983).
14. CMND 2923, Local Government Finance: England and Wales, (1966).
15. CMND 4040, Royal Commission on Local Government in England 1966-1969, (1969).
16. CMND 6453, Committee of Enquiry into Local Government Finance, (1976).
17. R.J. Bennett, 'The Local Income Tax in Britain: A Critique of Recent Arguments Against Its Use' Public Administration, Vol. 59 (1981)pp.295-311).
18. CMND 4741, Future Shape of Local Government Finance, (1971), and CMND 6813, Local Government Finances, (1977).
19. The Education Authorities Directory 1983, (School Government Publishing, Redhill, 1983).
20. R.J. Bennett, Central Grants to Local Governments, (Cambridge University Press, Cambridge 1982), pp. 103-130 describes the arrangements in detail.
21. F. Marslen-Wilson and A. Crispin, 'How much influence does the GRE have on LEA attitudes' Education, (16.9.83), pp. 232-233.
22. For example, their effects as reported in Education, (17.12.82), pp. 483-484.
23. See the overall perspective in Education, (12.2.82), pp. i-iv.
24. Jones and Stewart, (1983), p. 9.
25. T. Travers, 'Local Government, Planning and Land Act 1980' Political Quarterly, Vol. 52 (1981) pp. 355-361.
26. CMND 9008, Rates- Proposals for rate limitation and the reform of the rating system, (1983).
27. DES, Report by Her Majesty's Inspectors of the

Effects of Local Authority Expenditure Policies on the Education Service in England - 1981, (1982).
28. Society of Education Officers Occasional Paper No. 2, ' Education block grant: how it could work', Supplement to Education, 25.6.82.
29. CMND 8449, Alternatives to Domestic Rates, (1981).
30. See the many articles and views developed, particularly in Education during 1982.
31. Specific grants, to no more than 0.5% of total revenue expenditure, introduced from 1985-86 seem probable.
32. Ministry of Housing and Local Government, Management of Local Government, (HMSO, London 1967).
33. The New Local Authorites:Management and Structure, (HMSO, London, 1972).
34. C. R. Hinings, P.R.S. Ranson and R. Greenwood, 'The Organisation of Metropolitan Government: The Impact of Bains', Local Government Studies, Vol. 9, (1974) pp.47-54.
35. CMND 6845, A Policy for the Inner Cities,(1977).
36. T. Bush and M. Kogan, Directors of Education, George Allen and Unwin, London, 1983), pp.30-32
37. H.J.Hartley, Educational Planning-Programming-Budgeting:A Systems Approach,(Prentice Hall, Englewood Cliffs, N.J.,1968),pp. 129-137.
38. J.N. Danziger, 'Assessing incrementalism in British Municipal Budgeting', British Journal of Political Science, Vol. 6 (1976), pp.335-350.
39. A. Down, Inside Bureaucracy, (Little Brown, Boston, 1967), pp. 249-251.
40. R. Greenwood, C.R.Hinings and S.Ranson, 'The Politics of the Budgeting Process in English Local Government', Political Studies, Vol. 25 No. 1, (1977), pp. 25-47.
41. Department of the Environment Circular 14/81 Capital programmes (1981) and 7/82 Capital programmes, (1982)
42. F. Marslen-Wilson and A. Crispin, Education, (16.9.83).
43. National Advisory Council on Education for Industry and Commerce, Committee on the Effective Use of Technical College Resources,(HMSO, London, 1969).
44. DES Circular 7/70, Government and Conduct of Establishments of Further Education, (1970)

Chapter Four

RESOURCES AND THE CURRICULUM

A DYNAMIC CURRICULUM

From the vantage point of the early or mid-1980s the curriculum resource concerns of twenty years previously seem, if not irrelevant, certainly trivial. Then, schools were expanding their curricular provision, not protecting them from the exigencies of shortfalls in staff and equipment: colleges were deciding which new course to offer, not defending existing programmes against the onslaughts of the NAB or LEA. Yet, a comparison such as this, hides a paradox. Unit costs are higher than in the early and mid-1960s. Of course, a statement such as this demands qualification. Actual comparisons of expenditure per child, for example, over such a period are notoriously prone to relative price effects: while for further education, and AFE in particular, the emergence of new college and polytechnic structures renders meaningless a comparative costing exercise. Similarly, any effort to contrast the percentage of GDP utilised per client, or some other such measure, is certain to encounter methodological problems of estimating the number of clients, the real value of GDP or the rate of education expenditure.

However, one resource-based measure allows a stricter comparison. As compared to twenty years previously the pupil-teacher ratio has been lowered in both primary and secondary schools, from 29.2 to 22.4, and 21.2 to 16.4 respectively.[1] Clearly, to proceed from this fact to a statement about higher unit costs involves assumptions: about the relative values of teacher salaries, the provision of other resources or possible variations in teacher quality, for example. However, the basic issue that the average child should be in smaller classes, receiving

109

more teacher time than twenty years previously, is beyond dispute. Costs have to be higher. The paradox therefore can be sustained: there are less children for each teacher to deal with, unit-costs must be greater, but the priorities relate to curricular protection and the effects of retrenchment, rather than the development of new activities.

The contrast results from the totally different impacts of contraction and expansion, and the significant effects of resource situations during preceding years. By definition expansion attracts additional resources. Suppose a school has a starting PTR of 28:1, improving to 26:1, with 1456 pupils on roll, the staffing establishment would increase from 52 to 56. If the high ratio was retained an additional 112 pupils would still yield four extra teachers. The expansion may take different forms, but four more teachers bring with them specific interests and expertise, (selection procedures permitting) not found in the original staff. The school might be able to introduce a new subject into the curriculum, and there are four additional teachers to organize trips, coach teams and so on. Perhaps, most important of all, if the growth is sustained year on year, the school can anticipate and begin to plan how to utilise extra resources as they become available. In these circumstances the notion of 'disjointed incrementalism' (that is, expansion without direction and planning) becomes much less appropriate.[2] The aggregative element in resource acquisition is well illustrated in expansionary conditions: staff numbers increase, and with an effective recruitment policy, so do the range of skills experiences and disciplines in the school, as the current years resources build upon previous years: with a parallel development in non-teaching staff, books, equipment and buildings.

Conversely contraction represents disaggregation. Take the example of a school, now generously provisioned, with 1200 pupils on roll, a PTR of 15:1, and therefore 80 staff. As for expansion the retrenchment can occur in two ways, or more usually by a combination of both: either the number on roll (NOR) decreases to (say) 1125 with a static PTR, or for a constant roll the LEA increases the ratio to 16:1. In either case the staffing establishment would be reduced to 75. In practice, how the departure of five staff is achieved, and in particular which staff, lies outside the control mechanisms of the school (however well organized) and, in many situations, the LEA. The process of disaggregating the resources the school has accumulated over a number of years, often through careful planning, has a powerful streak of randomness. The economics teacher moves on to another school, the teacher of German opts for early retirement, and these posts are not filled because the school is then 40% nearer its staff reduction target: the remaining teachers prove insufficiently flexible and, almost by chance, the school curriculum alters.

In terms of relative staffing levels, it seems quite ludicrous to compare the school in the first example, PTR 26:1, to that with a ratio of 16:1. In the former situation there are 56 staff for 1456 pupils: in the latter only 1200 children and 75 teachers. Therefore the classes should be smaller and subject-range greater. Some caution is needed, though (particularly when the ratios contrasted are much closer) because of school freedom in determining average class-sizes, the availability of options and teacher contrast ratios. However, there can also be little doubt that the former school, the worse provisioned, will reckon itself to be more in control of curriculum planning. It can project on the basis of one, two, or more additional staff, what extra subjects can be introduced into the curriculum, or how remedial provision might be increased or, possibly, class-size reduced. By comparison, the other school might deal with a series of chance situations, resulting from the coincidence of the age-profile of staff, the likelihood of individual members moving elsewhere, and the ability and willingness of those remaining to retrain and adopt flexible work practices. More generally, an assessment of staffing levels, or any other resource, at some point in time is no more than a snapshot. It gives some indication of current standards of provision, but not the whole picture: this depends upon the present situation, what has happened previously and anticipations of what might follow.

In many ways the comparative example encapsulates the recent experiences of most schools and colleges and their efforts to resource their curricula in the contrasting environments of expansion and deflation. While resources may not be the sole factor in determining the curriculum offered, there can be no doubt as to their importance, and of the components in any resource-mix it is the availability of teaching staff which dominates. Simple logic decrees that the more teachers or lecturers employed, the greater the range of deployment possibilities. A Polytechnic with additional staff is more able to launch a new course or increase options within an existing one: a school with extra teachers can offer more choices to pupils or arrange smaller classes. However, according to this view curriculum design is no more than deploying staff effectively. The curriculum is, then a collection of activities or a range of subjects from which, and when appropriate, the pupil or student chooses a course. It is no more than a scheme, which can be described in a report or a statement about the arrangements of named activities. Yet, common experience contradicts this thinking. A theoretical example makes the point. Two schools or colleges have, on paper, identical curricular: the same range of courses and subjects are available, the choices that students can make are comparable, even the syllabi do not vary from place to place: but there is neither certainty, nor likelihood that the curricular related experiences of two pupils or students at the different institutions will be identical.

As far as resources are concerned the significant factor is that the two schools in question can have similar staffing ratios, identical buildings, and the same levels of other support services yet the curriculum in one may be broad, closely related to the needs of pupils, and meaningful to them in terms of education, training and employment prospects, while that in the other has none of these merits. More directly, there is a world of difference between a dynamic, responsive curriculum and a static, inflexible approach: even when provided by the same level of resources. Curriculum is therefore much more than a collection of subjects or a range of activities: it is also a series of processes in which quality matters. Similarly, the availability of teaching staff dominates the relationship between resources and curriculum: but it would be naive (and once more contrary to experience) to suggest that teacher quality is uniformly distributed. More likely a normal distribution pertains, with some excellent teachers and a number of incompetent staff, but with by far the greatest population clustered around average levels of competence: individually each teacher also has strengths and weaknesses. The crucial factor relative to accomplishing educational objectives is the utilization of the teaching resource, combining these individual and group characteristics: more than that, though, this resource, although dominant, is only one among several (non-teaching staff, equipment, buildings) and the combined deployment of all determine the quality of the curricular processes. The purpose of this chapter, therefore, is to consider the interactions between resource availability and curriculum implementation.

THE DOMINANCE OF THE RATIOS - PTR AND SSR

The qualifications about quality have to be made, and in practice are of immense importance, while the search for a desirable resource-mix is of considerable significance, but neither of these factors can disguise the fact that the number of teachers or lecturers the school or college acquires pervades every aspect of curriculum organization. A headteacher of a 1,000 pupil school, given the choice between a staffing establishment of 60 below average teachers and 40 high performers would probably select the larger staff: not so much, perhaps, because of the wider and more varied curriculum that might be sustainable, but because of the physical limitations (heightened, particularly in further education, by union restrictions) on what can be achieved by the smaller, more talented, staff. In addition quality of actual teaching or lecturing is not a static entity: it varies according to the number of classes taught in a given time, their size and composition. Of course a headteacher never has to make this sort of choice, but what the example demonstrates is the importance of the ratio of clients (pupils or students) to staff (PTR for schools, SSR for colleges) in any discussion of staffing relative to curriculum.

There are, in fact, four distinct reasons why the ratio is so focal. The first two, simplicity and objectivity, create the third by facilitating its conversion into an effective planning tool: all three explain its key role in management when, the distribution of resources and the monitoring of their utilization, require attention. Taking each separately:
1. Above all, a ratio is such a simple idea and so easy to understand. A school with 1,200 pupils and 80 staff has a PTR of 15:1. There can be a few arguments about the detail. Whether the headteacher should be counted, for example, the inclusion of pupils who join or leave the school during the school year (a problem particularly in secondary schools with fifth-form leavers) and the inclusion of absent or peripatetic staff, are all debatable

issues, but whatever is decided the effect on the ratio can only be marginal. Figures can, therefore, be calculated for all schools reflecting the position in mid-year. In practice, the numbers of pupils and qualified teachers is collected by the DES from Form 7 (schools) returns for primary and secondary schools (Form 11 for nursery schools). The actual number of teachers paid by the LEA, which will be slightly higher (because of peripatetic staff) derives from Form 618D returns.[3]

In further education calculation gives more problems. Part-timers, sandwich-course and block release students have to be converted into full-time equivalents FTEs. Colleges and LEAs may be unhappy with the conversion formula, but have no alternative other than to adopt them, because of the need for inter-authority consistency. However, the two main methods of calculating SSRs can still provide discrepancies. In the first, the FESR count of student enrolments in November, divided by the total number of lecturers employed (Form 618G returns of each authority) provide an aggregate SSR for each LEA. Obviously, these figures will not coincide with the returns from an 'annual survey' of a large sample of institutions performed by DES which, by considering total teaching hours throughout the year, provides college-based figures covering situations (new courses starting or finishing before the end of the year) not included in a 'snap shot' arrangement. While the calculations may be cumbersome, and conversion formula potentially contentious, these do not detract from the simplicity of the notion. The procedures can be difficult to understand, the ratio that results presents few problems in comprehensibility.

2. Linked to simplicity, are the advantages of objectivity. When as in schools, all pupils, and most staff, are full-time, and fluctuations in roll-size are small and monitorable, the PTR can be totally objective. The basis of the calculation is beyond dispute. Even when allowances are made for non-attenders, a methodology can be agreed (possibly involving class registers) and the calculations can be replicated and checked in different schools. Similarly, while the mix of full, part-time, block-release and other students produces a more complex situation in FE, a high measure of objectivity can still be maintained, so long as there exists a system for converting all modes of attendance to full-time equivalent students (FTEs). There may be disagreement about detail, based on course-hours or

whatever, but provided the methodology is clear and open objectivity continues. Universality provides a natural complement. If there are students and staff a SSR can always be assessed. An infant school may have a PTR of 24:1, the neighbouring polytechnic a SSR of 8:1, and while this represents a crude comparison of resource utilization, the contrast is marked and can be given high visibility.
3. The simplicity of the ratio provides the main rationale for its use as a planning tool. If a LEA projects a secondary school population of 17,000 and intends a PTR of 17:1 it will require 1,000 teachers. More important from a budget perspective if the average salary costs are estimated at £9,000 (usually estimated from the previous years figure with an allowance for inflation) then the expenditure on secondary school salaries can be budgeted at £9m. This type of calculation can be extended in the PESC forecasts to project spending levels in relation to likely pupil numbers and a desired PTR.[4] In 1984-85, for example, the 1983 Expenditure White Paper projected a total school population of 7.34m (allowances being made for specified participation rates among under-fives,35.0%, and above school-leaving age, 22.5%) and the employment of 390,000-395,000 teachers at a PTR in the range 18.0 to 18.3. In FE the use of SSR as a planning device for future staff numbers and salary commitments presents more difficulties because of the different effects of the various modes of student attendance but its efficacy is not reduced.
4. Simplicity and objectivity is most fully exploited when the ratios become management tools. On occasion even the universality can be utilised. Turning again to the discrepancy between an infant school (PTR 24:1) and polytechnic (8:1), it is significant that a main thrust of DES relationship with LEAs and colleges has been to increase SSR while, even with falling rolls and public expenditure reductions, policy towards schools has been more ambivalent. For schools as a whole the intention seems to be to hold the national PTR at around 18 or 19:1, a historically low level, after strenuous efforts to reduce it until the mid-1970s.[5] Although there appears no suggestion of a long-term goal to equalise ratios across all institutions, the medium-term intention in FE appears still to be higher SSRs through employing fewer staff, attracting more students and generally reducing per student expenditure (lowering the unit of resource). From a more detailed perspective, however, comparative school,

Resources and the Curriculum

college and LEA figures offer better prospects as monitors of resource use and factors in allocative decision-making. Take inter-LEA figures for PTR, which can be readily converted into a rank order (Table 4.1), and also comprise an important component in the resource-based profiles of LEAs (Chapter 1). The differences between generous provision (14.2 for ILEA and Brent, for example) and higher ratios (20.2 in Essex, 20.7 in Somerset) reflect enormous variations in per-pupil expenditures. If either authority with high PTR were to achieve national standards their salary costs would have to rise by over 10%, alternatively the more generously provisioned could reduce teacher salary expenditure by around 20% (provided employment policies made it practicable) and still have staffing standards no worse than the national average. Clearly such variations raise questions about the deployment of staff within schools - is the curricular broader, are classes smaller, do learning difficulties receive more attention, are the individual differences of children more effectively considered? - when the PTR is lower. Simple answers are impossible because of the autonomy with which schools deploy staff in relation to their own curricular design, but the dominance of the ratio remains.

Yet so long as LEAs have discretion over teacher employment, distributions about a mean PTR will continue. An authority with a high ratio will be pressurised, such is the visibility of that situation, by some councillor and teacher unions to employ more staff. The unions, in particular, functioning within a national perspective, try to establish a ratchet effect to drive PTRs downwards, with the only countervailing force (powerful though it is during contraction) being expenditure constraints. Differences therefore reflect local preferences and conditions powerfully reinforced by the historic situation in the LEA. Variations, of course, might be eliminated by an education block grant mechanism (Chapter 3), although it would take time before anything approaching inter-LEA uniformity emerged. Presumably, if input equity were sought, both at school and LEA level, and given the dominance of salary costs, then some sort of PTR consistency would be necessary. The situation that could result is well exemplified by ILEA experiences. Each school has some autonomy in determining teacher numbers (Chapter 6) but the resultant situation relative to PTR is readily monitored at District Level (Table 4.2) and, if necessary, within districts.

TABLE 4.1

PTRs Within Schools of English LEAs

	Prim.	Secd.		Prim.	Secd.		Prim.	Secd.		Prim.	Secd.
Barking	21.4	15.3	Oldham	24.0	17.5	Sandwell	22.9	15.7	Glos.	23.4	17.3
Barnet	20.6	15.0	Rochdale	22.9	15.5	Solihull	24.0	17.0	Hampshire	24.4	17.3
Bexley	24.1	17.1	Salford	21.5	15.5	Walsall	21.4	15.1	H'ford & Worc.	24.5	17.5
Brent	18.7	13.5	Stockport	23.6	16.7	Wolver'ton	19.1	15.2	Herts.	21.9	16.0
Bromley	23.9	16.2	Tameside	24.5	16.5	Bradford	20.9	18.9	Humberside	21.4	16.8
Croydon	22.3	16.0	Trafford	23.4	16.6	Calderside	22.1	17.3	Is. of Wight	22.9	18.1
Ealing	19.2	15.2	Wigan	21.5	15.4	Kirklees	22.6	17.7	Kent	24.0	17.5
Enfield	22.5	16.0	Knowsley	22.2	16.0	Leeds	23.1	17.5	Lancs.	24.4	16.7
Haringey	19.0	14.9	Liverpool	20.9	16.1	Wakefield	23.8	18.2	Leics.	23.7	16.8
Harrow	20.8	14.3	Sefton	22.6	16.9	Avon	24.3	16.9	Lincs.	24.7	17.0
Havering	23.3	16.1	St.Helens	23.5	16.0	Beds.	21.8	16.8	Norfolk	22.2	17.0
Hillingdon	23.1	16.5	Wirral	23.3	16.7	Berkshire	23.1	16.5	N.Yorkshire	22.2	16.9
Hounslow	20.4	15.1	Barnsley	22.5	16.7	Bucks.	23.8	16.7	Northamptons.	23.2	17.1
Kingston	22.4	16.7	Doncaster	21.8	16.6	Cambs.	23.5	16.8	North'land	23.4	18.2
Merton	22.2	17.5	Rotherham	22.9	17.2	Cheshire	23.3	17.1	Notts.	22.5	16.7
Newham	21.0	15.7	Sheffield	20.6	16.2	Cleveland	22.4	16.5	Oxon.	24.8	17.5
Redbridge	23.6	16.4	Gateshead	20.4	16.9	Cornwall	23.8	16.8	Shropshire	22.4	16.4
Richmond	21.6	16.1	Newcastle	18.3	14.4	Cumbria	22.0	16.3	Somerset	24.7	18.5
Sutton	24.9	17.1	N.Tyneside	20.5	15.6	Derbys.	22.8	17.4	Staffs.	22.4	16.5
Waltham Fst.	21.9	14.2	S.Tyneside	20.4	15.4	Devon	23.6	17.6	Suffolk	22.4	17.4
ILEA	17.5	14.1	Sunderland	22.0	16.2	Dorset	24.0	17.4	Surrey	22.2	16.5
Bolton	24.2	16.4	Birmingham	23.1	16.9	Durham	21.1	16.8	Warwicks.	22.8	17.5
Bury	23.1	16.1	Coventry	22.6	16.7	E.Sussex	22.5	17.4	W.Sussex	23.5	17.4
Manchester	22.2	14.8	Dudley	23.4	16.6	Essex	24.3	17.5	Wiltshire	23.8	17.6

Source: CIPFA Actuals 1981-82

TABLE 4.2

PTR in ILEA by Division (September 1979)

Division	Number of Schools Primary	Number of Schools Secondary	Total Number of Teachers Primary	Total Number of Teachers Secondary	PTR Primary	PTR Secondary
1	86	20	931	508	16.9	14.1
2	93	22	949	628	17.1	14.1
3	59	14	741	183	17.4	14.1
4	76	15	859	219	17.4	13.8
5	69	16	715	389	17.4	14.1
6	80	20	1044	285	17.8	14.2
7	88	20	1076	364	17.2	14.3
8	93	23	1054	424	16.9	14.2
9	95	15	1074	239	17.6	13.4
10	89	19	1127	299	17.3	14.3

Source: DES, Her Majesty's Inspectorate: Educational Provision by the Inner London Education Authority, 1980

Significantly, in a situation analogous to central funding, the differences between highest and lowest ratios (17.8:1 to 16.9:1 in primary schools, 14.3:1 to 13.4:1 in secondary schools) is much less than the equivalent discrepancies among LEAs. Therefore, because the ILEA has executive responsibility for the overall control of expenditure, in a similar way to which the DES might in block grant arrangements, the results are sanctioned by a single decision-centre. In contrast those in Table 4.1 emanate from a hundred or so separate centres, in which there may be pressure for conformity but not formal arrangements to achieve it. In either case the position of PTR as a needs comparator and resource monitor continues. It is difficult, for example, to envisage an ILEA situation in which District representation in allocative mechanisms would allow a substantial spread in ratios. Individual schools may have a figure away from the mean (in secondary schools, for example, the extreme range was 11.3 to 17.3:1) but such discrepancies represent adjustment situations - unanticipated pupil or staff changes.[6]

Following through the argument about separate decision centres would neatly explain variations in SSR among colleges.[7] It has some credibility of course, because of the element of resource independence possessed by colleges within LEA control mechanisms, much reduced in AFE activities by pool-capping and the development of NAB. However, even with much tighter restrictions, current levels of staffing reflect decisions made much earlier. More generally, though, SSR differences raise questions about the efficacy of the ratio as a management tool. It monitors the total deployment of staff by an institution at any one time. In colleges as complex as polytechnics, with different mixes of courses (making varying demands on staff time) and several modes of student attendance (whose importance is not uniform across colleges) identical SSRs would not be expected. However this raises two questions. First, how can some colleges function with low or high ratios, even when allowances are made for course and attendance patterns? The ratio can identify differences, but it cannot possibly attempt to answer this question. Second, when differences are identified what can or ought to be done? With a unified decision centre, for example, it might still be impossible to impose SSR uniformity, by recruiting more students or losing some staff, if the ratio of a particular college proves too low. The programme of activities might not be sufficiently attractive to recruit additional students, and there could be contractual obligations to staff. Over a period of time it should be possible to move towards inter-college consistency in ratios, using the SSR as the main distributive instrument, but with considerable risk of misallocation because no search has been made for an answer to the first question. To a large extent that is why derivatives of SSR have emerged, to consider the deployment of staff relative to students, courses and classes, so that arrangements leading to differences in ratios, and their elimination if necessary, can be more readily understood.

By contrast inter-school variations in PTR within an LEA are a less contentious topic. First, because differences which do emerge are more easily corrected. There may be difficulties in certain circumstances, a school with rapid NOR decline, for example, but in most situations there is a steady flow of staff leaving for one reason or another, and a precise estimate of pupil numbers. Second, as the basis of the calculation is simpler because the institutions are less complex, an objective of PTR uniformity across secondary schools in a LEA (say) gains more ready acceptance. As a result, LEAs pursuing consistency have fewer practical problems in achieving this goal in broad terms. Once again however the issue of the unitary decision-centre dominates. Unlike polytechnics, the final decisions about teaching staff for the schools of an authority are sanctioned by a single body, the education committee. As a result of the normal processes of micro-politics it is highly improbable that a school could sustain a generous provision, or be willing to accept less staff than its neighbours without some good reasons which were, at least, tacitly acknowledged by those involved in decision-making. Governors, for example, once alerted to an adverse situation are not likely to quietly accept a mugh higher PTR than a school down the road. Perhaps the LEA (as in the case of the ILEA[8]) can persuade those concerned that an objective set of needs criteria should be used to determine distributions, but this occurs in an authority already generously provisioned and where the inter-district differences in PTR that result are limited. More generally, staff, parents and governors will exert whatever influences they can, using the PTR as a main feature of their arguments, to correct what they would perceive as a deficiency. Of course, these efforts will not be wholly effective, with figures representing a snapshot, subject to fluctuations in pupil and teacher numbers (Chapter 6). However, the objectivity and the visibility of PTR as a measure of intra-LEA resource deployment militates against large inter-school variations in spending which can occur with other items.

The use of the ratios is not restricted to inter-institutional comparisons. Particularly when departments are separate, as in many colleges, with staff only working in one unit, the main problem in calculating intra-institutional ratios is to account for those students on inter-departmental courses and make allowances for service teaching. Obviously the methodology of calculating relative student loads between departments can always be disputed. Nor is a common ratio across an institution anticipated, for instance, because of the different demands made by lecture-based and workshop/laboratory situations. One of the first guidelines from the AFE pooling committee's suggested different target ratios of 7.5 - 8.5 for laboratory and workshop activities (Group 1 Faculties) and 9.2 - 10.2 for classroom-based work (Group 2 Faculties). The two bands being introduced to allow for the greater supervisory demands of the former students although the analogous study situation of library work for the other students did not contribute to teaching hours.[9] Originally these were no more than recommendations as pooling allowances were calculated quite separately. Particularly since the establishment of NAB the mechanisms for calculating institutional entitlements have become more sophisticated using a range of cost factors for each programme area. As a result the centrality of SSRs in these processes, because of its effects on salary, and therefore total, costs has increased.

Within schools, such inter-unit calculations are rarely attempted, not because they are impossible but, as most pupils study many subjects, an acceptable system of allowances is impracticable and the whole calculation highly cumbersome. In any case what appears to be a satisfactory method of comparing staff loads already exists, based on the number of periods of class-contact. If in each department the teaching contact ratios (TCR) (the number of periods with a class as a proportion of the total numbers of periods) are similar, then equal loading is assumed. However, in this context the TCR is much less revealing than PTR: for example two departments may have identical profiles of contact ratios among their staffs but because of larger classes one may be carrying proportionately a bigger pupil load and, if calculated, a higher PTR. For example, in a situation with average class size of 24 in geography and 12 in economics, the PTR supported by the former is, in effect, double that of the latter. However, if teachers in both departments are in contact with classes for 32 (out of 40) periods distributional equity might easily be assumed.

For different age-ranges PTR provides a monitor of staff deployment. This can be done by dividing the number of periods offered to the year group, (say 360 to Year One of a 9 form entry school) by the average teaching load (36 periods) so the time of nine teachers is utilized by 240 pupils, giving an operational PTR of 240 divided by 9 equals 26.7. This reduces with age-range, particularly as options are introduced.[10] It is a relatively easy matter to calculate. For schools with sixth forms the PTR there, in comparison to the rest of the school, introduces an important element teacher utilization. The basis of the calculation remains unchanged. In a 1,100 pupil school, with 100 in the sixth-form, and 72 staff, 360 periods are taught at sixth-form level and 1,800 in the main school. On this basis $\frac{360}{1800 + 360}$ that is 1/6th of all periods are attributable to the sixth-form, or the equivalent of twelve staff. The PTR for the sixth-form is therefore 100:12 (8.3:1), while that for the main school is double at 1000:60 (16.7:1). Of course both calculations can be criticised on methodological grounds. Is the division of staff, based solely on number of periods, reasonable? There is an implicit assumption that TCRs do not vary among staff working with the different age-ranges. Arising directly from this does work with sixth-form pupils occupy, in reality, the equivalent to the time of twelve staff? On one reckoning it is an underestimate of the time consumed by sixth-formers, as presumably their lessons demand more preparation and generate additional marking, as compared to those for the rest of the school. Perhaps the teachers concerned have more non-contact time. Alternatively, it is an overestimate to what would have been the calculated outcome had the product of pupils and periods displaced the periods only criterion for estimating staff time requirements. In this case the larger classes of the main school would be evaluated as taking a higher percentage of staff attention, yet the children would be comparatively disadvantaged by the large group situation. Nevertheless PTR remains as a highly visible monitor of teacher deployment, and evidence to support redistribution if it is thought, say, that sixth form work occupies too much staff time.

The process of disaggregation from LEA to institution to department in the use of the ratios can be taken a further stage. There is no reason, although it rarely happens in practice, why a student loading ratio cannot be calculated for each member of staff. The idea is probably more applicable in colleges than schools, particularly when staff are involved in a mix of full and part-time courses and different teaching arrangements. Two staff with similar class-contact hours may have quite dissimilar teaching loads, because of the relative size of classes and varying involvements in different teaching situations - formal lecturing as compared to supervising a laboratory. The way to reflect these dissimilarities in load is to concentrate on the student recipient of teaching activity. In any calculation of SSR one full-time equivalent student is assessed at exactly 1.0. That is the basis of the whole arrangement. Therefore, if a lecturer contributes 10% of the total teaching offered to a full-time student the resultant loading is 0.1: if the student is in a class of 20, this loading rises to 20 x 0.1 equals 2.0, if the class consists of part-timers (each of FTE 0.2) the loading would reduce 2.0 x 0.2 equals 0.4. By considering all the students with whom the lecturer is involved, whether in groups or individuals, an individual SSR for that staff-member can be calculated. Once more the system cannot be made totally objective. How, in the example cited, can one lecturer be assessed as providing 10% of all the teaching services given to that student: how will the remaining 90% be sub-divided among colleagues? These are matters for internal negotiation among staff. On this basis the average individual SSR for departmental staff must equate to the SSR for the whole department: and a viable method for monitoring the loading of staff has been provided.[11]

The range of situations in which PTR or SSR can be used to assist in resource management, therefore, vary from national comparisons of schools and colleges through to calculations of the teaching loads carried by individual staff. In the main it is the simplicity of the idea which creates the numerous opportunities, and while objectivity in an absolute sense may not always be available, allowances for part-time students in SSR calculations, for example, permit an objectivity which is visible and (if necessary negotiable) and an extension of usage to all circumstances where there are staff and clients. The ratios are therefore central in any consideration of resource management and the curriculum. Yet that very simplicity is, of course, the main disadvantage of the ratio, because of the issues which as a result can never receive attention. It is those which are considered next.

MANAGING THE CURRICULUM WITH PTR AND SSR

The ratios, are, therefore, focal because they are easily understood and, in most cases, simple to use: on account of their universality and, in many situations, objectivity: and as they provide invaluable monitors of resource use, which guide in resource allocations, and assist in calculations of staffing requirements and their costing. Yet, in this detailed consideration of the ubiquitous merits of PTR and SSR one dominant issue has gone unmentioned. It is all very well to talk of staff requirements, in relation to teacher numbers and their costs, or implicitly when considering ratios that might be used to adjust the supply of staff, but any discussion is inhibited until some clarification of these requirements has been attempted. More directly, whose requirements are they, and how have they been defined? If a school compares its PTR to that of a neighbour, or its own over time, all the measures are relative. The fact that the ratio might be rising says something about the general availability of resources: a lower PTR than that of the next school implies that somewhere in the decision-making process its requirements for staff have been assessed to be greater than that of the neighbour: but these judgements are not absolute. It all depends on the definition of requirement, and the criteria selected for that definition.

In using PTR and SSR as management tools the main disadvantage is that every school and college could make out a case for additional staff, while the ratios can give neither any indications of how the extra staff might be utilised nor the criteria against which the case is being made. Even when soon after their establishment some polytechnics had low SSRs the argument that the main problem of student shortage might be alleviated by more staff offering a wider programme of courses had some credibility. Whatever the circumstances, there is

Resources and the Curriculum

always some measure of support from staff, governors, parents, local councillors etc. for the idea that the school or college could benefit from extra teachers. This stems both from the view that with more staff the school or college could do a better job, and as an integral component in public resource allocation, from which the institutions cannot escape. If they do not lobby for additional resources then by implication they find current levels of provision satisfactory and are, in a competitive situation, highly unlikely to be able to increase these levels: more significantly, with retrenchment they must be candidates for reductions.

Take the situation in a secondary school, if more staff are employed, and with constant NOR the ratio declines from 17:1 to 15:1, then it should be able to offer additional options, organize smaller classes and put more staff into remedial work. In colleges with constant or rising student numbers and a SSR decrease then, almost certainly, analogous processes would result. In both cases it can be argued that the requirements for additional staff are no more than a restatement or an interpretation of educational needs. For the school mentioned, insufficient choice of options is provided for the children, their learning is impeded by large class sizes and opportunities for remedial work too restricted. Therefore a range of educational needs are either being overlooked or inadequately satisfied. A lower PTR provides, at least, a partial remedy. Clearly, a definition of needs depends entirely upon the individual making the judgement. One person may think that the particular school offers enough choice to pupils, has optimum class-sizes and gives sufficient attention to remedial activities: another would wish to maximise choice, minimize class size and expand the remedial work even if it means a reduction of PTR to 13:1.

While a statement of educational needs to be satisfied has implications for PTR or SSR, the value of the ratio selected, although reflecting an interpretation of needs, does not imply anything about them. It says much more about the demands for educational services, and the total level of resources available. A school or an LEA may have a smaller PTR than its neighbour: this does not mean that its educational needs must be greater nor, more important, that there has to be a greater chance of their satisfaction. An opportunity for smaller classes etc. exists, but that is not the intention of the exercise. Ultimately, educational

125

wants at which the lower PTR is directed, can only be considered in terms of more effective learning by the children.

The relationship between the ratios and educational needs is, therefore, tenuous. PTR and SSR are measures of resource input. As already demonstrated they can be extremely useful, but as managerial tools they have their limitations. From a management stance the key issue is, indeed, obtaining some agreement about the needs to be satisfied, and maximising the pursuit of this satisfaction by the most effective use of resource inputs. Clearly, a college with a reduced SSR can organize more activities and offer more lecturer time per student, but is the subsequent programme better or, more precisely, is progress towards the aims and objectives of the institution accelerated? Of course, the relationship between inputs and outputs is notoriously difficult to assess in education. In most situations precision is impossible because exact definition of intentions, in a manner acceptable to all involved, cannot be achieved. Usually a multiple set of goals are sought, involving processes, the fundamental component of which - the organization of human learning - is not well understood. In these circumstances there is an inevitable tendency to concentrate on those items where precision is possible: in this case the resources input and, more particularly, the PTR or SSR. A change in SSR from 9:1 to 8:1 offers no guarantees about more or improved outcomes by the college. To assume this as a certainty confuses the curriculum of the college as a scheme of subjects and activities, with a series of processes whose qualities in relation to student needs is the key element.

Nevertheless, it is perhaps inevitable that without formal assessment of outcomes that attention should be centred on the number of clients per staff-member as a substitute measure of achievement. In schools, fewer children per teacher gives a chance to spend additional time with each child, therefore facilitating the identification of individual wants and providing for their satisfaction. In addition, for each school, the ratio has to be considered in relation to tradition, previous practice, and expectation. As already mentioned, a school with a higher but reducing PTR is likely to perceive itself in a preferable resource position to another with a lower, but rising PTR. The nature of this perception is important. Viewing the curriculum as a series of processes, a main determinant of quality must be the attitudes of teachers (because of their dominance in these processes) which in turn are influenced by the actuality of the ratio (and its effects on their work situation) what it has been previously and what it could become. Teachers in a school of PTR 16:1 will be appalled by the possibility of a rise to 18:1, while 20:1 (even if there are no implications for job-security) might be regarded as quite tolerable. Yet, in another school, or at an alternative time, this last level of staffing could have been perfectly acceptable. In direct terms the perception of staffing provision can affect the quality of the process.

These factors however do not alter the main issue that PTR and SSR are no more than measures of input which, in themselves, have uncertain links with educational quality, nor do they throw any light on the issues of teacher deployment relative to the pursuit and accomplishment of educational objectives. For example, during the last 15 years or so, a thrust of government policy towards AFE has been to increase SSRs, but it is difficult to envisage that part of this intention, throughout the period, was to reduce the vigour with which educational needs were pursued. It may have been true, certainly for some of the time, that needs and their satisfaction were being redefined, or that the same range were being sought at lower cost, but that misses the point. A comparison between a national policy to reduce PTR and simultaneously increase SSR is significant and, more importantly in this context, it illustrates the increasing level of sophistication with which the ratios must be deployed if they are to provide effective tools for curriculum management. In colleges these processes are well developed, partly because of the more complex arrangements of courses and programmes (which does not occur in schools) but mainly as a response to pressures for higher SSRs. Therefore, the whole issue of using teaching staff, and the other resources of the college, to provide a range of activities has received more public attention than in schools. There, until recently, the PTR has remained supreme (largely because of policy to lower it and the resultant benefits to the school) but with the coincidence of fewer children and less resources refinements have been sought. However the differences in developmental stages of SSR and PTR are so great that separate consideration is demanded.

SSR AND THE COLLEGE CURRICULUM

Obviously the most logical way to begin discussing the curricular requirements of a college is with a definition of educational needs. What are they, which educational objectives are involved, what alternative routes happen to be available for their accomplishment, which of these is likely to be the most effective? Then having gone through these processes, while linking them with resource considerations, start to plan for the buildings, staff and other resources which will have to be deployed. In practice, except possibly with the establishment of a new college, this is not the order of events. Colleges have grown in response to needs, as expressed now (or some time previously) by the community, local authority, staff, government or whatever, but these wants are not constant. A new department has been set up in a college perhaps, because of the demands of local employers for certain skills. As these demands change, as well as the means for satisfying them, it would be unusual for yet another department to be introduced: it would be even more unusual for the original department to be closed down: more likely the department will have to adapt its activities to new circumstances.

The more realistic starting point, therefore, in discussing a college curriculum relative to staffing concerns fitting resources which the college already possesses (staff in post, etc.) to an interpretation of educational needs. The annual budget is vital, in terms of acquiring new and additional staff, but as already discussed in Chapter 3 many decisions have already been taken before that stage occurs. When a new need is identified the college can argue for more staff and with those that it attracts as a result of the budget processes, alongside other lecturers willing or persuaded to adopt different commitments, it provides the team that attempts to satisfy the additional requirements that have been generated. However, many older needs continue, and the total process is best viewed as a series of modifications with the college adjusting deployment patterns in the pursuit of a changing group of objectives. The speed of that adjustment depends upon institutional characteristics obviously, but also upon the availability of new resources, the rate of change in the needs, the pressures from community, governors and employers, and the ways in which the college chooses to

Resources and the Curriculum

interpret those needs. Therefore, it is a mix of college, community and education based parameters which shape the curriculum at any point in time.

Unlike a school, it would be misleading to even try and specify the curriculum (in terms of courses and activities) at a typical college, primarily because of the difficulty of describing such an institution. A local college of FE, concentrating largely on NAFE work, might be thought of as representative of a particular type of institution but individual variations are still considerable, reflecting the traditional strengths of the college and the industrial base of the area, which may well have changed. One college may have a large engineering department, another a predominating science faculty, (possibly with a specialism in (say) glass technology,)while a third college may concentrate on 'O' and 'A' level work. This lack of typicality arises from the high scope of further education as defined by the 1944 Education Act, ranging from part-time non-vocational courses to higher degrees by research. 12 In fact so wide is the spectrum that the only connecting strands are staff, students and the satisfaction of educational needs. Returning then, to the deployment of the first to meet the needs of the second the natural starting point remains SSR.

The actual calculation of a college or departmental SSR can present some problems. Many are of a technical nature but require consideration because of the likely effects on curriculum organization. Notionally, of course, the matter could not be simpler,

$$\text{SSR equals} \frac{\text{Number of Full-time equivalent students}}{\text{Number of Full-time equivalent staff}}$$

On this basis all that has to be done is to discover the number of equivalent full-time students at any time and divide by the complementary figure for staff. The difficulties centre on the work equivalence. It is not sufficient for a college or department, or even LEA, to have its own conversion formula from part to full-time, because the 'AFE pool', and inter-authority arrangements for payment demand a standardized national agreement. Therefore, allowances have to be available for every mode of student attendance, applicable in all maintained colleges.

Basically, four categories of students are defined, and the combined total from each category provides the aggregate student FTE of the college: (a) full-time students enrolled on three-term courses, each of whom is classified as one FTE: (b) sandwich course students x 0.9 (to allow for the time these students are not in college): (c) students on short courses (lasting less than a term) x 1.1 x Y: (d) students on other courses x Y. Where Y is the number of hours of tuition received by students in (c) and (d), divided by the average hours received by a full-time student during the year.[13]

Clearly any type of attendance can be included in the calculation from full-time and sandwich students through part-time day and evening study (for example on BTEC courses) MSC financed courses lasting longer, at 46 weeks, than the conventional three-terms (36 weeks) to non-vocational, evening only courses. If, for example, a student receives 60 hours tuition during the year (and the total for full-time students is 600 hours) the FTE is 0.1. Were the course to last less than a term this would be raised to 0.11. The FTE for staff is the number of full-time staff, plus the number of hours of tuition provided by part-time staff per year divided by the product of the number of weeks in the normal college year, and 18 in AFE, or 21 for NAFE (on the assumption that the average teaching hours per week of full-time staff is 18 or 21 respectively).

The calculation is, therefore, straightforward if tedious, although not uncontentious. There are a number of minor issues, to the extent that their effect on the SSR will be minimal, which require little further attention. Whether the most senior non-teaching staff should be included (usually not), the allowances to be made for essential non-teaching staff (such as librarians) and the 0.9 factor for sandwich students (which could only become more exact following detailed comparative studies of the hourly demands made by conventional full-time and sandwich courses), are all factors which only influence the final outcome marginally. However, two other components have a more substantial effect:
1. The argument that the demands upon staff of part-time students, relative to full-time, attract an underestimation through this methodology is difficult to refute. Few who have worked with both types of student would dissent from the view that, other things being equal, the hour by hour requirements of part-timers, when in attendance, are much greater. When at college for the day or evening the teaching sessions tend to be much more

Resources and the Curriculum

concentrated. Often a leisurely approach in lectures or tutorials cannot be countenanced if the course material is to be covered in the available hours. Yet these five hours, say, as compared to the 20 hours per week of a full-time student only attract a FTE of 0.25, raised to 0.275 if the course lasts less than a term. Some allowance is therefore made for the additional demands of short-duration courses but in the overall scheme it represents no more than an incremental response. Similar arguments for under-allowance apply to the marking and preparation duties generated by part-time students, and the administrative load created. Only in building utilization, particularly with evening only students using rooms which might otherwise be empty, are part-timers not discriminated against in SSR calculations: and even this assumes that premises are provided for full-time students.

In terms of curriculum organization the most likely effects of this under-estimation of the demands made by part-time students is to enhance the importance of full-time courses. From a departmental or institutional perspective there are obvious attractions in maximising the numbers of full-time students, irrespective of definitions of educational needs which may place more emphasis on short courses or those involving day-release. In addition to the benefits accruing from the method of calculation there are often perceived status gains among staff when working with full-time students. For AFE, in particular, work with full-time honours degree students will appeal to some staff much more than an equivalent series (in terms of student loading) of short courses which, almost certainly, will be more difficult to plan and not provide the same long-term guarantees of student attendance. The combination of factors, directing staff towards full-time students, becomes especially significant in any attempt to up-date the skills of the work-force and extend adult education (Chapter 2). Some of the elements adversely affecting part-time activities may be difficult to correct: allowances in the calculations are not.
2. Clearly an assessment of the number of hours students are in contact with a teacher is a dominant theme in the calculation. If (c) and (d) (above) are important contributors to total student numbers then the actual procedures to evaluate hours will have a considerable effect on the FTEs provided by part-time students. Undoubtedly this

occurs in colleges concentrating upon NAFE work. Here nearly 2.1m., out of a total population of over 3m., attend for evenings only, while 426,000 of those remaining are day-release students. Less than 10% are full-time students, although the equivalent figure in AFE (including sandwich courses) is higher at 55%.14 Yet, in some colleges, there may be as many as four methods of describing course hours: (i) those specified in course documents, for example, in CNAA validation exercises: (ii) those that are timetabled: (iii) those on returns to DES: (iv) the actual hours students attend lectures, seminars etc.15 The discrepancies may be small, but a 10% reduction in the calculation of part-time hours and a 10% increase in the comparable full-time figure would lower the contribution of FTEs from students in categories (c) and (d) by over 20%. If a college with a large part-time element wishes to maximise its calculated SSR it can face something of a dilemma. By increasing the hours of students in categories (c) and (d), and reducing those of full-time students, it can increase the FTE contribution of those part-time students, but at the risk of making the full-time courses less effective while reducing the contribution of full-time student hours to college staffing allowances and departmental grading calculations.

However the question of hours raises the more fundamental issue of the optimum timetabled contact between students and lecturers. A powerful argument can be presented that this should be left to the discretion of the lecturer, perhaps by negotiation with the students, provided that monitoring procedures are sufficiently developed to ensure that objectives are being accomplished. It is the lecturer who knows the work that has to be covered and, making professional judgements about the learning rates of the students, should be able to determine how many hours are required to cover the syllabus. In other words, what has to be done is the first consideration: how long it might take follows. There is a risk, however, that with so much concentration on hours (exacerbated by agreements about the weekly teaching load per lecturer) the initial concern will be the utilization of staff time. More directly, the charge can be made of over-teaching. It may appear paradoxical to raise this issue when an objective in schools is to maximise teacher availability per child, but there are advantages in allowing students time for private work and reading. As a result the discovery by a college that it is under-utilizing the teaching resource by 10% (lecturers only being timetabled for classes for 90% of the total agreed - 20 hours per week instead of 22 hours, for example)[16] must be considered with some caution. If the solution is to raise staff time with the same classes this would be much less satisfactory than the attraction of new classes and the formation of additional groups with the extra time.

Were alternative mechanisms to calculate SSR adopted, undoubtedly some colleges or departments would be relatively advantaged as compared to others. In what ways, though, would they be assisted? Certainly not in actual terms: a different scheme for calculating SSR, however much it may change that particular outcome, does not provide extra staff or additional students. A higher calculated SSR may make the institution appear more effective (as it is processing more students per unit of teaching staff resource) and can be a tool in arguing for resources. The development of the polytechnics in the early 1970s provides a useful example. Some colleges were well below the target SSRs of the pooling committee, largely because of inadequate recruitment. Not surprisingly such under utilization of a resource, provided both at considerable revenue cost and substantial recent investment, could only be supported as a temporary measure. Here, the argument presumably was that high expenditures in the developmental stages of a major project were to be expected, according to a graph of costs against time (Figure 4.1)

FIGURE 4.1   Development costs over time

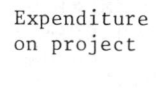

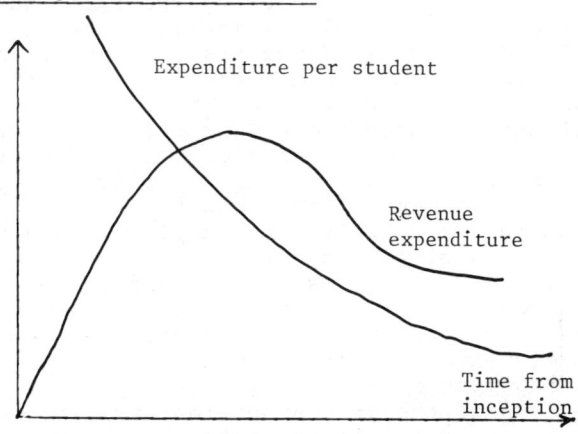

On this occasion low levels of student recruitment, and therefore the relatively high unit costs, disguised the opportunity it gave staff to introduce alternative teaching approaches and initiate course development, which might not have been available with greater student loads. In other words, the development costs were passed on to the taxpayer or ratepayer. Paradoxically in another situation the reorganization of secondary education, where 'slack' due to depleted recruitment did not occur, the client - the school child- had to sustain the development costs: as the new courses and approaches were introduced within existing and largely unaltered constraints on staff time.

However a situation involving under-utilization of resources, and high unit costs, could not be allowed to continue indefinitely. All that SSR demonstrates, in these circumstances, is too few students or too many staff. It says nothing about how the staff are deployed in relation to time with students or class sizes, nor the timetable commitments of students. In view of low rates of SSR a formula linking these factors attracted considerable attention from 1972 onwards.[17]

$$SSR = \frac{ACS \times ALH}{ASH}$$

where ACS is the average class size, ALH is the average hours per week lectures are with students and ASH is the average hours per week students are being supervised.

At any given time SSR is constant (the college has its complement of staff and students, and the methodology for calculating the ratio has been confirmed) so in itself it is not a device for raising SSR. What it can demonstrate, though, is the disposition of staff and students in relation to three main contributory variables, and the potential effects of adjusting any of the four factors. For while developed when ratios were judged too low, the relationships are still applicable in a different environment. If a department has to raise SSR from 10:1 to 12:1, for example, likely implications for class-sizes etc. or the number of courses to be organized, can be estimated, and by focussing attention on specific items a potential new dimension is added to curriculum management. In a course with an elective element attended by 100 students introducing more options will raise ALH but lower ACS because of the greater choice available and, unless extra students are attracted by the new options, SSR will remain static. In addition, by using more total lecturer hours available to the department, remaining courses might be deprived unless complementary adjustments can be made in their ACS or ASH.

From a curriculum management perspective the crucial issue is college control over the variables. With regard to the teaching hours of staff, choice is limited. Following union agreement the proportion of the normal 30 hour working week involving timetabled teaching and related activities (tutorial and supervisory work) as well as invigilating examinations etc., depends upon the seniority of the post. The actual contact hours required of each lecturer, being set by local arrangements between the LEA and NATFHE, within the following bands agreed nationally. Principal lecturers - 13-16 hours: Senior lecturers - 15-18 hours: Lecturer Grade II - 17-20 hours: Lecturer Grade I - 20-22 hours. In addition the college principal is allowed a certain level of remission hours, to be awarded to staff with particular administrative duties, such as BTEC co-ordinator.

Work in the college is classified by level:-

AFE	I	- Courses, or research programmes, where a first degree is a normal pre-requisite of attendance.
	II/III	- Courses leading to a first degree or equivalent qualification, with normal entry requirements of one or more 'A' levels.
NAFE	IV	- Courses above 'O' level or comparable standard.
	V	- Other courses.

with these categories being used to determine the staffing profile, by seniority, required in each department, calculated from a range of distributions of lecturer posts nationally negotiated. (Table 4.3). Combining course categorization and the recommended distributions of senior posts, with the appropriate figure of available teaching hours per lecturer, provides a mechanism for calculating the staffing requirements of each department and therefore the whole college.[18]

Clearly these arrangements inhibit college freedoms in maximising teacher contact-ratio, to raise ALH. Control over this variable is limited to ensuring that teaching loads of individual staff are near or at the top of the negotiated

135

TABLE 4.3   Recommended Distribution of Lecturer Posts in Further Education

Category of Work	Grade	Proportion of Posts Estabs. of Further Education	Colleges of Education Technical
I	Principal Lecturer	20%-30%	35%-40%
	Senior Lecturer and Lecturer Grade II	70%-80%	60%-65%
II/III	Principal Lecturer	10%-25%	25%-35%
	Senior Lecturer and Lecturer Grade II	75%-90%	65%-75%
IV	Senior Lecturer	0%-5%	
	Lecturer Grade II	40%-65%	
	Lecturer Grade I	30%-60%	
V	Senior Lecturer	0%-5%	
	Lecturer Grade II	15%-25%	
	Lecturer Grade I	70%-85%	

Source: DES *Scales of Salaries for Teachers in Further Education, England and Wales 1983* (HMSO, London, 1983).

Resources and the Curriculum

range. From a logistical perspective this presents problems and raises again the issue of overteaching. There is a similar lack of flexibility in relation to ASH. Suppose a college, maintaining other variables constant, wishes to attract more students, raise SSR, and offer students less teacher contact. Often it cannot as the number of hours of supervised study available to a student on a particular course is not solely determined by course-teachers or even the senior staff of the college. They may directly affect the outcome when it is decided to organize additional tutorial work, for example, but in the main it is a matter of influencing the negotiation process, involving the department, the agency sponsoring the student (where this is appropriate) and the organization which validates the qualification. A department will agree with BTEC, and probably the student's employer, the most appropriate time allowance for one of its modules: parallel discussions with MSC, or a professional institution, will determine the hours required by students on a retraining course or in preparation for a professional qualification. Departmental control over these matters is limited, and flexibility rare, with regional and national patterns setting norms of acceptability supported in many cases by the traditional arrangements established by past practice. More directly the likelihood of a college being able to achieve an overall reduction in ASH of 10% say, even if it wished to, is remote. The college finds itself locked into practices over which its controls are circumscribed. Therefore, as for ALH, ASH is less susceptible to adjustment by college staff than might have been expected. In fact many colleges and departments have to resolve a dilemma: if they wish to raise SSR they must minimize ASH, but the product of this, the weeks of the course, and the number of enrolments (that is the annual total of student-hours) is central in Burnham procedures, helping to determine both the grade of the department (and therefore the salary of the head) and the group of the college and, as a result, the salary of the vice-principal and principal.[19] In brief if it wishes to improve its position under Burnham arrangements it should (a) enrol as many students as possible (b) maximise the number of hours of teaching (to increase its claim for staffing, and raise the salaries of senior staff) (c) recruit students to high level courses (as they count proportionately more in college totals) and (d) teach students in small classes to increase teaching hours.[20]

To raise a college SSR it becomes increasingly clear that the most fruitful approach, if sufficient students can be attracted, is to increase ACS - the average size of classes (the total of student-hours divided by the total contact-hours of staff). Invariably class size is less than course size because option choices, individual tutorials and small group seminars, are all likely to be available, while in many practical and workshop situations courses have to be sub-divided. Some LEAs set minimum enrolments before courses can proceed. One set of recommendations suggests a minimum of 24 for full-time courses (including sandwich) 15 for part-time courses, with practical elements, and 10 for other part-time courses.[21] For NAFE activities LEAs have discretion over numbers, and indeed whether courses should run. Rules can be established by individual LEAs but are not mandatory. Undoubtedly in some authorities control mechanisms are under-developed with guidelines (when they exist) being disregarded, but courses regularly attracting small numbers of students can adversely affect subsequent allocations to a college or department. In AFE the Secretary of State, through NAB (originally using the Regional Advisory Council network) has the ultimate power to approve all work. In other words mandatory controls exist, but consistency in their application, as perceived by colleges, may not always be obvious. The pattern, established in 1983 emphasises the need for skilled technological or scientific workers, implying that DES will only approve new courses if they seem likely to satisfy this need or are otherwise essential for industry, commerce and the professions.[22] This clarifies the position to some extent, but from a resources perspective the main problem once a course has been approved (by DES or LEA) and recruits students, the college enters into a commitment with students who wish to continue, and an obligation, in terms of the marketability of future activities to itself, to support the course until its conclusion, irrespective of final student numbers. As students leave - and this is a particular problem for three or four year courses - ACS will decline, and an appropriate entry size, in relation to likely drop-out, determines the mean ACS over the duration of the programme. With ACS, unlike ALH and ASH, staff are dealing with factors over which they have some measure of direct influence. In most situations the likelihood of students leaving before course completion is not unrelated to the quality of teaching and support services, and student perceptions of how adequately the programme meets their needs. It is of little value, and may well be counter-productive, to start with large classes, anticipating high drop-outs: far better to sustain ACS by means of activities which attract and retain sufficient numbers of students.

This section began with the observation that the calculation of SSR could be complex. In one respect this complexity reduces the efficiency of SSR as a management tool, because acceptance of its usefulness also involves acquiescence to the assumptions and qualifications which are needed to support that use: in another respect the value of SSR is increased because that complexity encourages the development of refinements in the ways in which it can be applied. Therefore, ALH, ASH and ACS have all evolved as derivatives of SSR. Yet, having considered their inter-relationships, the issue of usefulness again emerges. If ALH is constrained by union agreements, ASH by tradition and negotiation with validating and supporting agencies then, in some ways, average class-sizes is little more than a surrogate for SSR. In other words if classes are small then SSR will be low and unit costs high, while to increase the ratio the only option involves raising class-sizes: but this is so self-evident it hardly requires derivatives or refinements to SSR for its justification.

The main point is that ALH, ASH and ACS are supportive monitors: indicators of how the main resource, of teaching staff, is deployed relative to students, and therefore within a framework imposed by SSR. Norms are published for the three minor indicators (Table 4.4) using the same upper, middle and lower quartiles as for SSR, so that colleges can assess their own position relative to others. However, the dominant issue is that those subsidiary measures, as befits indicators, follow and monitor the process of curriculum management, they cannot lead it. A college plans its programme of courses and activities relative to the availability of staff interests and expertise and, setting aside the matter of quality, that defines its curriculum. Clearly, the process of planning, and more particularly implementation, is tightly constrained by resource issues. A college cannot organize a course unless staffing, as well as buildings and equipment are available, but the starting point is some perception of educational needs and how these can

TABLE 4.4   National Distributions of SSR, ASH, ALH and ACS (1981-82)

			Lower Quartile	Median	Upper Quartile
POLYTECHNICS					
SSR	Group 1	Poolable	8.6	8.9	9.7
		Non-Poolable	7.3	8.6	11.0
	Group 2	Poolable	10.1	10.6	11.4
		Non-Poolable	7.4	10.0	12.1
ASH	Group 1	Poolable	19.5	20.5	23.4
		Non-Poolable	25.9	26.2	26.2
	Group 2	Poolable	14.4	15.4	16.6
		Non-Poolable	22.6	22.9	24.6
ALH	Group 1	Poolable	12.8	13.1	14.4
		Non-Poolable	13.5	14.6	15.1
	Group 2	Poolable	11.8	12.6	13.5
		Non-Poolable	12.1	13.9	15.5
ACS	Group 1	Poolable	12.3	14.2	16.3
		Non-Poolable	12.7	14.8	19.5
	Group 2	Poolable	12.3	13.4	15.0
		Non-Poolable	12.4	15.4	23.9
COLLEGES OF FURTHER EDUCATION					
SSR	Group 1	Poolable	6.5	7.5	8.7
		Non-Poolable	8.0	8.5	9.4
	Group 2	Poolable	6.8	8.5	10.3
		Non-Poolable	8.2	9.8	11.1
ASH	Group 1	Poolable	25.6	26.8	26.8
		Non-Poolable	27.3	28.6	30.3
	Group 2	Poolable	21.7	23.1	26.4
		Non-Poolable	25.5	28.0	30.0
ALH	Group 1	Poolable	14.4	15.9	16.8
		Non-Poolable	17.6	18.2	18.7
	Group 2	Poolable	14.3	15.6	17.0
		Non-Poolable	17.1	18.3	19.1
ACS	Group 1	Poolable	10.7	12.4	14.6
		Non-Poolable	12.2	13.0	14.7
	Group 2	Poolable	10.1	12.0	14.4
		Non-Poolable	13.4	14.8	16.4

Source: The Department of the Environment, Audit Inspectorate; Colleges of Further Education, Guide to the Measurement of Resource Efficiency (HMSO, London, 1983).

best be satisfied with the resources likely to be available, rather than calculations utilizing the two variables ACS and SSR over which the college has most control. Perhaps the most apt description is a series of interactive processes of matching programmes to a definition of objectives.

Therefore, the main items in curriculum management are the organization of courses to attract sufficient numbers of students, the likelihood of sustaining these numbers for the duration of the course, and the replacement of those activities which, because of their lack of attractiveness, do not appear to be adequately satisfying student needs in relation to the mix of resources the college has at its disposal or is able to acquire. It is a matter of maintaining the match between the needs and resources. The college can help define needs by marketing its courses to individuals or organizations (systematically approaching local employers, for example) and by introducing new courses, possibly following the identification of skill shortages or perhaps as a result of sponsorship by MSC or a local firm. However, if it defines them wrongly or pursues them ineffectively (because staff are inappropriately trained for the task, say) then market mechanisms come into play. Students leave (or do not join) courses, class-sizes decrease, SSR falls and unit costs must rise: in fact, auditors are asked to monitor procedures for introducing new courses, and the ability of colleges to attract and sustain student numbers, as well as the outcomes of ACS and SSR.[23]

In the actual mechanics of staffing a college curriculum there are two quite distinct approaches. In the first of these, Burnham arrangements are used to determine staffing requirements, following aggregation of the hours likely to be taught during the next year in relation to course level and the agreed teaching loads of staff. Figure 4.2 demonstrates the methodology. In this case the curriculum design is finalised during the LEA - college negotiation about course hours the LEA is prepared to support. This approach is more popular in colleges with a high proportion of NAFE work, because of the greater LEA freedom in sanctioning work at this level. Provided that there is LEA and college agreement that a course should be provided this can be incorporated in the calculations and there is no need for further support. In many situations there will be discussions with neighbouring authorities to ensure inter-LEA support for students: there may

FIGURE 4.2   Calculation of fe staffing needs by 'Burnham'
             methodology

In the example of a typical large department there are three
distinct stages:

(a) The course-hours per week are listed by category (p.135)

II and III	IV	V	Total
145.5	419.5	292.5	857.5

(b) The course hours per week are then allocated to lecturer
     post seniority (Table 4.3). On this occasion using mid-
     point of the Burnham distribution.

PL	17.5% II and III hours	
SL and LII	82.5% II and III hours	
SL	2.5% IV and V hours	
LII	52.5% IV hours	20% V hours
LI	45% IV hours	77.5% V hours

to give an hourly distribution:

PL	SL and LII	SL	LII	LI	Total
25.5	120	17.5	278.5	415.5	857.5

(c) These hours are converted into staff establishments
     using the recommended weekly teaching load by level of
     lectures (p.135)

Principal Lecturer	14 hours
Senior Lecturer	16 hours
Lecturer Grade II	18 hours
Lecturer Grade I	21 hours

Therefore staffing establishment

PL	SL and LII	SL	LII	LI
1.8	6.6	1.25	19.9	19.8

have to be reliance on a sponsoring agency (such as MSC) and in some regions machinery exists to avoid wasteful duplication of effort among colleges, but the basic situation remains unchanged. As a result of these circumstances, with ALH and ASH as integral components in the calculation of staffing needs, ACS becomes, in effect, directly proportioned to SSR, and the need to maintain attractive courses all the more important. As a result, however, if the Burnham arrangements are used as an allocative mechanism SSR becomes an after the event monitor of class-size strongly influenced by the ability of the college to retain students and the main determinant of unit costs.

The alternative approach uses SSR as the basic allocative tool, crude though it is, and award the college (or its department) staffing levels based on predicted student numbers for next year. A college attracting extra students may therefore be disadvantaged, but the main effect is the diffusion of curriculum management processes through the decision making mechanisms of the college and department. Take a college with a predicted enrolment of 1,000 FTE students and 100 staff. It is highly unlikely that each department will have a SSR of 10:1, indeed there is no certainty that this will represent a feasible college objective. First, there are the recommendations of the pooling committee and Audit Inspectors on differential SSRs between Group I and Group II faculties, which may influence college decisions: second, in some situations colleges might wish to protect certain departments with low SSRs as they introduce new courses: third, and most significant of all, lecturers are not readily transferable among departments. If it appears that during the next year one department will have a SSR of 12.1 and another 8.1 there is little the college can do towards equalization in the short term. Lecturer skills are usually so specific that transfer opportunities are minimal, and the only mechanisms available to correct such an imbalance are either to award more staff to the department with the higher SSR or raise the student quotas in the other. Clearly, these are implications for future staffing allocations, but even here (if there is a policy of no compulsory redundancies) flexibility depends upon the availability of additional staff or the chance occurrence of resignations. In other words the importance of SSR as an allocative mechanism, in an absolute sense, has to be modified by reference to a set of desirable target figures, which are strongly influenced by the practicalities of staff in post and student enrolments. In the same sense the derivatives of ALH, ASH and, in particular, ACS illustrate the actuality of staff and student deployment (relatable, of course, to targets) which can then be used as parameters in the processes of curriculum planning and implementation.

The least contentious explanation of the greater popularity of SSR distributive mechanisms in AFE colleges is that the resultant diffusion of decision-making to college and department, sanctioned by LEAs, balances the controls imposed by DES, CNAA and NAB. Also such colleges tend to be large, often involved in work not easily understood by non-experts, while the systems of government, as they have evolved, emphasize staff and governor autonomy.[24] It can be argued, on the basis of these inter-related factors, that LEAs defer to college-based decision-making because they are unwilling (or unable) to become associated with the detail of curriculum management. Without external controls though, it is doubtful whether LEAs would have granted such freedom, particularly given the high unit costs of AFE. In contrast with NAFE, if a LEA or a sponsor provides adequate resources a course can run and therefore tighter authority control of college activities through direct negotiation might be thought necessary involving fine detail of curriculum organization - the number of options on a course, the size of classes before they should be split etc. Yet, if there is validity in this explanation the school situation appears highly paradoxical.

PTR AND THE SCHOOL CURRICULUM

The main component in the paradox is that while the PTR has been the traditional method of determining the teacher requirements of a school (and continues with some minor variations in most LEAs) external controls on the utilization of staff in relation to activities are minimal. There is no need for DES permission to teach certain subjects for example: and nothing equivalent to CNAA or NAB. Certain regulatory requirements have to be satisfied (length of school day, number of days per school year, teacher qualifications etc.)[25] but their direct impact on curriculum management are minimal. So it appears that local authorities (and, for that matter, DES) have been content to award schools a certain number of teachers, based mainly on roll-size, and considerable latitude in how they might be deployed. This describes the practical situation as it has evolved: an uninitiated reading of s23 of the 1944 Education Act implies otherwise. According to this LEAs can control secular education in maintained schools, but even by 1945 the Ministry of Education model articles of government,26 adopted by most authorities, suggested that the LEA should only determine the general educational character of the school and its place in the local education system, while the governing body accepted responsibility for the direction of the conduct and curriculum of the school. Evidence since clearly demonstrates that this role of governing bodies has never been taken seriously, or regarded as important, and their duties were assumed by the headteacher and staff, giving them curricular powers in excess of the internal organization, management and discipline of the school mentioned in the model articles. Even with changes in the structure and functioning of governors in the Education Act, 1980 this distribution of curricular responsibilities remains largely undisturbed.

Detailed control, therefore, both in terms of medium and long-term and day to day management, resides with the headteacher and staff. If the school expects to enrol 1,000 pupils and the LEA has decided on a PTR of 20:1 then it will have 50 teachers during next academic year. Most will already be in post, representing a particular range of expertise and skill: for new appointments some LEA influence and control over job-specification and appointment is possible. In addition there are constraints imposed by LEA determination of building provision and distributive control of other resources, but these represent the limits of direct intervention. It may be that authorities view these and the curricular parameters erected by examination boards (supported by the influence of their own advisory services, and the conventions and orthodoxies of acceptable school practices) as adequate control mechanisms.

In the main this combination of factors appears to have been sufficient to constrain most schools within a generous curricular framework. As for FE the process of curriculum design is probably best viewed as matching available resources to educational needs by a series of approximations. Yet given the inter-school variations in both parameters and the absence of overt controls, curricular similarities are more visible than differences. Perhaps

Resources and the Curriculum

most of all in the first two or three years secondary education where a subject spread of English (5 - 7 periods), Mathematics (5 - 7 periods), R.E. (1 - 2 periods), P.E. (3 - 4 periods), Social Studies (4 - 6 periods), Science (4 - 6 periods), First Foreign language (4 - 5 periods) is offered to all pupils. The actual timetables are not identical: some schools teach separate sciences, for example, or Social Studies as History and Geography, but a clear pattern still emerges. In primary schools, with most of the time spent in class (children are rarely taught by another teacher for more than five hours per week) a subject based curriculum as for secondary schools does not exist, but within a broad curriculum the areas of language and literacy, and Mathematics, dominate.[27] Even the curricular differentiation which occurs in Years Four and Five of the secondary school, usually with children choosing one subject from a 'block' of subjects, still has a core of 50% time, on average (again dominated by English and Mathematics) and results in over 67% of 'O' level entries being concentrated among seven subjects.[28]

What these similarities hide, however, are enormous variations in content and approach. Ignoring external examination requirements, two neighbouring schools may each timetable four periods of Geography per week, but there is little likelihood that the same topics will be included. Almost certainly, this example could be repeated in all subjects at every age range. Teacher control, therefore, extends to content, approach, timing and organization. A LEA wishing to be more directional in these areas would soon discover the gap between what happens to be legally permissible (although never tested) and what is practically, and politically, feasible. Few LEAs (if any) have either the facilities, or the will, to design, implement and monitor the detail of curriculum management. As a policy it would necessitate substantial co-ordination, stretching administrative and advisory services beyond reasonable limits. Yet, since the mid-1970s moves to initiate more LEA curricular involvement have been quite apparent. The 'Great Debate' of 1977 was the overt starting point, with its overtones of under-representation of commercial, industrial and parental interests as compared to over-representation of teachers in educational decision-making, epitomising changed DES attitudes to curricular matters. [29] Undoubtedly the debate was legitimised by general societal disquiet about the quality of education, particularly in schools: but whether these concerns were genuine, in an educational sense, or represented a broader re-appraisal of public institutions in a country faced by economic decline is largely irrelevant in this context. The main point was that attention became more clearly focussed on teacher responsibility for curricular decision-making. New questions were asked: in primary schools, about the broadening of the curriculum following the disappearance of the 11+ examination: in secondary schools, about the erosion of external controls following comprehensive reorganization, the establishment of C.S.E., the emergence of Mode 3 examining, and the effects of the many curriculum development projects.

A pattern of DES sponsored local concern for the curriculum, therefore, evolved. At national level two main surveys of practice (for primary and secondary schools) were followed by statements of curricular policy from both DES and HMI.[30] Before this, LEAs had been asked to review and report on procedures for exercising duties and responsibilities relative to the curriculum in accordance with the Education Act, 1944.[31] A substantial re-orientation after over 30 years of apparent DES acquiescence to LEA delegation to school staffs. Later, Circular 6/81 pursued the same theme.[32] As a follow up to the DES document "The School Curriculum"[33] LEAs were reminded of their duty to secure the provision of efficient and sufficient primary and secondary education to meet the needs of their areas, and the ensuing responsibility towards 'the content and quality of that education'. More directly each LEA was asked, in relation to the document, (a) to review its policy for the school curriculum, and arrangements for making the policy known, (b) to review the extent to which practice in schools was consistent with the policy and (c) within resource constraints, plan future developments accordingly, with replies anticipated by the end of 1983. There is no compulsive element: 'The School Curriculum' does not set out to be a definitive and detailed statement of curriculum. The only suggestion which, if implemented, would directly effect the curriculum in most schools is for all pupils to study science to age 16: but even if it wished to, DES does not have statutory powers to enforce that viewpoint. LEAs could, if they chose: but most, if not all, seem reluctant to implement a specific policy. In many authorities suggestions for curriculum design have proliferated, syllabus guidelines for each range, and every subject-area, have been produced by working parties of teacher, advisers and officers, but invariably there is no need for the school to comply. 34 The extent to which recommendations are introduced remains the professional judgement of the staff.

In relation to staffing then, how significant are the changes? If the LEA continues to finance a school on a PTR basis, the authority can try to influence and cajole the headteacher towards a particular staff deployment: it can also rely on the effects of external constraints, but the ultimate decision-making about the use of teacher time relative to the curriculum resides in the school, just as it did ten years ago. Logistically, the school can continue to determine the subjects of any core, the time to be given to them and exercise the same freedoms in optional arrangements. It would be misleading, however, to underestimate the potential impact of the natural channels of influence which emanate from DES through the LEAs to schools. Many LEAs will respond to a DES initiative, or schools to the LEA, not because they have to, or are without ideas of their own, but as a reaction to the inherent merits of the new scheme. In other words they perceive advantages from an empirical-rational perspective. 35 Alternatively they may think it might be possible to build upon and extend other ideas, in conjunction with their own - in other words utilizing the 'normal re-educative' innovative strategy.

Also, intentionally or not, in designing their curriculum statements both DES and LEAs have the advantage of utilizing components within a power-coercive innovative thrust. LEAs and schools only want to be regarded as different from the rest for the best of reasons. Deferential factors, which permeate any hierarchical structure, are prominent. As a DES or LEA curriculum statement can translate into an orthodoxy, it requires a powerful LEA or school, with a well-defined policy of its own, to contradict conventional wisdom. If a school, say has a curriculum at variance with stated views it will continue to be supported by its constituents - parents, governors, employers - but only if it appears to be successful according to their criteria. If not, they will be obliged to pressurize for conformity. However, an even more important item in this change strategy concerns resources. The DES-LEA-school hierarchy contains a resource dependency: not necessarily in a direct sense - a LEA, for example, does not have to rely on its degree of

Resources and the Curriculum

compliance with DES curricular policy for its central government grant - but resource allocation involves subtle processes. A school which chooses to overtly contravene LEA policy, even when there is no compulsion to comply, disadvantages itself in competition for resources. Of course it would be impracticable for the LEA to stop its allowances, but in any contest for additions, or the avoidance of subtractions, it would almost certainly lose out to a neighbouring school.

In other words it is the acquisition of resources - particularly at institutional level - which dominates. Certainly since 1979, an interventionist government, leading (or propelled by) concerns for school outcomes has reminded LEAs (and through them schools) of their curricular responsibilities: and attempted to nudge them, comparatively gently, towards a particular view of the curriculum. In most respects this view is so general, and in some ways so vague, that it is difficult to take serious issue. It has been argued that DES publications and related activities mask a more sinister intention: some form of conspiracy in which the final goal is a centrally imposed curriculum.[36] This argument cannot be sustained unless (or until) there is also detailed specification of syllabi for each curricular area, standards to be sought at every level, and definitions of the most appropriate methodologies. Undoubtedly, were such restrictive arrangements to be introduced items such as time per subject, class-sizes, TCRs (with allowances for age-ranges, etc.) would also have to be centrally determined. With these items, and an effective mechanism for school by school monitoring, there could then be a centrally determined curricular framework, but this would not occur without a re-drafting of the educational legislation and, more important still, a total re-organization of the powers and functions of all participants - DES, LEAs, governors staff and unions.

If more firm (not to say rigid) controls do emerge, they are more likely to do so through a resource based route, rather than as a direct result of curricular concerns. This may appear to contravene the main thrust of this chapter that resources and the curriculum are intra-dependent. However, as Chapter 3 demonstrated, the introduction of an education block grant, undoubtedly accompanied by target expenditures, grant abatements etc. could so reduce the autonomy of LEAs that grounds for their continuance would be minimal. Certainly, the notion

of accountability to the local electorate would
shrink to the point of meaningless. The impetus for
such a grant (whose implementations seems unlikely
in the foreseeable future) come from some sections
in LEAs (but not the local authority associations)
and parts of the DES: mainly with a view to more
standardization of expenditure across LEAs, and to
strengthen the financial position of education within the local sector. With strengthening centrality
the issue of likely curricular controls requires
attention. Without LEAs would the DES to school
relationship reflect LEA-school patterns of light
control, or would DES attempt precise curricular and
syllabus specifications? In this context, though,
the key item is that tight control, if sought, could
only follow major changes in financial arrangements,
reinforcing the resources curriculum inter- relationship.

The direct action of MSC with TUEI in particular, [37]by-passing the traditional decision-making
routes in education, examplifies the dilemma of a
more interventionist DES. It could not have acted
with this degree of directness and rapidity, even
had it wished, with the current legislative provision. Significantly, legislation to permit some
measure of DES to LEA specific grants seems likely
in the mid-1980s. The intention being to facilitate swifter responses to new demands on education
services by adjusting marginal expenditures in areas
determined as important by government. However, it
would be naive to assume that increasing central
interest in curricular matters has occurred coincidentally with the emergence of a more difficult financial climate. For a start, declining resources
produces more personnel with a heightened awareness
towards how they might be used. Then, it can be
hypothesised, there is a causal link between perceptions of unsatisfactory educational outcomes and the
resources education is able to attract. The whole
movement towards more DES and LEA involvement in
curricular debates was lubricated by adverse reactions to the activities and work of schools: as a
result anyone, at whatever level, arguing in a competitive environment for more educational resources
does so (and this situation continues) against a
background of disquiet and apparent reductions in
consumer satisfaction. The level of resource dependency is, therefore, raised because with retrenchment the resources themselves become that much scar-
cer. In an expansionary situation it is unusual for
an institution not to receive some financial incre-

Resources and the Curriculum

ments on a year by year basis: all are relatively advantaged, and the dependencies relate to the degree of advantage. With contraction the institutional objective becomes the minimization of expenditure reductions that might effect the school, in a framework of global reduction. In this type of setting schools highly dependant upon LEA decision-making for resources are likely to perceive that they have no alternative but to respond positively to curricular suggestions from the authority. In a contrasting situation the nudge may need be no more than very gentle, particularly if LEAs with school support, evolve new methods of staffing schools.

The combination of retrenchment and increasing DES-LEA curricular attentions, therefore, focuses interest on the local authority method of staffing the curriculum. Up till recently an estimate of next years roll-size and the PTR selected by the LEA determined a schools entitlement. Some additional allowances often occurred if the school had particular difficulties (a high proportion of children from ethnic minorities, perhaps) or a large sixth form. Occasionally an aggregate ratio for the whole secondary school was replaced by an allowance covering each year group, using independent PTRs, with sixth forms, in particular, receiving separate consideration. Schools were highly satisfied with these arrangements because, in the main, they were doubly advantaged. First they became larger, often with proportionately more older pupils which attracted a greater staff entitlement: second, as part of the expansionary framework, PTRs were being reduced. Take a secondary school which over a period of time increases its roll from 1,000 to 1,080 with a simultaneous reduction in PTR from 20:1 to 18:1, that is a rise from 50 to 60 teachers. Clearly, it would be highly unlikely for the 10 extra staff to spend all their time with the 80 additional pupils: after all, this would mean a ratio of 8:1.

Four distinct strategies present themselves,
1. A reduction in the size of all classes, so that main teaching groups in the primary school fall from 30 to 28, say, while classes particularly in Years One to Three of the secondary school (when no options are available) also become smaller.
2. An increase either in the number of special classes (those for children with some form of learning difficulty or particular ability) or the teaching time awarded to these classes: probably, but not necessarily, involving additional children.
3. A rise in the teacher non-contact time for

staff, allowing more opportunity for lesson preparation, marking, and a range of curricular and other developmental activities.
4. An increase in teacher non-contact time but restricted to staff with particular responsibilities, such as deputy heads, senior teachers, heads of departments, pastoral care organizers etc.
For secondary schools (or any situation where children can make individual choices) there is a fifth strategy in which the range of options is raised: most often by providing additional subjects and increasing choice, less frequently by enabling subject combinations previously debarred.

What experience showed during expansion was that schools did not ruthlessly pursue one particular strategy to the detriment of the other. Each route has a natural core of supporters, on both educational and personal grounds. In an effective organization there has to be compromise. Additionally, the strategies cannot be exclusive. An increase in the number of children in special classes for example, reduces average class-size elsewhere. From a logistical perspective the FE formula of $SSR = \frac{ACS \times ALH}{ASH}$ can be simplified for schools to $PTR = ACS \times TCR$. For this particular secondary school a PTR reduction of 20:1 to 18:1 might have been achieved by lowering both ACS from 25 to 24 and average TCR from 0.8 to 0.75 - that is, two additional non-contact periods for each member of staff. The reduced ACS seems much less attractive. The evidence to favour improved educational outcomes with smaller groups is not clear at this level of difference. A study, for example, found no class-size effects either upon achievement measures (reading, vocabulary, mathematics problem-solving, art and composition) of children's attitudes and self-concepts in groups ranging in size from 16-37. In mathematical concepts there were gains with smaller classes, but it would appear that classes must be less than in this range to have a significant impact on outcomes.[38] Although teachers preferences for smaller classes, and the effects of this on their behaviour, attitude and performance, must never be discounted to follow through the logistical argument, a change in class-size from 25 to 24 will only raise the average teacher access for each child from 1.60 to 1.67 minutes during a 40 minute lesson.

However, the dominant feature, as compared to the situation in further education is the relative

Resources and the Curriculum

autonomy of school decision-making. There is no equivalent to the union agreement over teaching hours. Two surveys reported differences in secondary schools ranging from 0.68 to 0.84 as an average (1980-81), and 0.70 to 0.89 (although the latter figure was in a modern school)[39] Table 4.1 showed inter- LEA variations. Often the freedom that school mangements have to adjust average TCRs is not fully realised, with 100 teachers, and an increase from 0.75 to 0.8 (that is two additional lessons per week) teaching time equivalent to five new teachers is generated. Also no standard pattern of teaching remission for staff with additional responsibilities exists (nor, for that matter established practices LEAs or schools can turn to for guidance) although TCRs do appear to reduce with seniority - Deputy Headteachers average 0.45, Scale I staff 0.84 in secondary schools.[40] Yet, even within these broad parameters it was sometimes difficult for schools to appreciate how much of the additional flexibility during expansion came from increases in NOR. This was not so true for primary schools, but in the secondary age-range it could be a dominant factor because of the ways in which the school can utilize arrangements where a choice of classes exist. In the previous example, suppose 28 of the extra pupils join Year One to Three, and there are no options: perhaps one extra class has to be established and with a contact ratio of 0.8 the time of 1.2 of the ten additional teachers will be utilized. In the limit, with a wide-ranging setting and option system from years four through to seven, and available places in each class it could be feasible to slot each of the 52 extra pupils in these year groups into sets and options without forming new classes. In practice this may not be possible, nor desirable: compulsory subjects in fourth and fifth years are most likely, some classes may be judged full before expansion, certain options may be over-subscribed, but it remains true, nevertheless, that the school in this example has sustained freedom in using the time of the additional nine or so teachers. Even with a constant PTR it would still be entitled to four more teachers because of the 80 extra pupils, and while this, from a staff deployment perspective, may never be feasible, it would require inept organization for the equivalent of three teachers available for option work not to provide increased flexibilities and curricular opportunities.

In the cirumstances of growth to the mid-1970s

school decision-making dominated: that is, apart from the vital choice of PTR. Setting aside, the powers of influence and persuasion, this choice represented the limit of LEA intervention. Both parties appeared satisfied with this divided decision-making: schools for obvious reasons (so long as expansion was sustained) but, in retrospect, the attitude of LEAs is less easily understood. PTR provided them with an effective management tool to estimate total expenditure and allocate staff to schools with some degree of objectivity, but neither it nor any derivative were introduced as control mechanisms within schools. Perhaps schools were thought too simple organizations: possibly the drive to reduce PTR, with resultant problems (such as teacher shortages) was uppermost in their thinking: but the logistical techniques to aid curriculum management did not materialize in the school situation to anything like the extent of FE. However, it was not until circumstances changed from growth to contraction that the dual disadvantages of separate decision-making and limited evolution in the detail of resource utilization mechanisms became obvious. As soon as LEAs found themselves having to make PTR decisions (which in conjunction with NOR changes) did not benefit the schools, the need for some form of additional dialogue emerged. Simultaneously, schools became only too aware of the disappearance of previous flexibilities (and the accompanying curricular freedoms) and, more significantly, the rigidities which the ossification of decisions associated with past flexibilities had induced into their practices. The specialist teacher of a new subject introduced when the curriculum was expanding, for example, presents a problem unless (s)he is prepared to become less specialist in the new circumstances.

As falling rolls affected schools the majority of LEAs held ratios constant (if not reducing them marginally) although, of course, employing fewer teachers. Even in these circumstances unless the reduction in PTR has been sufficiently compensatory, schools must resort to the inverse of the strategies employed during growth. Experience already suggests immense practical difficulties. Turning to each of the strategies which emerge from the equation PTR = ACS x ATCR, and assuming a constant PTR. The first raising ACS may seem attractive logistically if not educationally but, particularly in secondary schools with a complex option system, it is unlikely and probably impossible, to increase class-sizes with fewer children while retaining the option arrangement intact. On this basis the Briault study[41] on falling rolls recommended a small number of large secondary schools to retain option systems intact. Without such a strategy schools find it increasingly difficult to staff subjects such as German, Needlework, Sociology, Drama, Metalwork, R.E. and Woodwork in fourth form options.[42] A reduction in time given to special work with particular children, or additional music lessons and remedial reading in primary schools for example, may present few problems but only if the extra teachers leave or can transfer to more general work in the rest of the school. Second, an increase in TCR will probably be necessary in any case to balance the natural reduction in ACS which follows from less children in the school. Also there is always the possibility that the 'cubed squared' law of administration which inflated time given to administration as the school grew will not be precisely reversed with roll-decline. It can be argued that as the school loses children problems increase disproportionately, and therefore more non-teaching time has to be given to their solution. Alternatively, senior staff who gained most in non-contact time and status as the school expanded may increase their teaching loads reluctantly with contraction, perhaps thinking it reflects upon their status particularly as from senior positions they are well placed to enforce their preference. Naturally, this demands an even higher TCR from other teachers.

What became increasingly clear to schools as they face their new situations is not only inter-relationship between the two strategies available to them (which makes the design of an appropriate scheme more difficult), but, of even greater importance, how the very flexibility which allowed each school to select its own composite strategy during expansion resulted, especially for larger schools, in a complex mix of additional arrangements, teaching patterns, option groups etc. which are not easily disentangled. Take the secondary school of the example starting from a NOR of 1,000 a PTR of 20:1 and therefore 50 teachers which expanded to 1,080, 18:1 and 60 respectively, but then returns to its original roll, retaining the new PTR, and therefore about 55 staff. As compared to the original situation the school appears advantaged, but it would have to increase TCR by 10% from the peak staffing to maintain the same curricular programme, and this assumes that the particular skills of the five fewer staff can be replaced from among those 55 that continue. Most likely, if the curriculum offered at maximum size is to be sustained, the school must be even more generously staffed, in PTR terms, as the roll declines. Even if, in more favourable financial circumstances, LEAs were able to do this the question of how generously would still be apposite. What activities are not now possible because of the five less staff? How does the curriculum with 55 teachers compare to that with the original 50 staff, and with that of other schools? Are there any central areas of activity with which this school cannot cope in its new situation? More generally, what are these central areas of the curriculum? Obviously in deteriorating economic circumstances, and when they are displaying increased curricular concerns, LEAs do not wish to - and probably cannot - accede to demands for lower PTR without, at least, asking these questions of individual schools, all as components of the major issue, in relation to the curriculum, of how schools should be utilizing the staff they deploy relative to educational needs.

INFLATING AND PROTECTING THE CURRICULUM

A degree of tension between resource suppliers (in this case LEAs, constrained by DES and Treasury) and curriculum providers is inevitable, and in many ways desirable. A school or college not lobbying for additional resources is often without ideas about what tasks it might perform differently or new activities it could introduce. The key item, of course, centres on the balance of interests. LEAs have a responsibility for achieving an equitable distribution of resources among all schools and colleges, and the determination of total expenditure. They also retain a justifiable concern to ensure that resources are used effectively in pursuit of aims and objectives with which they approve, and perhaps, nominate. In contrast, the school or college focus of attention is initially the acquisition of sufficient resources so that, according to the perceptions of staff, institutional requirements can be fulfilled, and then, for a variety of reasons (to do a better job, to do more things to reduce the load on staff, to raise status levels etc.) the maximization of resource acquisition.

The starting point in reconciling this clash of interests is clearly some delineation of institutional tasks. For schools, until quite recently, this amounted to no more than LEA specification of

Resources and the Curriculum

pupil numbers and age-range: with DES regulations over length of school day and school year: and the traditional boundaries of curricular acceptability. Presumably, LEAs thought this combination sufficient: indeed their own efforts to lower PTR suggests they reckoned schools to be under-staffed for these tasks. As compared to FE, the number of clients and their mode of attendance is tightly defined. A school can only attract additional children at the expense of other schools. Therefore, apart from children above the statutory leaving age, schools can only exercise limited entrepreneurialism. This is not so in FE. The regulations from 1944 (which ultimately limit what colleges can do) are relatively open-ended and over the whole possible range of activities only a minority of possible courses are ever organized, with few of the potential student population registered at any one time. The scope for college staff to recruit more and more students, by introducing new programmes, is therefore substantial. A successful and thrusting college could place immense pressures on its LEA for extra resources, if other controls were not introduced. Clearly, this is a factor in the evolution of the control mechanisms of NAB, CNAA, Burnham related calculations and LEA controls over SSR.

Perhaps the natural and ineluctable restrictions on pupil numbers represents the most pressing explanation of light local and central controls on school activities, and relativity tight scrutiny of FE work. Without restrictive parameters it is quite feasible that a college staff would define institutional tasks in such a way that twice the original staff would be required: both in terms of introducing new activities and using additional staff in an attempt to improve existing courses. This represents a perfectly legitimate interpretation of educational needs and how they can best be satisfied but solely from a staff perspective. Obviously they are exercising professional judgements, but it is impossible to separate these from improvements in self-interest factors, such as job-protection and creation. Undoubtedly, the result, without LEA (and DES) limitations, would be curricular inflation: both in terms of high unit-expenditures, because of staff perceptions about the desirability of small classes and willingness to accept high developmental costs, and as a result of the enormous programme of activities, to satisfy a wide spectrum of educational needs.

In the new circumstances of retrenchment the need of institutional staff is for curricular protection. From their particular perspective this represents a perfectly understandable sentiment. The peak curriculum, according to their perceptions, was going some way to satisfy educational needs, and these have not necessarily been reduced because of fewer pupils or a lower college enrolment, and certainly remain unaffected (and possibly raised) by an adverse financial climate. The real problem for the institution is that while it may have accumulated staff during growth in a reasonably logical way, based upon the requirements of potential developments, reductions must occur haphazardly as teachers happen to resign. When a key teacher leaves, a school often has no alternative but to ask the LEA for some form of protection, through a lower PTR. As this occurs the LEA has legitimate queries both about the flexibilities with which remaining staff can be deployed, and the basis on which the relevant curricular areas are seen in relation to the totality of the institutional task. Significantly, as soon as a school or college looks to the LEA for curriculum protection, and a dialogue becomes established, the whole basis of the relationship is changed.

What both schools and LEAs require is some definition of staffing needs, based upon the number of classes, their size, the subjects to be taught and the number of lessons. There is no reason why this cannot be done in both primary and secondary schools. In the former case the number of basic teaching groups as well as the demands for supportive expertise in number work, language development, music, drama etc. would have to be specified. With this information, and desired TCRs staffing requirements can be formulated precisely, not only in terms of the total number of teachers but also relative to particular specialisms. For a secondary school with a first year of 125 children mentioned in the previous example, perhaps four classes of 27 would be formed, with a smaller group of 17 requiring specialist remedial attention: each of the five classes needing forty periods per week tuition in specific curricular areas. This process of calculating by specialism, and by year, when repeated throughout the school provides a precise delineation of teacher need. This can then be considered alongside staff availability, and shortage (or surpluses) in particular activities identified. (Table 4.5)

While the school might have protected the

TABLE 4.5 Staffing needs and deployment in a secondary school

(a) Staff deployment by year-group

Year	Pupils	Periods (per week)	FTE Staff	FTE Staff / Pupils
1	198	280	9.3	0.047
2	202	280	9.3	0.046
3	210	320	10.6	0.05
4	215	405	13.4	0.062
5	224	410	13.6	0.061
6	64	195	6.4	0.1
7	37	170	5.6	0.15
Total	1,150	2,060	68.2	

(b) Staff needs by subject

	Periods per week proposed	Periods per week possible	Potential Flexibility	
Chemistry	115	108	[+8	−24]
Physics	110	96	[0	−28]
Biology	135	152	[+15	−12]
Mathematics	273	254	[+6	−28]
English	285	302	[+29	−12]
French	95	98	[+8	−4]
German	25	30	[+5	−10]
Computing	105	75	[0	−45]
History	54	68	[+28	−15]
Geography	56	72	[+34	−16]
CDT	175	180	[+5	−35]
Home Econ.	154	160	[0	−12]
Music	38	45	[0	−6]
Drama	44	30	[+20	−8]
PE(B)	60	64	[+4	−6]
PE(G)	56	68	[+6	−2]
Art	92	110	[+12	−15]
Remedial	144	126	[+28	−34]
Bus. Studies	44	48	[0	−12]

Note: Potential flexibilities measure the ability (and willingness) of staff not designated to a subject to teach that number of periods (+ ve), or staff nominated for a subject able to teach elsewhere (− ve).

curriculum by participating in such an exercise, it is at the expense - if that is how the school perceives it - of being totally explicit over staff deployment in relation to subjects and courses on offer, class sizes, the availability of choices, teacher contact ratios etc. In many ways the calculation resembles that in FE when Burnham arrangements are used to assess requirements for lecturing staff. The keynote in both environments is negotiation. A LEA trying to limit (or reduce) total expenditure, and maintain equity among institutions, while demonstrating its own concern for curricular activities, will not readily sanction curricular schemes which it disapproves or thinks inefficient. It is, for example, most improbable that 'A' level situations with one student could be negotiated. LEAs may be able to tacitly support arrangements about which they are only vaguely aware, irrespective of unit costs, they cannot do this when knowledge of such arrangements is integral to resource distribution procedures.

Potentially, however, LEA awareness can go far beyond individual items in discussion with schools. The end-point of negotiation is either agreement or imposition of a particular view by the dominant partner. The resource dependency of schools on their LEAs, particularly during retrenchment, should not be underestimated. Ultimately LEAs can impose their curricular frameworks, using the resource parameters implicit in the arrangements described. There are advantages, in relation to an inter-school equity for example. Those schools which gained most by inflating their curricular during expansion could claim they needed most protection with contraction. Given that the political processes are unlikely to be too dissimilar in the contrasting circumstances - that is, schools which developed effective lobbies during growth will not surrender their advantages with retrenchment - they could well be successful. Unless, of course, the LEA demands from each school a precise quantification of requirements for teaching staff, interprets these requests by negotiation, relative to class-sizes, subjects offered, programme availability etc., and then arbitrates to determine individual school allocations. Although more cumbersome and time-consuming than using PTR mechanisms LEAs can exercise duties implied in Circular 6/81, for example, in a more interventionist and directional manner than previously.

Unless developments of this nature occur, it becomes difficult to understand why individual LEAs have generated so much interest by sponsoring working parties on the curriculum, publishing guidance documents etc. Presumably they wish to establish a consensus, but have then baulked at the introduction of mechanisms to ensure implementation. More puzzling still, according to a survey by the local authority associations, many LEAs are either introducing or considering some form of curriculum-led staffing, often at the instigation of school staffs or the teacher unions.[43] In other words, such are their demands for curricular protection, they appear willing to re-negotiate the balance of curricular interest to achieve it. One compromise which would appear to leave those interests undisturbed has the disadvantage of illogicality. Here, as occurs in some LEA's, the LEA determines the staffing for a secondary school through detailing the curriculum by subject it ought to provide, given its size and pupil profile, while the school retains its traditional autonomy with regard to curriculum design. It may result in some protection depending, obviously, on the nature of the model curriculum in comparison to that which the school chooses to pursue. In practice, for a school with 60 staff, this might amount to no more than one additional teacher. Therefore, unless the LEA intends to be generous (which it could be using PTR) it is both an ineffective and illogical procedure for staff allocation.

It is ineffective because it represents only a minimal improvement on PTR: being less objective potentially more unfair, and little better at matching resources to tasks. The element of unfairness arising from curricular criteria which are tacitly optional, but whose satisfaction may advantage a particular school because of the chance way in which its curriculum at any time fits alongside that specified by the LEA. It is also illogical to staff schools according to an imposed model curriculum and then allow them to adapt the staffing awarded to their own individual, and perhaps, idiosyncratic, pattern of working: when a direct individual school to LEA negotiation, of which these idiosyncracies would be a part, could be available. The school, and its constituencies (pupils, parents, staff and governors) has to define tasks as part of its role of curriculum provider: ultimately the LEA, as resource provider, must sanction these tasks, the resources to be used in their accomplishment and arbitrate between all schools. Direct negotiation would seem to be the only rational and defensible method of reconciling the differing interests of the two parties. It need not mean an erosion of school freedom or the imposition of a uniform set of arragnements in every school. In fact were this to happen it would defeat one of the main objectives of the exercise. In crude terms the school defines what it wants to do in its own particular circumstances, tries to convince the LEA, which adjudicates among all its schools while working within an expenditure limit and in relation to a curricular policy. In other words it is the freedoms and the flexibilities of direct negotiation which are sought. Ideally such negotiation should not be restricted to the number of teachers. If schools have increased control of their whole resource situation (Chapter 6) discussion would then take place within a framework of the total resources, over which the school has influence. Teacher numbers would be a dominant facet, but related to others.

Paradoxically it takes the exigencies and problems of a harsh financial world before the advantages of a logical system for allocating teachers (or distributing total resources) are realised, when such an approach would have been even more appropriate during a time of rapid expansion. Had it been utilized, then, to allow a more coherent expansion, many of the difficulties that have to be overcome may never have occurred. Undoubtedly, without contraction, the position of PTR as the main distributive technique would have remained unchallenged. In terms of protecting the curriculum an institution is most vulnerable to rapid changes in financial support when a dichotomy between resource and curricular dialogues exists. The most direct example of this type of situation occurred in AFE during early experiences with capping the pool. Here a polytechnic, for instance, found itself having to reduce planned expenditure at short notice by over £1 million (a few weeks before the start of the financial year).[44] The real cause of vulnerability is the slowness of response, generated by a high level of committed expenditure (mainly on salaries), the long-time scale of activities (courses planned, or already running) and the politicisation of decision-making (many groups regard themselves entitled to a stake). Ironically, much of the difficulty is exaggerated by autonomy. Schools, for example, given more resource freedom by LEAs may have to be protected from some effects of unexpected changes in committed

expenditures (Chapter 6). If the relationship with
the authority is wholly financially orientated (the
college, with NAB etc., determining curricular and
the authority resource availability) and the LEA is
unwilling, or unable, to make good an unexpected reduction in income from the pool, the institution can
be forced into a series of short-term measures (elimination of building maintenance, abandonment of
new courses, non-renewal of temporary contracts)
which owe more to political flexibility than the
satisfaction of educational needs.[45] In other words
the reductions that do occur either cause least
disturbance to interest groups, or effect items
which do not have powerful supporters. The view
that in having to lower expenditure an institution
will develop a more rational decision-making procedure (as compared to a period of expansion) when
relating resources to curriculum provision cannot
be supported if reductions have to be made swiftly
and cannot be anticipated. In such circumstances
the focus will be on saving jobs, college, faculty
etc: with the emergence of irrational decisions,
effected by chance occurrences such as staff leaving.
More so if resource and curriculum determinations
are considered separately.

THE CURRICULUM AND OTHER RESOURCES

To ignore resources other than teaching staff
in consideration of curricular provision would be
both demeaning to non-teaching staff who are obvious contributors to the teaching and learning
processes (however indirectly) and imply that a
teacher or lecturer could work equally effectively
whatever the state of the buildings and however
much equipment or support facilities there happens
to be available. Clearly, factors such as these
effect not only the work of teaching staff - in
terms of attitudes and teaching methodologies -
but also the detail of the curriculum. A school
with only four science laboratories, for example,
is inhibited in its science curriculum as compared
to a similarly sized school with twice the space
for laboratory work. However, the issue of teacher
availability still dominates. Science can be taught
in an ordinary classroom. It may not be taught as
well: the facilities for demonstration and experi-
mentation undoubtedly will be limited, but without
a teacher the lesson cannot be taught at all. The
issue of whether the teacher has science qualifications - the match between teacher expertise and

Resources and the Curriculum

curriculum needs - is dealt with more fully in Chapter 5.

Another example from a FE college emphasizes the point. Suppose the College has language laboratories serviced by a technician. Were s(he) to leave, almost certainly the sessions would continue: lecturing staff might have to do more technical work and, perhaps because of this, their teaching would suffer: repairs would take longer and, in all likelihood, reduce availability to students. Yet in curricular terms, the technician, as for all other non-teaching resources, remains no more than a facilitator: the prime resource continues to be the lecturer without whom sessions would have to be abandoned. Significantly, facilitators when not available, or misused, rapidly translate into inhibitors (a caretaker on strike, for example) which prevent, or radically alter, curricular processes. Three main categories of resource demand attention.
1. Buildings 2. Other staff and 3. Equipment (including books and consumable materials).

For schools the impact of falling rolls has lessened problems associated with building availability. It stands to reason that fewer children require less space. However, while there may be less difficulty in finding a place for every child, other problems still arise. LEAs, for example, are under pressure from DES to take surplus places out of use to reduce costs, often placing them in opposition to local communities wishing a particular school or facility to continue. Yet in secondary education if no action is taken 40% of costs by 1990 could be premises related, rising from 20%, and therefore threatening other expenditures.[46] Closing part of a school, for example, saves not only building up-keep costs but also perhaps four-fifths of the expenditure on non-teaching staff (cleaners, caretakers). Also declining rolls mean that the case for new school buildings is inevitably reduced-aside from the dramatic reductions in capital expenditure generally - except in the special circumstances of (say) a new town: so that even if old buildings are closed the average age of schools may still rise. Ironically, from a solely cost-cutting perspective, it often is more attractive to shut new schools, where debt charges are invariably high, if the proceeds from sales prove sufficient to pay off any outstanding loan.

Clearly, both reducing the number of pupil-places, and substantial limitations on capital spending, have curricular implications. In broad

Resources and the Curriculum

terms, if a LEA opts for a smaller number of large schools, as suggested[47] then they should be able to provide a wider curriculum than a larger number of smaller schools. This is not a judgement about school effectiveness, but a statement of fact. Restrictions on capital projects, however (including relatively small alterations) may only have minimal effects on the curriculum, provided it is intended to continue more or less unchanged. That, though, is the key: when the provision of buildings moves from facilitator to potential inhibitor.

Take the case of a school with 34 classrooms, 8 workshops and 8 laboratories: that is 50 "work stations", ignoring any games facilities. The first and most obvious restriction concerns the fact that there must never be more than 50 groups timetabled for any single lesson. With declining rolls this may not present a problem. Perhaps the school has to lose space, and gives up five classrooms: it still retains 45 work stations which with a declining NOR may appear adequate: but not, however, if the guidelines in 'The School Curriculum' are followed to allow every child to study science up to age 16, or a higher proportion of practically based activity is sought for low achieving fourth and fifth year pupils. In circumstances such as these there may be times during the week when non-classroom facilities are insufficient. Of course the school will cope, by arranging science lessons elsewhere and retrenching on plans to increase the number of workshop sessions, with possibly more activities away from the school: but at the potential cost of introducing the innovations less effectively, and significantly, of erecting barriers which may deter the implementation of such schemes. If some staff are doubtful about new arrangements for whatever reasons, it is easy for them to utilize arguments about the non-availability, or limited suitability, of premises to persuade themselves, and others, that the innovation should not be attempted. As a result the teaching methodology becomes excessively classroom-based and orthodox teaching methods prosper. This inhibitive tendency of building provision is obviously reinforced when, as in FE colleges, additional programmes for large numbers of new students have to be introduced relatively quickly. Not only is there a space-shortage but the easiest, and least costly, work-stations to find, yet probably the least appropriate for young unemployed, are traditional classrooms: inducing conventional teaching methodolgies which have

already been rejected by many of the students.
It could be misleading to sub-categorize non-teaching staff into two distinct factions because the divide is never totally clear in every situation. In fact CIPFA statistics use three main categories - educational support (auxiliaries, teaching assistants and technicians), premises related (caretakers and cleaners) and administrative (clerical staff). However, caution is necessary as some employees (cleaners, caretakers and maintenance staff) can have little direct influence on curricular processes (although with fewer employed, because of less premises, salary savings might be available for other expenditure) while others (secretarial and clerical staff, for example) as well as direct educational support staff, do impinge directly on curricular processes. For in some part of their work they perform tasks which otherwise would be left to teaching staff, if done at all. The secretary types and duplicates a work-sheet, the auxiliary takes a small group in the infant school for additional reading, the technician sets up a class experiment, and in each case, the teacher should be freed to do other things. That is the intention: based upon the dual principles of professional staff being competent (and allowed) to perform certain tasks, and the necessity, or desirability, of support from others so that they receive maximum attention. In practice such a precise division of labour into professional tasks and non-professional support cannot be achieved. A teacher (or lecturer) no matter how assisted, does many things which could be done equally well by auxiliary staff. The giving out of equipment, the maintenance of records of student work, and the marking of registers, being three typical examples. A clear separation is not attempted: firstly, because so many activities of this type are regarded as integral to the teaching and learning processes, with potential inefficiencies if overt divisions were to be made: secondly, it transcends the delicate area of professional responsibilities and practices. A teacher or lecturer has higher status and is better paid than any support staff, resulting from a longer period of training and higher qualifications. According to the professional this state of affairs should not be disturbed either by precise definitions of who should do what (which could erode the scope of the professional job and result in arguments for fewer posts) or closer integration of professional and support staff-activities so that

Resources and the Curriculum

their work becomes indistinguishable. As far as financing the curriculum goes, the central item concerns the appropriate mix of staffing - clerical, technical and teaching/lecturing. Of course, a teacher should be better prepared and the lessons more effectively organized if (s)he had a full-time secretary to duplicate worksheets, design visual aids etc. Learning rates would probably be increased, but with scarce resources additional support staff invariably means fewer teachers: unless that support is free, for example, when parents go into a primary school to assist with reading schemes. Because of the sensitivities already alluded to, the optimum combination of professional support and voluntary services to maximise curricular processes within a limited expenditure is not a topic which has received a great deal of attention.[48] Decisions have to be made during the formulation of the budget but without a clear differentiation and costing of tasks and responsibilities. The size of non-teaching establishments tends to be low, particularly in schools. In the secondary sector, for example, a school with 60 teachers may employ three or four clerical staff, much of whose time will be specifically directed towards school administration unconnected with curricular activities. With the development of computer soft-ware to facilitate this administration more clerical time may be freed. Indeed so little consideration has been given to the most desirable teacher-clerical resource mix that a LEA discovering free time would be attracted to reducing the number of clerical posts, rather than employing the personnel in a teacher support role. At primary level, a ten teacher school might have one secretary, wholly employed on administration, and no technical assistance: while in the secondary sector the teacher to technician ratio is likely to be even higher than the equivalent teacher to clerical figure. National expenditure figures make this point clearly, with the salaries of Educational Support Staff taking only 3.2% of total costs in primary schools (2.4% in secondary schools), premises related staff 6.4% (5.2%) and administrative/clerical 1.8% (1.7%) as compared to teacher salaries figures of 69.0% (67.5%).[49] In further and higher education these ratios are reduced, as demonstrated by the institutional profiles of expenditure (Table 6.1), but the proportionately more support staff reflects a greater complexity of administrative tasks, and additional sophistication in the educational support services (computing, audio-visual, technical etc.) rather than a reflective policy of offering individual lecturers additional clerical and technical assistance.

The actual process of determining establishment levels for support staff either occurs in the LEA, normally by use of arbitrary criteria such as size of school and number of teachers, or at institutional level when a budget is submitted to the authority for approval. From the perspective of pursuing the best allocative mix, allowing a school or college to nominate its preferred disposition of teaching and other staff has many attractions. The staff, have the premier position from which to assess what ought to be done, and the number of secretaries and technicians (relative to teachers) which would most assist the relevant curricular processes. At school level this sort of consideration was an important factor in persuading some LEAs to test the feasibility of more school financial autonomy. There is no reason why consideration of support staff levels should not be integral to direct LEA school negotiations over teacher numbers: as both resources are so crucial in teaching and learning. In fact from an inter-LEA perspective variations in per-pupil expenditures on this resource mix are far in excess of (say) differences in PTR. Take the figure of 3.2% for expenditure on educational support staff which in per-pupil terms given an average national expenditure of £18. Yet actual spending per child on this category is as high as £53 in ILEA (£44 in some other London Boroughs) but as low as £1 in Gloucestershire. The top to bottom differential factor in secondary schools is lower, but still in excess of 12. Within LEAs inter-schools differences are less marked but still exist. In other words, very large variations in resource mix happen but with little monitoring of intention and effect.[50]

Yet against the potential advantages in institutional determination of resource mixes the factor of teacher domination in decision-making cannot be ignored. Particularly with resource shortages, the perception of many professionals will be directed towards maximising their own numbers, but at the cost of distorting the resource mix by squeezing the employment of support staff. However, as different methodolgies evolve, with more practical-based activities and greater use of audio-visual techniques, the area of potential overlap between professional and non-professional competencies steadily increases. Most pressing of all, the rapid

Resources and the Curriculum

curricular changes folowing the introduction of micro-computers will almost certainly continue, particularly as appropriate software packages become more available and cheaper. As this happens, individual learning situations multiply, the traditional role of the teacher assumes less relevance, and the importance of distinguishing between professional and other support staff becomes even less significant. In these circumstances a lobby to maximise teacher numbers lacks all credibility, without an awareness of the total range of skills required - teacher, programmer, maintenance technician etc. - in relation to the learning programme envisaged.

What books and equipment (the third of the non-teacher resources) exemplifies, again, is the variations in LEAs spending commitments. In per-pupil terms the spread of expenditures may not be so great as for the Educational Support Staff category, but an average figure of £16 for each primary school child includes £40 for the ILEA as compared to £10 for Durham: in secondary schools the mean of £29, encompasses Waltham Forest at £45 per head in contrast to Leeds at £15.51 Additionally, as for the other two items, shortage, or absence, of any of them benefits orthodox and traditional approaches to the curriculum. In terms of non-teacher requirements by far the least demanding of situations involves a conventional room, a single group of children or students, and a methodology concentrating upon teacher directed talk, complemented by some blackboard work. The need for support staff is nil, and for equipment minimal. However, as in the case of buildings, the real dilemma, heightened during contraction, is the effect of any shortages on attitudes towards the development of new curricular strategies. In the limit an innovative approach becomes impossible, if the requisite collection of support facilities cannot be provided. Without the likelihood of acquiring the course-books and equipment there is no point in teachers planning an alternative science curriculum, or of FE lecturers contemplating a new workshop programme, unless tacit assurances emerge that the essential machines will be made available. Significantly computer controlled machine tools for use in colleges are being financed directly by the Department of Industry, so as to short-circuit the normal resource procedures. Even when courses can be introduced without additional assistance, there must always be a chance of both teacher frustration, resulting from an inability to do the job properly, and reversion to more traditional teaching processes. Clearly, there are intermediary situations, primary schools being good examples, where staff are prepared to improvise, make apparatus, up-date out-moded cards, and so on. Perhaps this accounts for the lower capitation allowances in these schools, but there are obvious limitations in what can be achieved, imposed by the willingness of staff to supplement deficiencies in provision and the complexity of whatever is required. Staff construction of apparatus for a primary school science programme may be feasible: a similar exercise with an 'A' level Physics course presents a different order of difficulty.

During expansion it was often possible to persuade staff to introduce alternative teaching approaches, the various Nuffield science packages being good examples, because of the additional funds such schemes could attract from the LEA. The fact that they could be inequitably distributed was perhaps less important than their availability.[52] With retrenchment such possibilities are minimised almost to the point of non-existence: indeed there is every likelihood that allowances for books, science apparatus as well as consumable items such as paint, paper etc., will be reduced disproportionately to, say, staffing because these items lack a natural lobby within the system. Teachers and lecturers will protect their own jobs, support staff will act similarly but, apart from specific pressure groups such as the book publishers, equipment expenditure lacks sponsors. Some empirical evidence does support this view,[53] in that the percentage of total expenditure in primary schools on books and equipment decreased from 3.5 to 2.8% (4.2 to 3.6% for secondary schools) between 1974-75 (the first year of the new authorities) and 1980-81. From a more qualitative perspective, HMI survey local authority expenditure policies and relative to books and equipment, report situations in many LEAs which appear to be satisfactory (without defining in detail the criteria for that satisfaction) but comment upon adverse situations in some authorities and the cumulative effects of retrenchment on these expenditure categories.[54] For items lacking real support and presenting easy targets, the real danger is that budget after budget will include a gradual erosion in commitment.

THE EDUCATIONAL-RESOURCE INTERACTION

Only when the processes both of financing the

curriculum and the curriculum itself have been considered in detail does the ubiquitousness of the effects of resources on education become clear. Yet in schools and colleges at all levels two items emerge subsuming all others. The first, and most important, concerns the balance of interests between resource suppliers (DES, LEA and Treasury) and curriculum providers within the institution. The second, and related, matter involves the optimum resource mix within each school or college so that the pursuit of whatever aims and objectives have been identified is maximised. A host of subsidiary issues follow naturally - about the definition of tasks, responsibilities for their determination, and choices about resources required in their performance, as well as evaluation of this performance. Undoubtedly, interest in these questions and the two major items has been exaggerated by the rapid transition from a lengthy period of sustained growth to a contracting or, at best, a static environment. What expansion did demonstrate overwhelmingly (not in every school and college, but in sufficient to place the matter beyond dispute) was that given the opportunity staff would expand the curriculum to utilize whatever resources became available. Extra options could be offered, new courses might be introduced, additional remedial classes established and more small group work initiated: with explanations and motives for such increases ranging from the creation of more teacher job-opportunities, through raised status- levels and 'empire building', to the more effective satisfaction of educational needs.

It would be misleading to imply that the provision of additional resources, even at the peak of expansion, had reached a 'saturation level' attracting institutional profligacy. Contrary examples can be quoted: low SSRs in AFE, small sixth-form groups in some LEAs, depressed ATCR in a few schools, and unused equipment: but in such cases it could always be argued that under utilization of resources represented some interim stage likely to disappear as the appropriate scheme became fully developed. However, what this, or any other, explanation cannot disguise are obvious inequities in such examples. While one school could support high non-contact time, and still retain small teaching groups, another might be struggling to sustain the most basic of curricular structures: similarly, situations of unused equipment can be compared with those where funds were not available to buy the

171

equipment. The fact that such contrasts occur in different LEAs is to an external observer of little importance. To them the crucial element, with the distributional arrangements that seem to exist, centres around the level of resources that will be acquired by the generously provided, when the least well off achieve adequacy. Yet, were all the issues related to equity resolved, the matter of supplies provides balance is largely unaffected. Contraction demonstrates that this matter is not something internal to education. At all levels numerous parties have a legitimate interest in the outcome, and not just as passive observers.

As might be expected during shrinkage resource suppliers become ascendent, with the influences of the curriculum providers waning. With this move, opportunities for LEA (and DES) curricular interventions increase. Previously a clear (and disadvantageous) dichotomy in decision-making existed, with resources being the concern of suppliers and curriculum matters remaining the prerogative of the institutional providers. As a result there was insufficient consideration of the interactions between resources and the curriculum. An advantage of the new circumstances is that combined discussion about the two elements, both among and between the two parties, receives much more prominence. Even with the increased dominance of the suppliers, for practical as well as political reasons, the likelihood of this becoming total in both resource and curricular spheres is minimal. Were this not so, the need for dialogue would be eliminated: but it would seem that DES and LEAs have neither the will nor the facilities to achieve this intention. Instead it is the perceptions of the suppliers of what ought to be done relative to resource availability (substantially altered by the views and actions of providers about what can be done) which permeate the curricular-resource relationship.

However, this still leaves unanswered the question of resource mix within the institution. The logic of allowing institutional freedom in determining priorities for buildings, other staff, equipment and professional staff is compelling. The defects however, concern professional control and the practical detail of decision-making. When the environment is in a state of flux, with alternative teaching methodologies steadily evolving, the optimum resource combination may well be very different to that which the inflexibilities of practice and tradition permit. One solution which might alleviate these rigidities, of increasing resource levels, is both highly unlikely and proved ineffective, relative to this particular objective, in the past. Alternatively, a maximisation of staff freedom to choose between another member of staff or additional equipment, say, might be the best route towards resource deployment strategies most appropriate for changing circumstances. There is a risk that, with professional domination of decision-making, preferences which reduce the significance of the professional role, and in the medium and long-term these are the most likely changes, will be overlooked. Yet to impose external solutions on institutional situations which depend upon professional sensitivities and judgements is likely to be still more counter-productive. The actual processes of decision-making, if they become more sophisticated involving negotiation about the resource-mix for each institution, will be more complex and time-consuming. In these circumstances the ratios of PTR and SSR as well as their derivatives, become more prominent as monitors, but less important as distributive guides.

In all of these considerations, however, the main intention is the provision of a dynamic curriculum whatever the total composition of resources. Currently, and for most of the foreseeable future the main component will be the individual teacher or lecturer working with a class. So far professional staff have been viewed largely as a single entity. Clearly they are not, and therefore the next Chapter considers the influence of resources on their job tasks and performance.

NOTES AND REFERENCES

1. DES, Statistical Bulletin 2/82 (January 1982), and Ministry of Education, Statistics of Education 1961 Part one,(HMSO, London, 1962).
2. M.Wright (ed.), Public Spending Decisions, (George Allen and Unwin, London, 1980), although original notion from D. Braybrooke and C.E. Lindblom, Strategy of Decision,(Macmillan, New York, 1963).
3. DES, Statistical Bulletin 2/82, (January 1982).
4. CMND 8789, (1983), The governments expenditure plans 1983-84 to 1985-86, (1983).
5. DES Reports on Education, Pupil and Teacher Numbers, (No.80, December 1974).
6. DES, Her Majesty's Inspectorate, Educational Provision by the Inner London Education

Authority, (1980).
7. District Audit, Colleges of Further Education Guide to the Measurement of Resource Efficiency, (Department of the Environment, 1981).
8. ILEA, Allocation of Resources and the Alternative Use of Resources (AUR) Scheme.
9. Memorandum of the Pooling Committee on SSRs in AFE, (1972).
10. DES, Aspects of secondary education in England, (HMSO, London, 1979), pp.62-63.
11. W.F. Dennison, 'Equlizing Staff Teaching Loads- The Number of Students Serviced Approach', Educational Administration, Vol.9,No.1 (1980), pp. 68-85.
12. Education Act, 1944, s 41-47.
13. District Audit, Colleges of Further Education Guide to the Measurement of Resource Efficiency, p.11.
14. J. Pratt, T. Travers & T. Burgess, Costs and Control in Further Education (NFER Publishing, Slough, 1978.
15. DES, Statistics of Education:1979 Further Education Vol. 3, (HMSO, London, 1982),Table 3.
16. Coombe Lodge Reports, Vol.15, No.12, (1983).
17. V.J. Delany, 'Costing in Further Education', Further Education Staff College Reports, Vol.6, No.18 (1974), pp.853-860.
18. DES, Scales of Salaries for Teachers in Further Education, England and Wales 1983, (HMSO, London, 1983), pp.16-17.
19. DES, Scales of Salaries for Teachers in Further Education, pp.19-22.
20. Coombe Lodge Working Paper, D.W. Birch & J. Latcham, (1979), Determining College 'Establishments': Burnham v. The Student Staff Ratio.
21. District Audit, Colleges of Further Guide to the Measurement of Resource Efficiency, p.29.
22. DES, Circular 4/83, Arrangements for the Approval of Advanced Further Education Courses in England, 1983.
23. District Audit, Colleges of Further Education Guide to the Measurement of Resource Efficiency pp.30-31.
24. DES Circular 7/70, Government and Conduct of Establishments of Further Education, (1970).
25. S.I. 1086/1981, The Education (Schools and Further Education) Regulations 1981.
26. Ministry of Education, Administrative Memorandum No. 25, (1945).
27. DES, Primary education in England,(HMSO,London 1978).

Resources and the Curriculum

28. W.F. Dennison, Education in Jeopardy, p.120.
29. CMND 6869, Education in Schools, (1977).
30. DES, Aspects of secondary education in England, and DES, Primary education in England.
31. DES Circular 14/77, Local Education Authority Arrangements for the School Curriculum (1977).
32. DES Circular 6/81, The School Curriculum,(1981).
33. DES, The School Curriculum, (HMSO,London,1981).
34. Examples quoted in W.F. Dennison, Doing Better for fewer: Education and Falling Rolls, (Longman for Schools Council, York, 1983), pp.11-16.
35. W.G. Bennis, The Planning of Change, (Holt, Rinehart and Winston, London, Third edition, 1976), pp.22-45.
36. B.Salter and T. Tapper, Education, politics and the state: the theory and practice of educational change, (Grant McIntyre, London, 1981).
37. See, for example, 'Technical and Vocational Education Initiative for 14-18 Year Olds', Coombe Lodge Report, Vol.16, No.5 (1983).
38. E.N.Wright, G. Eason & J.Fitzgerald, 'An Experimental Study of the Effects of Class Size', American Educational Research Journal, Vol.17, No.2 (1980) pp.141-152.
39. DES, Aspects of secondary education, p.63, and I.Butterworth, Staffing for Curriculum Needs, (NFER-Nelson, Windsor,1983),pp.33-35.
40. DES, Aspects of secondary education, p.58.
41. E.W.H. Briault and F.Smith, Falling Rolls in Secondary Schools, (NFER, Slough, 1980).
42. G.Bardell, Options for the Fourth, (Schools Council, London, 1982.
43. As reported by the Association of County Councils.
44. S.S. Ferguson, and D.J.Robertson, 'Abrupt contraction and disrupted relationships: a case study of Liverpool and the capping of the AFE pool,'Educational Management and Administration Vol.10, No.2,(1982) pp.181-185.
45. W.K. Allen, 'The Unmanageable Contraction of Public Sector Higher Education': Coombe Lodge Reports, Vol.15 No. 11 (1983), pp.460-469.
46. DES Circular 2/81, Falling Rolls and Surplus Places, and N.Bartmen and T.Carden 'Falling rolls and building costs', Education (16.10.81), pp. i-iv.
47. E.W.H. Briault, Falling Rolls in Secondary Schools.
48. Scottish Education Department,Ancillary Staff in Secondary Schools (HMSO, Edinburgh,1976).

49. CIPFA, Education Statistics 1980-81 Actuals, (1982).
50. J.R. Hough, A Study of School Costs, (NFER, Slough, 1981), pp.122-144.
51. CIPFA, Education Statistics 1980-81 Actuals.
52. E.M. Byrne, Planning and Educational Inequality, (NFER, Slough, 1974).
53. CIPFA, Education Statistics 1980-81 Actuals, and CIPFA, Education Statistics 1974-75 Actuals, (1976).
54. DES, Report by Her Majesty's Inspectors on the Effects of Local Authority Expenditure Policies on the Education Service in England-1981, (1982).

Chapter Five

TEACHERS AS A RESOURCE

MATCHING STAFF TO THE CURRICULUM

The logical starting point in staffing the curriculum, as for curriculum design itself, should be a statement of client needs. Once this is converted into a group of aims and objectives, processes leading to their accomplishment can be constructed. Possibly, this order of events could occur with the establishment of a new school or college, but even here factors such as the previous experiences, and likely competencies, of newly recruited staff impinge upon an ideal world. This starting point, therefore, is not normally sought: instead a gradual process of evolution permits a matching of clients needs, as defined, to the curriculum providable by the group of staff who are in post. To characterize the whole arrangement as a chance affair would be misleading: but at any time the staff possess a particular set of experiences, and a unique collection of skills, and it is the combination of these within the environmental constraints of the institution which sustain the curriculum. Clearly, the selection of individual staff has been based on satisfying needs and meeting certain objectives as they exist at the time, but these alter and there is no guarantee (and, before the introduction of systematic staff development policies, no attempt to ensure) that staff interests will mirror these changes. As new staff are recruited it should be possible to modify the curriculum that can be offered. Simultaneously the interests and commitments might be adaptable, but the matching of staff to the curriculum can never be other than a series of gradual adjustments. More so with contraction, when staff leaving and those that can be replaced depends upon the opportunity

of resignation and early retirement.
There are two distinct levels at which the match between teachers and the curriculum becomes critical. The first is national, involving the overall relationship between the supply and demand for teaching staff. The second occurs within institutions: the balance among staff in post, those that the institution is in a position to recruit, and the curriculum it would choose to offer. At both levels the natural tensions between resource suppliers and curriculum providers manifest themselves. The question of how many teachers are needed, particularly in relation to the provision of training facilities, if not rhetorical, raises innumerable issues - about desirable ratios, the likelihood of teachers in training wanting to enter the profession: or qualified staff no longer teaching hoping to return, and wastage rates of staff already in employment. Clearly, a specification of intended PTRs, as in the PESC projections, strongly influences the numbers to be employed for a year or two ahead but, as a result of the other factors mentioned, need not be the only determinant of the number of students in teacher training.[1] A profile of trainee numbers since the early 1960s, and their opportunities for employment, illustrates the problems of matching supply and circumscribed demand over any period of time. The emphasis up to the early 1970s was on achieving rapid expansion in new entrants, to deal with large increases in pupil and student numbers by the introduction of permanent facilities. Simultaneously, the labour market was buoyant, inducing high wastage rates. As the extent of the demographic down-turn became apparent in the 1970s, largely coincidentally, the influence of resource suppliers rose, and the notion of maintaining a match by employing all completed trainees wanting to teach thereby further reducing PTR, became redundant. Training facilities, often recently commissioned, were taken out of service,[2] demonstrating that at the macro-level, trained and trainee teachers do not enter a free market for employment or training. It is tightly constrained by DES dominated, LEA determined, mechanisms. At the micro-level, however, if employment prospects reduce elsewhere, new entrants do find themselves in competition from increasing numbers of previously qualified personnel wishing to return to teaching. For example, just over 50% of vacancies in primary schools, and about a third in secondary schools, are filled by returning teachers.[3]

Of course, the shorter the length of training, the quicker the response rate of the system to changes in demand for staff, whether arising from demographic factors or financial contingencies. The time lapse between a realization of over-production and reductions in out-put being a significant contribution to teaching unemployment in the 1970s. This factor, alongside the wider employability of graduates in other occupations, explains the greater emphasis on one-year PGCE training courses rather than B.Ed. qualifications. It is planned that the 1985 entry of new recruits to training will consist of 75% PGCE students to 25% on B.Ed. courses for secondary schools (with those percentages reversed in primary schools)[4]. However, the introduction of shorter training does not reduce the tensions between suppliers and providers. To a certain extent it strengthens the position of suppliers, as more effective controls over output, and reduced likelihood of over-production prevents the lobby from curriculum providers to employ surplus staff either on moral grounds or to utilize the investments that have been made in their training. However, providers have a genuine concern about the effects of such changes, designed to influence the availability of new staff, on the qualities they bring to the job. In the simplest of terms a teacher requires (a) a knowledge of, and some experience related to, the subject(s) or curricular area(s) with which they are to be involved, (b) a knowledge of, and some experience with, the teaching methods to be employed, and how these can facilitate student learning, (c) a concern for individuals, their particular needs, and a commitment to both the general teaching/learning situation and the circumstances in which this will occur, and (d) an awareness of how the processes of the classroom and institution fit into a broader environment, with community, regional and national dimensions. It can be argued that item (a) is less important in a primary school (say) or that (b) happens to be of limited relevance in AFE. According to this view learning in the primary school is more dependant upon teacher awareness of the most appropriate approaches, and empathy for the needs of children, than in a secondary school or FE, because the actual subject matter is less sophisticated and more readily comprehensible. Conversely, a lower priority for (b) arises from the greater skills and experiences of students in AFE. They should be much more capable of assisting their own learning, through independent decision-making.

This is reflected in practice: in FE, for example, nearly 54% of staff have no formal training in education (over 73% in polytechnics) as compared to schools in which only 21,000 out of a total teaching force in excess of 400,000 had no training.[5]

These arguments have some validity. In essence they imply that the older the pupil or student, the more likely previous experiences can be utilized to overcome deficiencies in teaching methodology: and as curriculum differentiation becomes increasingly important during the secondary school the greater the emphasis on teacher knowledge in specific subject areas. From the perspective of staffing-curriculum match this raises a significant issue. For primary schools the dominant theme relates the actual number of teachers to total requirements. More directly, the range of skills, knowledge and techniques required does not vary too much. Of course there are differences in demands made upon a teacher of 'top' juniors compared to a reception class situation while specific expertise is developed in language, mathematics, music etc. but as most teaching is class-based, a more ready transferability of tasks exists here, compared to elsewhere. With separate curricular areas and subject specialisms a new dimension is added to the problems of maintaining the staff - curriculum match.

Clearly, a supply-demand balance (however defined) or even an over-production in total number of teachers, does not guarantee sufficiency in every subject area. Often there are problems with new subjects emerging (information technology in the 1980s, for example). Traditional patterns of recruitment may be ineffective, either because developments are so recent that few potential staff can be recruited, or (and this can happen in longer-established subjects) salaries and working conditions do not attract lecturers with adequate experience. As a result the curriculum (and the teaching processes if inadequate staff are recruited) can be distorted. This has been a particular problem which has caused concern in secondary schools since 1945, because of the chronic shortage of teachers in some subjects - notably mathematics and physical science. [6] In the main it has been viewed as an institutional difficulty - a school unable to fill a Physics vacancy. This constitutes the second critical level in balancing staffing and curriculum. However, caution must be exercised in describing shortage. In absolute terms definitions are impossible. First, because a standard curriculum is not

specified. Some schools offer more teaching in
'shortage' subjects than others, however more is
delineated - option availability, teaching periods
per week, or even class-sizes. Whether the reduced
teaching in some schools arises from lack of staff
availability or a positive decision to give 'shortage' subjects less curricular priority requires
clarification. Second, as links between teaching
subjects and teacher qualification are not specified
(in theory every teacher can offer any subject)
under or non-qualified staff can be persuaded to
fill timetable gaps. Of course, in the limit if no
teachers make themselves available a subject will
not be taught and disappear from the curriculum.
Conversely, if teachers in a specialism become dominant (Classics in the public schools and early
grammar schools, for example) they may well use
their influence to perpetuate these arrangements.
The emergence of subjects such as Drama, Economics,
and (more recently) Computer studies may demonstrate
some external pressures for curriculum change, but
they also show the potential fluidity in subject
priorities as influenced by the micro-political
situation in the school.

To be more precise however, it is possible to
delineate four main types of shortage.[7] First, and
most obviously, the problem of unfilled vacancies
arises. A school advertises for a mathematics teacher and cannot find suitable applicants. If this
occurs in science a number of other issues result.
If all pupils were to study the subject up to 16,
as recommended by DES,[8] then the number of vacancies would rise. Additionally, as the percentage
of time awarded to the subject is usually less than
that to the other two subjects (Mathematics and
English[9]) in core curricular, were it given equal
status still more staff would be required. One
solution, because Science is a collection of usually
separate activities, would be to use a potential
surplus of Biology teachers, but the under-emphasis
on Physical Sciences would prejudice the objectives
of the whole exercise. Second, in any shortage situation, some alleviation is usually possible by mis-
matching previous teaching experience or qualifications to actual duties. The young teacher with
a degree in Geography, intending to build a career
in that subject, can often be persuaded to take a
few periods of lower school mathematics. From an
organizational perspective, the progress made by
the children, the job-satisfaction of the teacher,
and the quality of the teaching, will be of less

priority than the fact that a shortage problem has apparently been overcome. Only institutions with limited concerns for performance appraisal could tolerate such an arrangement.

The remaining forms of shortage are more subtle. In the third, teachers of shortage subjects become overloaded either through a heavy timetable commitment (high TCR) or teaching large classes (an inflated personal PTR). Again in relation to science, a practical activity, the issue of optimum class size is raised. In Scotland, for example, science because of this practical element, receives the same consideration as workshop based activities and therefore smaller classes.[10] Were such arrangements to prevail, either TCR's for science teachers would have to rise, or the fourth type of shortage could occur. Here, an under-provision of teaching time exists either through having too low a proportion of pupils attending (limited availability in options, for example) or the subject having too small an allocation on the timetable. Again, though, the issue of what constitutes under-provision requires attention. Because of curricular freedoms science or mathematics (or any other curricular area in which there appears to be shortage of staff) will not figure equally prominently on the timetables of all schools. Turning to mathematics, for example, the percentage of total teaching time in four schools over a four year period varied from 9.8 to 13.7% (the equivalent figures in science showing a bigger range 10.0 to 17.9%).[11] No allowance is made for class-sizes in these statistics, and one possible way of rectifying this omission involves calculating the teaching time per pupil in each subject - a measure of the time with a teacher available to the individual pupil within a teaching cycle (usually a week) expressed as a fraction of a single lesson. Here, in main school mathematics, it can vary from 0.19 to 0.26 (0.46 to 1.07 in the sixth-form, although more likely to be influenced by class size) and 0.11 to 0.23 (0.56 to 1.65 in the sixth form) for science.[12]

Perhaps a more pertinent question than that about overcoming shortfalls in provision, given the difficulties of defining shortage, would be concerned with equalizing the flow of potential staff to curricular areas. With more applicants to teach history (say) than some other subjects, there are far-reaching implications with regard to the relative qualities of teaching staff, if the selection procedures have any effectiveness. In other words a college tutor or headteacher selecting from 100 applicants rather than ten (say) should be able to make a better choice. In a market situation, the effects of such imbalances could be overcome by paying teachers of defined 'shortage' subjects higher salaries. Overlooking both the practical difficulties of such arrangements (exaggerated by Burnham) and the organization defects relative to the school of two (or more) levels of teacher, that solution would only work if low salaries was providing a disincentive to potential entrants. What limited evidence exists for Physics suggests more intrinsic reasons for dissuading graduates from teaching than financial factors.[13] More important, if the market mechanism is pursued, issues related to levels of commitment, and the processes by which payment levels contribute (or not) to job satisfaction require consideration.

However, the most far reaching issue of all, relative to shortage, concerns its potential cyclical and long-term aspects. If the profile of new entrants to teaching is skewed, in terms of curricular interests, they will tend to reinforce any bias during their careers. For example, in primary schools, if the commitments of staff primarily cover language and creative activities, because mathematics, science and technical expertise is underdeveloped or not available, there are potential influences on the interests the children themselves will develop.[14] In fact all forms of shortage can be demonstrated in such a situation, except (probably) for an unfilled vacancy, but lack of match between teacher, knowledge and curriculum (possibly resulting in low quality teaching with little enthusiasm) and limited timetable provision, would dominate. Clearly, there are profound long-term implications if such a skew is not corrected. Some subjects will be under-developed, others over-developed,[15] at both primary and secondary levels, but without any absolute standards to define shortage of staff in terms of curricular objectives whether at national or local level, the school response must be to employ the staff it can, and organize the curriculum which emerges from the mix of staff and client interests, modified by external forces.

If a school (or LEA) does decide a shortage exists some apparently straightforward ameliorative methods are available. The use of peripatetic specialist staff, freed from all other duties: the introduction of teams of teachers, led by one specialist: the integration of some areas of school-work with activities in a local college: the retention of shortage subject staff in the classroom rather than promotion to administrative positions. The degree to which such arrangements can be implemented in the face of the practical difficulties and opposition they produce, depends upon a mixture of school and LEA policy, the determination with which they are used to overcome any difficulties, and chance (the proximity of a local college, or the appeal of a school to shortage staff, for example). More important, this combination of factors raises the issue of responsibility for curriculum match, particularly in resolving shortage difficulties. If schools or colleges have sole responsibility for curriculum design, then a natural corollary is that they should solve their own staffing difficulties. In effect, by designing the curriculum in a certain way they have created the problem. Yet a LEA cannot abrogate its duties to that extent. Previously, even with institutional autonomy, it may have tried to assist if a school had particular problems: with a new curricular relationship evolving a more positive stance is demanded of LEAs (and DES) not only for balance between supply and assessed demand for teachers, but also relative to the staffing of defined curricular.

SELECTING, TRAINING AND DEVELOPING STAFF

For schools, increasingly, selection of most potential teachers will occur at ages of 18 (for B.Ed. degree) and 21 or 22 (for PGCE courses). In FE a more complex pattern of recruitment will continue. Some recent graduates (trained and untrained) are recruited, but other staff enter lecturing after industrial, commercial or other experience. Often they will have come through the FE system themselves.[16] Basically, therefore, two separate entry routes emerge: the first in which little is demanded in the way of pre-entry experiences, skills and knowledge other than 'A' levels, can be contrasted with the second where these qualities, assumed to result from graduation and/or job performance, constitute prerequisites. In the former case the intention is that training should provide whatever qualities are required, while in the latter situation, where initial training exists, the methodologies relating to teaching or lecturing receive most attention. As a result of these different practices, though, there can be no simple answer to the question of when a person is selected for teaching. Someone entering school teaching, for example, participates in three or four selection procedures - on entry to training, on successful completion, and when applying for a job (and on finishing probationary service). In the context of questions about criteria used in any of these selection processes, again, there can be no simple answer. It is extremely rare to utilize objective measures to assess suitability for teaching. Degree or 'A' level performance, and an interview to assess commitment and personal qualities, normally suffice. Given the absence of clear agreements about the characteristics of good teaching, or any consensus about the qualities sought from intending staff, it would perhaps be inefficient to do extra. This does not imply that selectors do not attempt rigour when they choose. If they have six candidates of apparently equal worth the fact that they take time to select two (say) gives confidence to those chosen and allows the other to think their cases have been thoroughly considered. The real disadvantage in the selection function, diffused as it is between training institutions and employers, arises not from the absence of objective criteria (the subtleties of the teaching and learning processes do not permit otherwise) but the under-development of processes to monitor the work of staff. In other words the only way to assess whether selection arrangements have been effective in relation to individual staff is to evaluate subsequent performance, and utilize probationary service sanctions, when necessary. More directly it is the fourth of the selection procedures which should dominate.

The objectives of training have to be focussed on the four requirements of a teacher or lecturer. DES in designing criteria for the validation of initial courses for teachers reduces these to three:[17] 1. A two-year full-time study of the subjects to be taught (including graduate studies), 2. A study of teaching methods related to chosen subjects and differentiated by ages of children, 3. A practical base of experience. An intention to move to situations in which staff qualify to teach specific subjects to certain age-ranges is implied. There are obvious advantages in being able to target training more precisely, although the supply and demand situation for staff would become more difficult, compared to arrangements in which a qualified teacher, in theory at least, can work in any subject with every age-range. Yet, though there appears a close match between requirements of staff and training criteria further scrutiny is demanded. Even an item as apparently self-explanatory as the desirability of two-year (or graduate) study of subjects to be taught hides potential inadequacies. Having satisfied this criterion, a teacher has gained some knowledge of the subject to be taught, although not necessarily about specific topics, unless there is consistency between school and college curricular. They have also shown themselves to be capable, and displayed a commitment, if not necessarily an enthusiasm, to the subject. In other words graduate status has given both a general and specific credibility and (possibly) confidence to the individual, and a general range of competencies, although not precisely focussed on likely tasks. In fact, a concentration on teacher knowledge of the subject, if it becomes over dominant, induces two possible disadvantages. First, it raises the importance of a cognitively based model of the curriculum: the notion that the main task in teaching or lecturing is to convey a certain body of knowledge. In certain situations the ability of staff to transmit information is an important attribute, although in the long-term likely to become less central with the evolution of computer-based instructional methodologies, but rarely provides the sole objective in any learning arrangement. Alternative skills and interests have to be developed by a teacher if learning is to be maximised. Second, that knowledge may have been up to date when the teacher received it: the probability of it remaining in that condition is remote. Basically, graduate study should provide a foundation so that the teacher is in a position to update knowledge and be aware of changes in the subject area.

Clearly, curricular differentiation from upper secondary schools onwards, with increasing sophistication and complexity of subject-matter (particularly in AFE) reduces the generalizability of any comments about the absolute necessity of a teacher keeping informed relative to areas of professional responsibility. The situation of (say) an AFE lecturer in electronics, a teacher of 'A' level history, and someone responsible for mathematics work in a primary school, are totally different in relation to the rapidity with which content in their fields change. However, to focus solely on content fails to appreciate the full significance of the other three qualities required by a teacher. In these cases the rapidity of change in electronics is by far the highest, and the demands on the lecturer

Teachers as a Resource

will be greatest, but significant variations in practices and methodologies in the teaching of junior school mathematics do occur. More likely, than in the electronics example, they will be associated with the processes of learning rather than content, but in relation to the collection of skills and knowledge required of the effective teacher that is of limited importance. More centrally, in each of the situations, the issue of the teacher remaining alert to task performance, and the factors likely to effect and modify this, should be predominant. Those factors may emanate from the subject matter itself, the teaching/learning processes, the needs of the clients, or the environment of the institution, as affected by both internal and external pressures: and such is their scope (as increased by the range of potential interactions) that any initial training, no matter how effective (and whether primarily directed towards subject content or teaching methods) can only have direct influence on task performance during the first few years of work. Initial training, therefore, must be viewed, not as an end in itself, but a preparation for further development.

As important as the changing circumstances in which staff work, is the certainty that individuals alter their attitudes and practices with maturity and experience. Of course it is easy to extend these arguments about the limited impact of initial training, as compared to long-term development, to the point of its redundancy (or irrelevance in professional areas where it has received little attention). Such a view misses the main point: the intention is to achieve a situation in which teachers enhance their usefulness as a resource in such a way that they support their own further development. This comes about from two sources - initial training and other pre-entry experiences. In many FE situations, industrial or commercial experiences are a more important feature in the profile of new staff than any specific training qualifications. The benefits of lecturers moving from other occupations relate to the whole range of experiences, attitudes and practices introduced into the college. As intended many will be specifically directed towards the immediate work situation, but other advantages are obtainable by way of 'spin-off' benefits. For example, topics are considered from an alternative perspective, or problems receive different attention, because of the new frames of reference brought by staff with non-educational experiences. Occasionally, such situations lead to conflict, but the importation of these additional experiences provides a dimension in college decision-making, particularly in relations with external agencies, which is generally not available to schools. In the main, potential staff are selected and trained, after minimal (if any) non-school experience. As curricular are not vocationally orientated a direct analogy with staff recruitment in FE becomes impossible, but schools have a disadvantage, especially relative to client needs, that few staff know from first hand, for example, the circumstances of a 16 year old leaver. More generally, teachers who have not worked outside a school find it more difficult to appreciate external perceptions about the work of schools. Of course, it does not have to follow that because a teacher has other experiences job-effectiveness must necessarily rise. There are so many other factors which intervene, but non-educational activities can broaden the base on which initial training and further developments can be established in satisfying the requirements for a teacher.

The fundamental reason, therefore, which ensures the importance of staff development concerns the fact that the teaching staff employed by a school or college do not constitute a static entity. Even if the same group of individuals continue working in one institution, they change, learning (and unlearning) knowledge and skills, showing differing levels of commitment and motivation, and varying degrees of confidence in managing their own job-situations. All of these items being subject to powerful external influences: while the interactions ensure not only the potential fluidity of the staffing situation, but also the necessity of response if the institution is to exert its own influences over the environment. The most obvious response for (or from) institutions that they need a programme to develop staff provokes a host of questions. Some are highly practical. Who should be involved? What form can a programme take? While others are more searching, about the objectives of such an exercise or the relationship to future institutional environments, they all centre around some model of organizational behaviour. At one extreme stands a professional notion. Here the main intention is for the employee to gain satisfaction from the work itself. As a result the quality of that work should be maximised and the primary function of the organization is to provide a climate and working arrange-

ments to permit and sustain the achievement of this
satisfaction. In these circumstances entire responsibility for any developmental activities resides
with individual staff, who through the exercise of
professional duties are aware and alert to their
own needs and whether this involves course attendance, additional qualifications, extra reading or
simply more time for reflection. In other words the
self-development mode is dominant. The organization
provides a framework and some constraining parameters but little else.

In total contrast the bureaucratic model views
development as an organizational responsibility.
With jobs strictly defined, and positions specified in a hierarchy, the organization (or, more
correctly, senior staff) would determine the form of
training so that staff are prepared for both current
jobs and others as they became vacant. From the
perspective of the other, it is easy to castigate
either approach. The professional model may appear
highly appealing, relying as it does, on personal
motivational factors, heightened by commitment to
the work. Clearly, such a person is in an advant-
ageous position to assess the desirability of developmental activity. If the approach functions effectively it would seem to be unrivalled, but what
happens if the functioning is imperfect or, more
subtly, mechanisms are not activated to search for
potential deficiencies? More directly, in these
circumstances much is left to chance, particularly
where monitoring facilities, either through lack of
market mechanisms or appraisal procedures, receive
inadequate attention. Yet, imposed development,
either because its intentions or timetables are not
those which an individual would necessarily have
chosen, has limitations. There are motivational
disadvantages: in the limit individuals sell their
time to the organization, in return for payment because commitment levels have been so far reduced.
The extrinsic rewards of the job dominate, when
staff should be obtaining considerable satisfaction,
through intrinsic benefits, from task performance.
In such situations within schools and colleges, it
is highly improbable that staff will pursue alternative educational outcomes or search with any vigour
for new client needs requiring satisfaction. Of
course, it would be quite misleading to imply that
the imposition of staff development activities would
produce such organizational deficiencies. The fact
is that were it necessary to utilize impositional
arrangements as the only route to staff development,

numerous defects must already exist in the organization and little chance that centrally determined and administered development policies will prove a remedy.

In most schools and colleges a professional model of development has been self-evident, but related, in the main, to the needs of individual staff: while the organizations themselves have displayed a mix of professional and bureaucratic features. The autonomy with which staff have exercised many of their responsibilities, can be contrasted with the hierarchical structures of headteacher, college principal, head of section etc. which in turn contrasts with the fact that most, if not all, positions in the hierarchy are held by teaching/lecturing staff still performing professional duties. The status of non-professional managers and administrators tends to be low. Within such arrangements individual determination of developmental activities both in content and objectives, has been predominant because of its links with upward mobility of staff. More directly, a teacher attended a course, or whatever, and while this may have benefitted their work in the school, often a more significant intention related to improved chances of moving to a higher status post.

With contraction, and therefore less opportunity for mobility, two opposing reactions emerge: either less individually directed activity because motivation declines in line with opportunity or, conversely, increased efforts to improve prospects relative to the availability of fewer opportunities. In broad terms what contraction means to the individual is an increase in the bureaucratic strictures and some reduction in the availability of professional freedom, resulting both from a longer time-period working in the same institution, and reactions forced upon it by changed circumstances. In the context of developmental strategies the organization has to merge the potential benefits of the professional model to perceptions of its own needs. Essentially there are two foci. The first of these involves the individual, and utilizing professional commitment, to maintain a match between the four requirements of a teacher and task performance even in a rapidly changing environment. The potential procedures are numerous - private reading, study release, courses (in and out of the institution) further qualifications etc. The second focus is the institution. It, most effectively using all staff through participatory modes, has to determine what is needed from staff to pursue its objectives, and the ways in which individual development plans match and mismatch (and will therefore have to be modified relative to organizational requirements). Yet, in concentrating on these two elements, and their links, it is easy to overlook the most important component of all, without which the efficacy of any developmental strategies would be considerably reduced. For both the individual and the organization there is little point in directing activities towards task performance until an awareness of the quality of that performance exists. Therefore an appraisal system is essential: without it the main thrust of developmental exercises become obscure. Clearly, practical problems arise in an occupation, such as teaching, where there is no tradition of formal appraisal, and practice permits an individual, having completed probationary service, to assume job-tenure, irrespective of a lack of any self-initiated development. However, as selection and training have to be inefficient processes (because of the paucity of definitive criteria) and because changing circumstances likely to be encountered during a career make developmental activities prerequisites for sustaining teacher effectiveness, the evolution of appraisal mechanisms to provide a framework for individual and organizational development becomes a key issue.

USING THE RESOURCE

The utilization of the teacher resource to achieve maximum effectiveness invokes perceptions of over-directional management. The ensurance that staff are with a class, that lectures run for the scheduled length, and that non-contact time does not become free (non-working time) all relate to the mechanistic aspects of staff deployment. In an organization with refined professional attitudes such items may represent non-issues, but an important logistical component in the management function must continue whatever the state of staff commitment to their work. At the simplest level timetabling provides a plan for staff deployment: from a different perspective, its preparation, and the compromises between interest groups it includes and the outcomes of educational and finance-based decisions it represents, are central to the whole curricular-resources debate within institutions. In other words, while the final product may seem to concentrate on logistical items about teacher work-loads, class size, lessons per subject etc. the processes of production cannot exclude a series of issues related to the objectives of the institutions. In fact, the utilization of staff-time can be considered at three over-lapping levels. The first involves the institution in monitoring actual staff deployments when a plan has been introduced: while the second includes all activities related to the preparation of that plan (in the form of a timetable or whatever). The third level in many respects subsumes the other two, being closely related to the previous section, in that the logistical-mechanistic may often appear to dominate in any discussion on utilizing staff, but it is the quality of task performance, as influenced by training and developmental activities, which provides the more important determinant of outcome.

At the second level, in particular, a marked contrast between FE and schools procedures exist. There is no equivalent in schools to the detailed specification of weeks in the year, contact time, and hours per lecturer of FE (Chapter 4). Such arrangements can present problems in organizational terms and sustain curricular constraints, but they provide a framework. In schools, controls tend to be lighter, related to the minimum length of day and sessions per year.[18] Those studies which have been attempted to look at the working pattern of teachers (restricted in number because of the industrial 'work study' connotations) have demonstrated considerable variations. In junior schools in the late 1960s (and it is unlikely that the situation will have changed dramatically since then) a mean teaching time of 288 minutes per day was observed rising to over 300 minutes in some schools, but less than 265 in others.[19] Most secondary schools have established a pattern of seven or eight sessions, varying in length from 30 to 40 minutes. In other words, differences in length of school day of around 10% exist. The most direct question arises of whether this matters? What effect, if any has a longer school day on outcomes? Are schools with shorter days more time efficient, in relation to inter-lesson changeovers, or do they attempt to compensate with additional homework? Surprisingly, these topics have received comparatively little attention in educational research. However, the most imposing question for organizational managers, whether in schools or FE, concerns the extent to which the arrangements that have evolved are the result of tradition and practice, as compared to systematic efforts to achieve solutions to problems. Again a potential conflict between individual and organizational interests emerges. Returning to the junior schools study, an attempt was made to differentiate between teaching time and the use made of their own time by teachers during the school day. On average, just under 50% of class-time was given to actual teaching, with the next highest category involving class organization, but the most interesting feature was the high standard deviation, implying a range of work-patterns.

In a professional organization such variations are only to be expected, but they pose a dilemma for the management function. One intention must be to maximize delivery time, that is the time staff spend with pupils or students - although there has to be some doubt about this maximisation in certain FE situations, given the potential advantages of student private study. Yet, if managers pursue this goal they must impinge upon areas of professional freedom, and in doing so threaten some of the advantages accruing from autonomy. Take the example of an organization which decides to lower contact-ratios (or hours taught) by allowing larger classes, but on the assumption that sessions will be better prepared, or that new materials and approaches can be developed. Clearly, such a school or college relies on the fact that bigger groups will be more than matched by improved educational outcomes. In what ways though should the organization try to monitor the activities of staff in such changed arrangements without infringing unnecessarily an individual work pattern? More directly, how can the organization ensure that the additional non-contact time allocated to staff has been used in the ways intended? Indeed, if a complete professional relationship between organization and individual were sought, it would be argued that this type of question is largely irrelevant. The individual teacher, because of knowledge of the situation and commitment to the work, should be capable of making decisions about preparing lessons. The business of the organization is to establish parameters, and allow the individual freedom to exercise judgement.

Yet, the issue of how effectively teaching staff utilize their time is the most important item in any consideration of educational resources, because of the dominance of salaries in expenditure patterns. Improvement in the ways staff organize themselves, or procedures they adopt to perform the same tasks in shorter time, raise the efficiency of the institution. In practice, the topic of time management by individual staff has not received a great deal of attention. One response to suggestions that it should is that teachers are too busy or, more particularly, because so much of the working day has timetable constraints, insufficient flexibility exists to make this a worthwhile topic for discussion. The lack of flexibility argument requires clarification. Almost all job situations have regular duties attached,[20] and in this respect education is no different. From a quantitative standpoint few staff are timetabled in excess of 25 hours per week (others a good deal less) and, given the normal commitment to lesson associated activities, this still leaves time when teachers should be reasonably free to organize thier own time. The implication when staff talk of lack of flexibility concerns the effects of external influences on their working arrangements. In the limit such are the demands imposed that individuals find it impossible to do anything other than react to the situations and circumstances in which they find themselves. However, a person who displays entirely reactive characteristics in this way, makes no attempt to control the working environment. They are as tightly constrained, even in an environment they might claim to be professionally orientated, as someone in a bureaucratic organization, only the restrictions are provided by the pressure of events rather than organizational rules.

It is much easier to point out to staff who claim to be busy that they have lost control over their working situation, than to suggest remedies they might be able to successfully implement. The first difficulty is not so much to convince them that they have a problem (time pressures usually make this clear) although appraisal procedures may help to clarify views, but that potential solutions may be available. Schedules of how time is spent, and the time that appears to be wasted, performed by (or on) an individual highlight many issues. Away from lessons and lectures numerous items demand consideration. Questions about discussions with other staff - are they structured, do they take too long, do they cover topics already considered, have all teachers with a legitimate interest been involved (if not will they have to be repeated) - all require attention. Meetings may be overlong by general consensus, yet rarely are both starting and finishing times published, or the agenda structured to demonstrate the length to be given to each item.

Invariably, suggestions directed towards effective time management are simple: they cannot be otherwise. The fact that much self-inflicted frustration could be avoided if staff, instead of thinking about tasks not done, ordered priorities and performed them singly, rather than attempting several jobs simultaneously, is no more than common sense. Yet the importance of such apparent banalities, and their potential relevance, cannot be overstated if staff are unable to make time to reflect on what they are doing, or reconsider their priorities on a regular basis. In situations where staff find themselves unable to create time for proactivity - to modify teaching approaches, introduce alternative course structures, search out for changes in client needs etc. - both they and the institution will have stunted development, and the most important resource utilizes itself ineffectually. 21

PAYING FOR TEACHERS

Over recent years, several experiences have demonstrated the problems in comparing salary levels in teaching and lecturing with those in other occupations. In a market economy the simple answer to such questions is that supply and demand factors should provide the main determinant. As a potential solution the market place has two main defects in this context. First, salary levels may strongly influence the numbers entering teaching (and presumably effect quality) but have minimal impact upon the larger numbers already in post who, because of their service and lack of other experiences, are effectively debarred from other occupations. More directly, in any negotiation, management (DES and the local authority associations with the Treasury) have a strengthened position because they are dealing largely with a captive market, more so with high unemployment elsewhere in the economy. Levels of payment may effect commitment to the work, but for the vast majority of staff has minimal influence on availability for work. Second, because the teaching force is so differentiated, with huge variations in the extent to which skills and expertise can be transferred to alternative work-situations, a full market approach to the recruitment and retention of staff would need to reflect such disparaties in differential salary levels. Perhaps, such a mechanism, if implemented, would help overcome long-standing shortages for some types of staff, but the effects of large salary differences on staff attitudes within institutions would demand careful consideration. It would be difficult, for example, to sustain a participatory or collegial environment if one teacher was paid double that of another while performing essentially the same job and carrying a similar level of responsibility.

Therefore, putting aside relative payment levels not because it is an unimportant topic - according to PESC forecasts teacher salary increases can significantly affect expenditure on other items[22] - but as it easily develops into an irreconcilable debate about job-satisfaction, responsibilities, security of tenure etc. Additionally, apart from some specific shortages, market forces (defective though they can be) seem well capable of supplying an adequacy of staff in a country with high unemployment. More significant, from a resource utilization perspective, are the distributional elements in rewards to individuals, and the effect of factors such as length of service and responsibilities on payment and the organization of the institution. So different are the arrangements that schools and FE demand separate consideration. In schools, the procedures for determining salary levels, emanating from the Burnham primary and secondary panels,[23] can be traced back to the separate sectors of elementary and secondary school teachers before the Education Act, 1944. The number of pupils weighted according to age, determines the number of points available to each school (as well as the salary of the deputy and headteacher), with these points, distributed among staff, raising individuals above the basic Scale 1 post - 1 point for a Scale 11 etc. up to Scale 1V and senior teacher levels. (Table 5.1). The skew in favour of older children results from the earlier arrangements, in which only selective schools had pupils above the minimum leaving age,[24] and although less marked than previously still allows a predominance of promoted positions in a sixth-form college as compared to a middle school (say) or any school with a high proportion of older pupils.[25] Although such arrangements disadvantage certain schools (in particular, primary and middle schools and also secondary schools with few or no sixth-form pupils) they were generally accepted. So long as expansion continued staff could move from Scale 1 to Scale 11 etc. as additional points were generated. In such circumstances the need for a career grade was eliminated, as a teacher remaining on Scale 1 would either have been inept or unambitious. A climate of mobility was sustained by these procedures, with

TABLE 5.1   Unit-Totals, Points Scores for Schools, other than Special

Unit Total+	Points Score range	Highest Scale for Teachers	Group of School for Head and Deputy Head Teacher Purposes
up to 100	0-1	2	1
101-200	0-1	2	2
201-300	0-2	2	3
301-400	1-3	2	4
401-500	2-6	2	4
501-600	3-8	3	5
601-700	5-11	3	5
701-800	7-13	3	6
801-900	9-15	3	6
901-1000	10-17	3	6
1001-1100	11-21	3	7
1101-1200	13-23	3	7
1201-1300	14-26	3	7
1301-1400	15-28	4	8
1401-1600	17-33	4	8
1601-1800	21-37	4	8
1801-2000	25-40	4	9
2001-2200	30-44	4	9
2201-2400	35-49	4	9
2401-2700	41-55	4*	10
2701-3000	47-60	4*	10
3001-3300	52-65	4*	10
3301-3700	57-74	4*	11
3701-4100	62-79	4*	11
4101-4600	68-83	4*	11
4601-5100	75-90	4*	12
5101-5600	81-96	4*	12
5601-6000	88-103	4*	12
6001-6100	88-103	4*	13
6101-6600	94-109	4*	13
6601-7100	101-116	4*	13
7101-7600	108-123	4*	13
Over 7600		4*	14

* Including Senior Teachers
+ Each pupil under 14 counts 2 units, under 15 counts 3 units, under 16 counts 4 units, under 17 counts 6 units, under 18 counts 8 units.

Source: DES, Scales of Salaries for Teachers: Primary and Secondary Education, England & Wales 1983 (HMSO, London, 1983).

inner and intra-school movement, as staff transferred to new or additional responsibilities.

With contraction, of course, a system which previously had appeared attractive was soon proven defective, and disadvantageous to payment levels and career aspirations of staff. Progress through the Scales became much more difficult as schools found themselves, with declining rolls, having to reduce the number of promoted post positions. Many, when a Scale post holder left, had to use the opportunity to lower the total number of points to levels specified in the Burnham agreement. Adverse financial circumstances prevented the most obvious solution of raising the allowances per pupils, but even this would have been little more than a minor palliative, unless extended throughout the period of population decline. Public expenditure retrenchment was not the only factor which created additional problems: the age and seniority profile of the teaching profession, resulting from previous recruitment policies, had a similar impact. (Table 5.2). As can be seen the high levels of recruitment of the 1960s, and through into the early 1970s, (involving many staff who await some form of promotion) have a marked effect: less obviously but exaggerating any 'log-jam' factor was the relatively rapid promotion available during that period, and therefore the likelihood that many senior positions were filled at that time by teachers still in mid-career.

Even without the problems highlighted by contraction, there is little difficulty in specifying more inherent defects in the arrangements. There is for example, no attempt to delineate the additional responsibilities or duties expected of a Scale 11 postholder, and no definition relating to the extra tasks associated with the more senior positions of head of house or departmental head. To a large extent resolution of such issues has been left to institutional discretion. One school may have many Scale 11 positions as a policy, another might have concentrated points in more senior positions. From a management perspective any system of payment requires two dominant characteristics. First, it must closely relate to the fundamental task of the organization, teaching in the classroom. If possible, it should also assist in improving the quality of that teaching, by utilizing assessment of performance, and commitment to work, as part-determinants of salary. At present arrangements for probationary service, completed after the first professional year, are no more than a device to sift out the

TABLE 5.2 Actual and estimated age-profile of teaching force 1977-1995

Figures for England and Wales, in six-year intervals

	Age-range			
	Under 30	30 - 39	40 - 49	50 and over
1977	35.6	24.8	22.5	17.1
1983	21	34	26	19
1989	14	32	30	24
1995	16	19	39	26

The details for 1977 are actuals, from 1983 onwards estimates.

Sources: DES *Statistics of Education Volume 4 Teachers 1977* (HMSO, London, 1979), and DES *Reports on Education No. 98 Teacher numbers - looking ahead to 1995*, (March 1983).

least competent, or most inappropriate staff. Far better an initial placement category, lasting perhaps several years, with subsequent progress to a main career grade restricted to staff of proven competence, and accelerated promotion up this grade available for high-performers. At the top of this grade, so as to avoid an eventual 'log-jam' and to assist in monitoring motivation and morale, more increments could be added for those individuals who appeared to merit special payment for classroom performance. Second, because of the additional responsibilities that some staff must carry, a method of payment has to be devised which relates salary to responsibilities and duties while allowing the organization a management structure best suited to the pursuit of its aims and objectives. In this respect schools are perhaps unique in that the award of a certain number of promoted positions, because of size and pupil age-profile, provides a collection of posts and with these they must construct their management systems. It would be more logical, and in keeping with other types of institution, for each school to specify a structure, containing an allocation of responsibilities among individual staff, to be followed by an allowance negotiatiated with the LEA to remunerate staff for these extra duties. In other words, in addition to the main professional grade, staff such as heads of house would receive payment related to their responsibilities. In preference to a school's aggregate allowance for extra responsibility posts being related to NOR (which would be little better than current arrangements) it could be based on a LEA willingness to finance the proposed arrangements, relative to the characteristics of the school, or even be a component in the school's budget presentation in a situation of financial autonomy. (Chapter 6).

As a result of the intentions sought, other advantages could accrue from such arrangements. The perceived need of staff to move from Scale 1 to Scale 11 etc. for salary, status or whatever reasons would be eliminated. Similarly, the necessity of schools having to devise reasons to award staff promoted positions, alongside the distortions this can provoke in the organizational structure, could cease. Also much clearer definitions might be sought relative to the responsibilities associated with more senior positions throughout the school. Of course, any attempt to introduce arrangements along these lines would need to resolve a large number of potential problems. The role of the school and LEA in decisions about movement of individual teachers on to the main career grade, and the rate of progression through that grade, are potentially contentious issues. Given the mobility of staff among schools and authorities, there would be a need for consistency, in the criteria to be applied. That feature would also have to permeate procedures for LEA allowances to schools for additional responsibility payments. The necessity of definitions, in this context, to align responsibilities with payment does not have to produce rigidities. That is the problem with current arrangements which are potentially restrictive, particularly during contraction, in that a school having embarked upon a staffing policy, even some time past, has little freedom to adapt to changing circumstances, while allowing large variations in the duties expected of a teacher at a certain promotion level.

Whatever the apparent benefits, however, of any new arrangement they must be perceived as sufficient to overcome the conflicts within the management-teacher union environment to which they are focal. Unions, for example, might be most attracted by a career trade, because of pressures from their own members approaching the top of Scale 1, particularly if the uppermost point of this grade was above Scale 11 rates. In contrast, they would be much less inclined to accept a time-lag before the establishment of individual teachers on the career grade, and the notion of accelerated progress linked to performance. Their natural inclination would be to argue for automatic transfer to the career grade and maximum rates of progress, therefore militating against the use of the payment system to raise performance levels. From the management perspective the main problem is to achieve structural change at minimal cost, given public expenditure constraints. As modifications which would make even a few personnel worse off have no likelihood of implementation, alterations are needed which bring responsibilities into line with payment, but at minimal additional cost, certainly in the short term. A career-grade would satisfy this criterion, by eliminating the cost of promotion of Scale 1 to Scale 11, and, more long-term, the increase in salary expenditures (depending, of course, on the detail of lower and upper points, number of stages etc.) could be relatively small. There would be some difficulties, for example with current Scale 11 holders carrying specific responsibilities, particularly in primary

schools. They might anticipate an allowance, but
their extra duties could be viewed as integral to
the commitment expected of career grade teachers.
It is the assimilation of more senior post-holders
which presents most potential problems, in relation
to issues such as payment levels compared to responsibilities, and salaries awarded to career grade
staff. Difficulties exaggerated by the fact that
when additional resources were available to facilitate substantial restructuring for example, with
the Houghton Report (1974), opportunities were
foregone.[26]

If anything, the salary structures for FE
lecturers are even less appropriate to prevailing
circumstances than those in schools. Some implications of the arrangements for curricular organizations have already been considered (Chapter 4).
Perhaps more surprsing, to an outsider, would be
the inverse relationship between seniority and contact hours with students. The intention, to allow
senior staff more time for administration, is clear,
but an intention (if it exists) to link the system
of rewards to the promotion of lecturing quality
remains obscure, not to say discouraged. In other
words if a lecturer demonstrates high performance
in teaching and receives promotion, the next position must (by management-union agreement) involve
less teaching. In practice the situation is usually
less simple, because of another section in the
agreement which relates proportions of promoted
posts to categories of work. One view would be that
some differentiation into levels is essential, because of the range of work involved, to provide a
fair system of rewards.[27] On that basis a lecturer
working with degree students should be paid more
than a person lecturing on 'O' level courses, because of the greater scope of the job: under current
arrangements they also have less contact hours. Indeed, two basic scales do exist, in some respects
analogous to the career grade suggested for school
work. In AFE work (Categories I, II, and II) because of a virtually automatic progression from
Lecturer Grade II to Senior Lecturer, all staff eventually achieve the latter status. By contrast for
NAFE (Categories IV and V) somewhere over half the
staff (in the limit up to 85%) are employed at
Lecturer Grade I level. The similarities with potential modifications to the school arrangements
cannot be taken too far, particularly in relation to
good teaching. There is no entry grade as such in
FE and a complete absence of attempts to relate

payment to performance. From a personnel standpoint the extreme of two disparate, yet clearly defined grades, with a salary differential of 40%, has considerable implications.[28] Particularly, when with assigned rates, a maximum 5% of staff working in NAFE can expect Senior Lecturer positions. As a result 'academic drift' is encouraged by both salary and status factors, in that staff benefit, irrespective of any educational or motivational reasons, from working on higher level courses. A trend assisted by examining boards and professional institutions wishing to see their courses up-graded.

The development of higher level qualifications as a response to technological change was developed in Chapter 2, and while a facilitating salary structure is desirable, it still must function effectively in its own right. Given the arrangements it is understandable that individuals, unions, departments, professional organizations and validating bodies will try to use the system, to a greater or lesser extent, in support of their own interests. An example, that staff can do so, is the fact that while NAFE constitutes over two-thirds of all work less than one-third of staff hold Grade I positions. Similarly, the steady increase in the proportion of Senior Lecturer posts to Grade II positions (24% to 30%, respectively, in 1976 reversing to 31% to 24% in 1980) does suggest that some institutions allow staff to invoke the promotion 'bar' criterion of 50% AFE work liberally, and move advanced work from lecturer to lecturer: for having once negotiated that bar, staff do not revert below it, even if they return to less than half-time on AFE activities.[29] Specifically, the divide between the demands of AFE and NAFE work does not appear to be sufficiently clear to justify the salary differentials it generates: more generally, it questions the whole issue of relating job-content to payment. It is difficult to dispute that a main objective in any system of payment should be to link the size of the job (the range of tasks involved and the demands made by each of them) to remuneration. In these arrangements that association becomes difficult, if not impossible, because of the gradual reduction in teaching hours with seniority: possibly resulting in departments with many senior staff, as a result of their profile of courses, having to find non-teaching activities. In this context there is little guidance from Burnham and related agreements, other than statements about teaching and non-teaching hours. A more appropriate starting point would be greater consistency over teaching hours, and clearer definitions of administrative loads enabling the establishment of a relationship between job-size and pay. A single salary scale (as suggested for schools) would be impracticable both because, in effect, two already exist, and the enormous range of work-situations involved.

There are, however, two situations pushing both unions and management towards a major restructuring. The first involves the rapid expansion in 'low-grade' work (Category V) discriminated against in the salary arrangements yet likely to provide an increasing proportion of students. Second, and related to this expansion, the probability that other agencies will wish to become involved and, with more flexible pay arrangements, be able to sustain a more competitively priced service. However, while such factors may facilitate the establishment of new arrangements, they do not assist in the design of alternative salary structures. A single salary scale would be too inflexible, while two, with an arbitrary divide, have obvious deficiencies: in addition, some allowances have to be included for organizational duties as they contribute to job-size. The main difficulty results from the complex range of teaching and supportive administrative activities, often within a single institution: which constitute FE. It must be questionable whether a single set of arrangements, let alone one salary scale, can deal efficiently and equitably with all the situations that occur. On this basis, the argument for greater institutional control over salaries so that they can be more effectively related to lecturing performance, administrative duties, and the size of the total job, has considerable significance. Some inter-institutional consistency would be necessary, but not sufficient to prevent colleges negotiating with LEAs and NAB, over aggregate salary levels and their distribution.

NOTES AND REFERENCES

1. T. Blackstone and A. Crispin, How Many Teachers? Issues of Policy, Planning and Demography, (Bedford Way Papers, 10, Heinemann, London, 1982)
2. D. Hencke, Colleges in Crisis, (Penguin Books, Hermondsworth, 1978)
3. CMND 8836, Teaching Quality, 1983, p.4
4. CMND 8836, pp.13-14

5. DES Statistics of Education, Volume 3, Further Education, 1979, (HMSO, London, 1982)
6. T. Blackstone and A. Crispin, How Many Teachers? pp. 54-57
7. I. Butterworth, Staffing for Curriculum Needs: Teacher Shortages and Surpluses in Comprehensive Schools, (NFER-Wilson, Windsor, 1983)
8. DES, The School Curriculum, (HMSO, London, 1981) pp.15-16.
9. DES, Aspects of secondary education in England, (HMSO, London, 1979)
10. Scottish Education Department, Consultative Committee on the Curriculum, (HMSO, Edinburgh, 1977)
11. I. Butterworth, Staffing for Curriculum Needs, pp. 88-91
12. I. Butterworth, Staffing for Curriculum Needs, pp. 40-44
13. J. J. Wellington, 'Straight from the Horse's Mouth: Physics Undergraduates' Attitudes to Teaching', The Durham and Newcastle Research Review, Vol.10, No. 49, (1982) pp. 21-22
14. DES, Primary education in England: A survey by H.M. Inspectors of Schools, (HMSO, London, 1978)
15. The delineation of four types of shortage can be mirrored by four forms of surplus: see Butterworth, pp. 17-19
16. L. M. Canter and I. F. Roberts, Further Education Today, (Routledge and Kegan Paul, London, 1979)
17. CMND 8836, p.19
18. S.I. 1086/1981, The Education (Schools and Further Education) Regulations 1981
19. S. Hilsum and B. Cane, The Teachers Day,(NFER, Slough, 1972): also see S. Hilsum and C.R. Strong, The Secondary Teachers Day (NFER, Slough, 1978)
20. H. Mintzberg, The Nature of Managerial Work, (Harper and Row, London, 1973)
21. M. Pedler, J. Burgoyne, and T. Boydell, A managers guide to self-development, (McGraw-Hill, London, 1978)
22. CMND 8789-II, The Governments expenditure plans 1983-84 to 1985-86, 1983, p.46
23. DES, Scales of Salaries for Teachers: Primary and Secondary Education, England and Wales 1983, (HMSO, London, 1983)
24. W. F. Dennison, 'Points, Unit-Totals, Age-Weighting and Promoted Posts - their effect on the Development of the English Schooling

System', *British Journal of Educational Studies*, Vol.18 No.3 (1980), pp. 225-239

25. For example in a middle school each child contributes two units to the schools unit-total: the equivalent figures in a sixth-form college are six or eight units per pupil
26. CMND 5848, *Committee of Enquiry into the Pay of Non-University Teachers*, (1974)
27. CMND 7880, *Standing Commission on Pay Comparability: Teachers*, (1980), para. 77
28. DES, *Scales of Salaries for Teachers in Further Education, England and Wales 1983*, (HMSO, London, 1983), p.12. The figures being £9,735 and £13,443 per annum at the maximum point of the respective salary scales
29. Evidence provided by management side of Burnham Further Education Committee.

Chapter Six

RESOURCES, PLANNING AND THE INSTITUTIONS

CHARACTERISTIC FEATURES

From a managerial perspective comparisons between education and industry can be both naive and misleading. Usually contrasts are founded on the assumption that education is badly managed and much would be gained by the adoption of industrial practices, often they fail to specify which industries (and practices) could provide reproducible models of managerial effectiveness, in relation to which sectors of education. Invariably, the issues of environmental compatability receive inadequate attention, the fact that practices and attitudes have been conditioned, and to some extent imposed, by the nature of the basic task.[1] In education the most important parameter being the intangibility of any final product. Children leave school with examination passes, students graduate from college, but to use such figures as a single measure of output, compared to a factory's production or a sales forces marketing figures, represents a gross over-simplification. To take one example, a staff appraisal scheme successfully developed in a situation where objective measures of an individual's job-performance are possible, cannot be readily transferred to a school. Without substantial modification it will be subject to suspicion, hostility and ridicule: far better, in these circumstances, to design a new system which utilizes, with a view to strengthening, the working arrangements of the actual school.

However, an argument that the managerial processes of education are sufficiently unusual (and in some ways unique) to merit special attention can be defended: what cannot is a view that nothing of value might emerge from studying other activities. In the case of staff-appraisal, the fact that many organizations have considerable experience about the link-ups to be established with staff development and retraining, for example, suggest that a school or college systemitising its appraisal activities could learn something. Similarly for resource deployment, a complete transfer of ideas or techniques adopted elsewhere into education would be inappropriate and unhelpful. Most obviously schools and colleges do not have to provide a profit and loss account or a balance sheet: indeed there is no charge (as such) to clients for services. In many schools, nothing more than an approximate match of income and expenditure is required. Resources are a key item, but not expressed in financial terms. Yet it remains impossible to construct guidelines for analyzing resource distribution and utilization methodologies without considering arrangements in other organizations. At the very least criteria have to be established relative to good practice. It may be that the arrangements in education have been strongly influenced by a separatist tradition - so different are the conditions, so atypical are the factors requiring consideration, that education staff have neither found the inclination nor the time to look to other types of organization for assistance in solving their problems - but a continuance of this isolationism lacks credibility.

If, for example, the education system were compared to a large firm it would be relatively easy to categorize. It is highly decentralised with head office (DES) having little direct power, although considerable influence: relatedly, the branch offices (LEAs) and retail outlets (schools and colleges) are best viewed as responsibility centres. Democratic accountability within the local government system demands this perceived status for LEAs: the pursuit of profesional autonomy has achieved and maintained this situation in schools and colleges. Taking this model of the firm Chapter 3 considered the procedures by which resources are allocated to the institutions and the deficiencies in these processes that emerged, particularly with contraction. In Chapters 4 and 5 tensions between resource supply to the institutions, and the uses to which these resources could be put (the curriculum) and the main participants in that utilization (the teaching staff) were discussed. In this chapter the analogy of the school or college as a responsibility centre within a decentralized structure is developed, more specifically in the context of resource deployment relative to the pursuit of institutional purpose.

Of the characteristics which differentiate educational institutions from other organizations, four dominate in resource matters. The first of these concerns the labour intensity of their work. Salaries take a high proportion of all resources, and therefore reduce flexibility. The second occurs because of the long-time scales involved. Schools and colleges are committed to programmes, often for years ahead, and as financial issues have much closer horizons, the planning function necessarily becomes more difficult. Third, is the underdevelopment of management control activities relative to resource matters. While fourthly, arising directly from this, value for money considerations receive little attention. Both of these final characteristics being attributable to the non-financial base of educational management.

FLEXIBILITY

The main feature emerging from any analysis of institutional expenditures is the dominant position of salaries (especially of teaching staff) (Table 6.1). These figures represent averages.[2] Considerable variations exist at institutional level, arising from previous expenditure freedoms. However the general pattern remains. The fact that teacher costs become proportionately less important with advanced level teaching simply reflects a greater number of clerical staff (justified by an increased administrative load) and more technical support to service sophisticated equipment. In the context of flexibility two issues arise. The first concerns the potential rigidities that high expenditures induce: the second the resultant limitations on freedom in the deployment of non-staff resources. A further item on the appropriateness of the mix between staffing and other resources has already been considered in Chapter 4. It is interesting that a few public authorities, particularly in North America, have recently experimented with resource allocation systems based on the concept of 'zero-base budgeting'.[3] In this an item is not included in the current budget simply because it appeared last year: every item has to be reviewed and the case for its reinstatement argued. Initially this seems a thoroughly commendable prospect: with the elimination of the arrangement by which the previous budget becomes the next spending plan, with the exception of a few minor additions or

TABLE 6.1

Institutional expenditure profiles

	Schools Primary %	Schools Secondary %	Evening Institutes %	Colleges NAFE %	Colleges AFE %	Polytechnics NAFE %	Polytechnics AFE %
Teaching staff	70	69	65	57	57	49	49
Non-teaching staff	13	11	16	20	20	25	25
Premises	12	12	12	9	9	11	11
Supplies and services	4	5	4	9	9	10	10
Establishment expenses	1	1	3	5	5	5	5

Transport has been omitted because compulsory provision and inevitable distances make a comparison unhelpful.

These are notional figures; there will be inter-LEA and inter-institutional variations.

Source: T.M. Hinds ' The Rising Cost of Falling Rolls' Proceedings of the Eighth Annual Conference of the British Educational Administration Society 1979, (1980).

Resources, Planning and the Institutions

subtractions. A new flexibility seems assured and apparently guaranteed. For a school or college such a system could not work because of the proportion of expenditure committed to teacher salaries. A zero-base exercise is pointless if the LEA wishes to retain existing teacher numbers (which actually means more or less the same personnel) and none of the staff choose to leave. A policy of reviewing the employment of staff in post every year (say) even when the authority can make staff redundant is impracticable. In fact, LEAs insisting when a teacher leaves (for whatever reason) that the post is reviewed, rather than automatically filled, utilizes 'zero-base' principles, so far as circumstances permit.

However, the clearest example of staff cost rigidities arises when institutions are forced to reduce expenditure: for example, the planning exercise in AFE to lower college spending by 10%. What Table 6.1 demonstrates above all is the high proportion of fixed costs and, as a result, the difficulties of achieving such a target. In effect, with national salary agreements, a 10% reduction in expenditure on teaching staff salaries relies upon persuading 10% of the staff to leave - by resignation, retirement, redeployment or redundancy. A task exacerbated by 'no redundancy' agreements in many authorities, the effects of relative price movements (raising the real cost of salaries) and incrementalism (staff on salary scales automatically entitling them to an increase). Were no teaching staff to leave, a 10% reduction in total expenditure could only be achieved from the 45% of other costs, lowering them by almost a quarter. In practical terms this might well be impossible if the college were not to close, as a proportion of this expenditure is effectively irreducible because of the need to heat, clean, and maintain buildings, for example. Similarly, non-teaching staff have contracts and in this case even if building upkeep costs were eliminated, a target 10% reduction in total expenditure would still not be achieved.

In the context of schools and colleges, a clear separation into fixed and variable costs is impossible. In fact, conventional understandings of these terms require reworking. The main problem concerns the definition of fixed items. Salaries appear to fall within this category, but some staff do leave, and others can be made redundant (if necessary). Building costs are also not necessarily fixed, as some can be closed, and reductions in expenditure on up-keep may always be possible. In contrast variable items present fewer definitional problems: essentially a reduction in spending, in this category offers comparatively few organizational or political difficulties. What happens, unsurprisingly, with a 10% reduction is the identification of variable costs: they comprise the easy targets. As a result, the contracts of temporary staff are not renewed, non-essential building maintenance postponed, equipment and books fail to be bought, small capital projects abandoned, while simultaneously non-controversial, but minor savings in fixed costs (simply energy conservation measures, for example) receive attention. Provided they give the required reduction in total expenditure there is no need to go further and consider the main fixed costs. In these circumstances the institutional priority has become the actual achievement of expenditure reductions while mimizing their impact on organizational members, even if this involves incompatability with educational goals. At best these are modified: at worst they remain unchanged when the resource situation render them inappropriate and unattainable.

Decision processes of this nature are not restricted to education. Whatever the circumstances the tendency in organizational decision-making is towards a minimization of problem situations. A critical perspective would view this as a search for an 'easy life': more perceptively, attention is scarce in any setting - enough problems demanding attention are generated in the normal course of events that potential and fresh difficulties should not be sought. On this basis, therefore, a decision to dismiss temporary staff is unavoidable even when this means losing effective teachers, offering subjects suited to the curricular policy of the college, while retaining some permanent staff who do not possess such desirable attributes. As a result, the inevitable conflicts and repercussions that would follow enforced redundancies are avoided. Only when no alternative exists, in this case all temporary staff dismissed and every other potential reduction explored without the target contraction achieved, would this route be followed. Possibly, the avoidance of confrontation is more attractive in education than some other environments, because of the paucity of institutional and personal performance measures (the contribution of an individual to the organization is difficult to assess)but, in more general terms, contraction demonstrates the problems in adverse conditions faced by organizations with a

Resources, Planning and the Institutions

high level of fixed costs (or committed expenditures). Such difficulties do not arise during expansion (or increased sales) as the non-committed (non-fixed) element becomes proportionately less significant. However, this does not follow if growth is used as an opportunity to introduce a new range of inescapable commitments.

In fact this is precisely what occurred in education. Additional staff were employed, buildings opened and courses introduced, so that while the percentage of committed expenditures did not change appreciably, the actual total of fixed costs in any one year was much higher. Undoubtedly a strong case can be made for this state of affairs as a desirable product of the labour intensity of educational processes. They demand a high level of individual teacher-client contact using staff committed to the tasks of teaching and learning and this is only achievable by employing well qualified, adequately paid staff, protected by security of tenure. The processes also need permanent (as well as adequate) buildings, and a continuous introduction of new courses as pupil and student needs change. However, in the facilitation of such arrangements decisions are possible without the full implications of their effects, over time, being realised. The employment of a new teacher, for example, affects the current budget, and the decision occurs within that framework but, by such a choice, there is potential impingement upon future budgets: in personnel terms, the expertise offered by this extra employee in terms of age-range, subject specialism etc., and the level of individual flexibility that might be achieved, as the needs of the school or authority change, are long-term issues.

In the context of resource distribution an important effect of high commitment levels is to concentrate attention upon expenditure at the margins. In institutions, as well as during LEA budgetary procedures, choices about additional teachers or incremental spending on equipment (at minimal cost compared to total expenditure) consume most time. This helps explain limited teacher interest in resource matters: the perception that most of the important decisions have already been made following the joint influences of the labour intensiveness of education and overall budgetary constraints. According to this view the dominant part of the job is teaching or lecturing: the financial circumstances in which this occurs are important, but only if they impinge upon task performance. In other words resource issues should be left, as far as possible, to those competent (and paid) to deal with them, provided there is sufficient institutional control over curricular situations. With attitudes such as these prevailing, it comes as no surprise when schools do not produce budgets. Their resources are strictly rationed by the LEA: so many teachers to be employed, so much to be spent on books and equipment, while any building costs are usually the direct responsibility of the LEA. At least FE colleges produce their own budgets although with strict LEA controls and little assistance in decision-making autonomy over such matters as virement and 'end of year' balances. Additionally, the processes of budget preparation and expenditure control are potentially complex, and having to follow rules provided and interpreted by the local authority reinforces college dependencies. However, the institutions by accepting this subordination have created a clear dichotomy between resource and curricular responsibilities. Yet such a divide breaches an important principle in organizational management. The idea of 'unity of command' may be out-dated,[4] and in circumstances such as matrix management require modification,[5] but there is little to recommend in an arrangement where one group determine most curricular issues separately from discussion about resource matters: when the availability of resources, and the curriculum they provide, are integrally linked.

Any moves to reduce this divisiveness must be set against the practical difficulties likely to be encountered. While recent developments suggest that LEAs want to be more influential in curriculum matters they seem to have neither the inclination nor the facilities to directly infringe upon many of the traditional autonomies of professional staff. If that is the case any alignment must come through more institutional responsibilities for resource matters, but any arrangements have to ensure that control of total expenditure, and its distribution among the institutions, remains with the LEA. What makes this condition more vital is the tendency of staff to allow, and encourage, the curriculum to expand and use whatever resources might be available. The prime difficulty, however, is to establish the likely efficacy of any new scheme, for even if it reduces the resource/curriculum divide it must also facilitate more effective choices, without demanding too much staff time for activities which must always remain less central to them than the

Resources, Planning and the Institutions

main teaching/learning task.

The pursuit of extra flexibility through offering schools greater autonomy has been attempted by a number of authorities. By awarding schools more freedom, a closer inter-relationship between resource choices is intended. Perhaps, the best known arrangement involves the ILEA and the Alternative Use of Resources (AUR) scheme.[6] Introduced into secondary schools in 1970, and primary schools two years later, each school was initially allowed to freely allocate up to 5% of its total resources - a figure notified before the start of the year. It has already received a basic quota of teaching and non-teaching staff (dependent upon NOR): over and above these allocations the school had to determine the deployment of additional resources, either by employing additional staff (notional salary figures were used), or by purchasing books and equipment or selecting any combination up to the 5% limit. If circumstances changed during the year (a non-quota teacher left) the pattern could be readjusted, and facilities existed to carry over end of year balances. Experience has led to some modification in the scheme, but the main thrust of the arrangements remains unchanged.[7] Currently, each school has a basic entitlement to teaching and non-teaching staff, calculated on a PTR basis (although with some additions for special difficulties and falling roll situations) and determined by the authority. For secondary schools, unable to claim extra support, this involves a PTR of 17.1, which the school cannot raise, but can lower by choosing to employ extra teachers. For this purpose funds are supplied in two ways: a school allowance allocated to every school on a capitation principle, and additional resources calculated both from NOR and the schools position on an index of need. This includes criteria based on the children's background (family size, parental occupation, disturbed behaviour etc.) for primary schools and, additionally, quality of building factors (including floor area and age) for secondary schools. The total funds acquired after a separate calculation each year, expressed in money terms, are then used to buy any combination of additional teachers, additional non-teaching staff, school requirements (books, equipment, educational visits etc.) or minor works that the school determines. For staff notional salary figures are still used, for other items actual expenditures are required, and having been told their various entitlements each school notifies the authority of its

215

spending intentions. In effect, they produce their own rather limited budget.

Undoubtedly ILEA is affluent by the standards of other authorities, a primary school (NOR 275+60 part-time Nursery places) may find itself allowed (in total) £12,000 for example. Possibly, it may decide to employ one additional teacher, use £4,000 for school requirements, and still have sufficient funds for extra secretarial assistance. For a large secondary school (NOR 1250) total allowances of £74,000 would enable the employment of three more teachers (notional salary £18,000), several non-teaching part-time staff, and additional help in music, and still leave nearly £40,000 for school requirements. More generally, the spread of expenditure across all schools (1978-79) again indicates the importance of teacher costs, taking 60% in primary (67% in secondary schools) of the total of freely allocable resources. For primary schools the next highest category was the salaries of 'helpers' at 19% (secretaries in secondary schools at 10.5%) while in both sectors around 10% was awarded to school requirements.

It would not be difficult to dismiss this particular scheme on the grounds that it can only work because of the relative wealth of the ILEA. As a result, schools are spared difficult choices because all they do is supplement already generous staffing provisions, while still retaining adequate resources to meet school requirements for books etc. In some authorities this degree of freedom could only be achieved by lowering considerably the basic entitlements - that is raising PTR and possibly having to dismiss quota staff. To some extent this argument is valid: the suitability of AUR as a model transferable to other LEAs must be questionable. Significantly, a whole range of school-based expenditures are ignored. At least two LEAs (Cambridgeshire and Solihull) have initiated feasibility schemes, involving a few schools, to include many more expenditure items. For both arrangements the starting point was an estimate of the individual costs in main sub-headings, of participating schools. Often finding this information presents difficulties, as there has been no obligation upon LEAs to maintain separate accounts for each school.[8] In the Cambridgeshire (Local Financial Management) scheme the estimated figures for the previous year were then used to calculate, after inflationary considerations, the schools allowances for the first year of the feasibility exercise. During 1982-83, for example, permissible expenditures ranged from £165,000 for a primary school (NOR 367) to £1.31m. for a large secondary school (NOR 1821), and by specifying these figures the LEA retained control of the total budget. From its allowance the school had to meet all expenditures on staffing: rent and rates: heating, lighting, cleaning materials etc: furniture and fittings: books, stationery and equipment (including administrative requirements): examination fees: postage and telephone: and educational visits, staff travel etc. To satisfy finance office requirements, and to maintain schools alertness to their financial position, spending was coded into major sub-headings (virement being permissible) with regular statements about payments, but the prime responsibility of the school remained the allocation of total expenditure into these categories and its restriction the maximum specified by the LEA.

There are many similarities with the Solihull (School Finance Autonomy) exercise.[9] Again previous expenditures were used to produce school budgets, although with a 2% overall reduction, to compensate the LEA for the cost of establishing the scheme. The school then organizes its own spending within the LEA determined limit. Shortly after introduction numerous issues had been raised by both arrangements. Some were technical, and unsurprising, as an expenditure control system devised and dominated by the authority, to cover all schools, had to be adopted to monitor a more autonomous situation in individual schools. Simultaneously, teachers had to learn unfamiliar and changing procedures. Occasionally, for example, a school paid an invoice and assumed it had been debited, when the sum was not included in the next computer print-out of its financial position as compatability between school and Finance Office procedures had not been established. For both parties initiation and familiarization certainly involve more time than previous arrangements: whether a functioning system would make the same extra demands has yet to be established, although in schools this seems highly probable on account of the additional tasks which would have to be permanently accepted. Then, there is the issue - basically technical, but far-reaching in its implication - of which expenditures should be a school's responsibility. If total inclusivity is sought, to extend the scope of autonomy, then a number of items over which the school cannot possibly have control must appear. Yet, this may limit rather than increase freedom. Any loan charges on the buildings or rate bills, for example, could be part of the school administered budget being, in effect, fixed charges. However, were circumstances to change with a rise in interest rates (say) the school would have no option but to pay and make compensatory reductions in other expenditures. Therefore, the argument to restrict autonomy to items over which the school has some measure of control is powerful. Yet additional interest charges have to be met by the LEA and to cushion autonomous schools from their effects could disadvantage other parts of the service including, in this case, schools outside the feasibility exercise.

This example epitomizes two dilemmas of LEAs pursuing autonomous situations. First, they have to protect schools, not so much against the inadequacies and spendthriftness of staff (although this is always a potential problem) but in case the coincidence of a high level of committed expenditure and unanticipatable events, eliminates all possible freedom. In these circumstances schools are in an analogous situation to FE colleges asked to make a 10% reduction in expenditure, or the polytechnic forced to reduce spending by £1m. just before the start of the financial year (Chapter 4). It could happen had a school to replace several teachers on maternity leave or long-term sick pay, that money would not remain for books or to meet other variable costs without LEA protective measures. Such an outcome becomes proportionately more likely in small schools. In fact, they will have additional problems because of the few support staff available to administer the scheme. Some parts of the additional duties will be size dependant, others will exist however small the school and with a few teachers and a part-time secretary (as in a rural primary school) financial autonomy may be quite impracticable. Even for large schools on administrative assistant (or bursar) may be essential. Basically, the second dilemma concerns inter-school equity. Schools will pursue savings by reducing previous expenditure which could then be used for other items: this idea is central to the whole arrangement. Some will be achieved by deliberate actions, involving all staff (reduction in heating or telephone charges, for example) others, however, will be chance savings, as when a senior member of staff leaves to be replaced temporarily, if at all, by a junior, less well paid teacher. More potential savings can be cited, possibly generated by school policies, as when payments to relief teachers are reduced through raising the job satisfaction and minimizing the absences of regular staff. In most respects the problem for the LEA is the obverse of protectionism. If schools are allowed to retain all savings, from whatever source, then some schools may be unduly benefitted and, within a limited total LEA budget, others must be necessarily disadvantaged. Yet, the motivation to achieve savings will clearly be diluted if those making them are deprived of the complementary advantages they seek. In Solihull the solution is to award schools 75% of savings but, in the context of equity, that is not the end of the matter. In fact, the nomenclature itself may be somewhat misleading. Essentially, savings are a choice by the school to transfer resources as circumstances permit,and the implementation of new arrangements allow,thereby introducing a new expenditure pattern. A difficulty arises if this pattern provides the guide for the next allocation: as a school could easily find itself with a new budget imposed, which effectively penalises it for downwards adjustments in total expenditure, and alterations to the resource mix, it has already achieved.

Undoubtedly, these difficulties would be less if schools, like FE colleges, had to produce their own budgets instead of relying upon previous estimates. This is the logical extension of autonomy, with the school articulating its resource needs relative to the curriculum and the LEA assessing and responding to those in relation to the demands of other institutions and services. Ideally, the arrangements would combine the best features of the FE system, involving staff in the assembly of the budget, a sub-committee of governors and a dialogue between college and LEA, with the additional freedoms, particularly to adjust spending patterns as circumstances change, which are beginning to emerge with autonomy. A school cannot participate in such an arrangement without demonstrating how resources acquired will contribute to the pursuit and accomplishment of educational objectives. It would find it difficult, as well, to co-operate without creating opportunities for staff to become involved in decision-making. In this way staff interest in resource matters, particularly as they effect the curriculum, could be raised by participation with some staff-development objectives realized. Also the potential advantage accruing from a greater alignment between curricular and resource decisions producing a more appropriate and more responsive mix of resources should not be underestimated. There is no certainty that this mix will be less dominated by teacher costs than would have occurred with traditional procedures: indeed with contraction substantial change is highly improbable. However, by offering institutions the choice between another part-time teacher, more equipment or additional secretarial help, through spending less on building upkeep (say) while permitting resource commitments to be adjusted as regularly as the situation permits, flexibility in resource deployment is maximised. Additionally, because variable expenditures (such as that on books) is so small, relatively minor adjustments to the overall spending pattern can lead to disproportionate changes in low expenditure items. Therefore, if textbook spending stands at 4% of total and a further ½% can be added through modifications elsewhere it is raised by 12½%. In a static situation, clearly another item must be reduced to compensate, and no certainty exists that any reduction will occur in teacher salaries. In fact, that can only happen as the labour intensity of education lessens with technological developments in the teaching/learning processes. With that, but not before, a major reduction in the inflexibility of the spending pattern might result.

PLANNING

The second characteristic of institutional resource procedures involves the under-development of the planning function. Fundamentally, a problem arises because the time horizon of schools and colleges, based on course length is longer than the annual financial cycle of local authorities. Therefore, when a school begins a three year 'O' level course, or a college a two year BTEC course, it is tacitly and, as far as the students are concerned morally, committing itself far ahead when resources are only guaranteed to the following March. The assumption is, of course, that the necessary resources will be made available at the appropriate time: indeed, during contraction, schools and colleges often have argued that their irrevocable commitment to incomplete activities should safeguard them from expenditure reductions. In fact, there is no obligation upon LEAs to consider resource use for more than the year ahead, and during retrenchment, an important objective (and sometimes the dominant goal) in allocative exercises has been to produce a politically acceptable budget, both in terms of content and total expenditure: often this task has proved so difficult that other considerations have been ignored. In other words the problems of the following years are considered when that proves necessary, but not before.

It is easy to castigate the resultant attitudes: that they place less importance on long-term planning and reduce forward thinking for example, or encourage decisions committing the authority to expenditures which will exaggerate problems requiring solutions twelve months ahead. However, given the annual nature of the RSG settlements and the continuing financial restrictions on local authorities, reasons for a twelve month time horizon can be appreciated. Ironically, government in presenting these obstacles to local planning is simultaneously responsible for the larger PESC expenditure projects. The translation of this mechanism from a planning to control orientation has been reported (Chapter 3) with forecasts and commitments subject to frequent adjustment: although it must remain doubtful, even without these fluctuations, whether local authorities could interpret anything more than general intentions and overall trends from PESC forecasts, and until these are converted into the specific figures of RSG, LEAs do not know their precise awards. Therefore, without a more predictable and long-term system for calculating government support emerges, the impetus for local authorities (and LEAs) to extend the cycle of their financial management is highly restricted.

What then emerges is a rather curious situation in which LEA and institutional staff find themselves producing academic projections, often with a time-scale of several years, on the assumption that the resources they commit themselves to will become available at the appropriate time. A separateness of academic and financial thinking is therefore encouraged, coinciding in the annual budget event when activities meriting support for the next twelve months are nominated. Apart from the government sponsored uncertainties already mentioned, two other factors help explain this separateness. The first is another example of teacher reluctance to consider issues in financial terms. Understandably in the discussions of a new course, for example, syllabus construction, teaching arrangements, examination procedures etc., dominate: but this should not mean, as invariably it does, the exclusion of items concerning what the course will cost in staff time, support materials, building requirements etc. or, at best, their consideration as minor issues following, and separate from, the main deliberations. The second factor, which encouraged the establishment of attitudes associated with the first, was expansion. It could be argued that as institutions received more resources, there was no need to co-ordinate academic and financial planning. All that had to be done was an ordering of priorities, so that depending on how much each cost, and the additional resources made available a readjustment of preferences could be achieved every year. The formulation and pursuit of policy objectives by DES often appeared to support this view. For example, the scheme inititated in 1966 to expand higher education outside the university sector did not attempt any assessment of the future resource demands it would make on the main providers the LEAs.[10] Later an additional increase of 150,000 FTE by 1981-82 was suggested, again without adequate discussion of the resource implications of such growth.[11] Similarly, the expansion of nursery education was first mentioned in the 1972 Education White Paper,[12] followed by a policy statement which envisaged 15% of three and four year olds in full-time, and 35% in part-time education, by 1981-82.[13] Significantly, specific estimates of participation rates were not reflected in precise resource considerations other than an implied reference to RSG settlements.

It was, however, the introduction of comprehensive schools which most clearly demonstrated the lack of concern for the future effects emanating from current choices. On both occasions that the policy of secondary school re-organization was introduced (1965 and 1974)[14] only the briefest public discussion took place about additional capital expenditure required for new buildings: and, no consideration was given, either to the time-period needed to acquire these resources, or the impact additional loan charges might have on revenue expenditure in following years. Needless to say, other costs, such as those for retraining teachers to work in the new schools, did not receive attention.

In all of these examples what expansion seems to have circumscribed is an awareness both of the likely impingement of one priority upon others (even with the generation of additional resources) and the alternative routes available in the pursuit of most aims. Invariably, these are amenable to some form of analysis, combining both resource and educational components. A LEA, for instance, which embarked upon an ambitious building programme, following these various DES initiatives, prejudiced other capital projects, as well as incurring substantial loan charges which would further increase the fixed expenditures and reduce flexibilities in later revenue budgets. On the issue of analysing alternatives, re-organization again provides a significant example. Besides the fact that the full accommodation costs were never considered, a first statement of policy suggested that one route to implementation, based on 'all through' 11-18 schools was the most appropriate.15 Yet in terms of buildings it was probably least suitable, requiring most new accommodation because of the mismatch between desired outcomes and the existing distribution of premises. However, no attempt was made to substantiate the argument about appropriateness, which was presumably based on educational grounds and, even were that argument supportable, no thought given to balancing educational resources or any other interests in an analysis to demonstrate a preferred scheme.

Although expansion may reduce the need to coordinate educational and resource planning, the arguments favouring integration are difficult to refute. Each of these initiatives demonstrated, as they developed, the difficulties encountered if the close association between the respective educational and resource parameters are not appreciated. Of course, it can be argued that these developmental problems were simply the result of the environmental change from growth to contraction. In this context that argument omits a key issue. The insitutions, in particular as they expanded, had no choice but to assume that the resources demanded by their additional commitments would be made available. They did not, therefore, have to consider or produce a coherent growth strategy, but as they were forced to retrench, with the elimination of the common element sustaining their forward thinking - an extension of educational programme - they found themselves devoid of any strategy. In these circumstances the main thrust became the protection of existing activities within a shrinking budget: but that was (and in some institutions remains) an interim stage, while attitudes adjust to situations in which expansion is not the norm and procedures evolve more appropriate to static or declining expenditures. What becomes abundantly clear about these new conditions is that if the institution wants to be innovative by responding to variations in client needs and changes in environmental factors by modifying courses and methodologies, combined educational and resource planning becomes imperative.

The basic reason for this conclusion hinges on the rigidities inherent in the resource usage patterns of schools and colleges. If these are to be modified it cannot be other than by an incremental process taking much longer than the budget year. Such modifications are not essential prerequisites for innovation in a no-growth situation. It may be that a school or college with declining resources can still promote a dynamic curriculum. However, with attitudes still influenced by situations in which the stimulation of change was synonomous with the acquisition of additional support (extra teachers, more equipment) a facility to adjust the resource mix (a part-time teacher replaced by a technician, for example) is of potential assistance in initiating and sustaining different arrangements and new processes. Any new distribution may not appear significantly different but with high inflexibility a small variation may have disproportionate impact. Reducing building costs by 1% of total, as the previous section indicated, perhaps permitting a rise in expenditure on teaching materials of 50%. In fact a large measure of inter-institutional and inter-LEA variations in spending patterns has emerged because of marginally different decisions taken over a period of years.

However, schools cannot introduce this capacity into their decision-making if their resources, and their control over them, is strictly rationed by the LEA. The logic, therefore, if educational and resource planning are to be co-ordinated, is for an extension of institutional autonomy. This argument is, of course, only valid so long as schools and colleges retain current levels of curricular responsibilities: were these to be subsumed by the LEA the case for the co-ordinating function (which must reside with the same unit) would transfer to it. In current circumstances, though, the institutions are far more suitably placed. This does not make the LEA redundant. It must approve institutional budgets and, in particular, establish expenditure limits: it has to monitor both the spending of each institution and task performance: and it will have to adjudicate about rivalries with resource implications - when two colleges compete to run identical courses or attract the same students. The key item, the total allowable spending, can only be predicted with certainty for the next year, and though this makes subsequent planning tentative, it also obviates the possibility that a detailed scheme, combining education and resource factors, will so commit the institution to a particular course of action that it will be unable to react to changing conditions and events. Staff leave, for example, and a college has very little control over this process, but it can have over the rapidity and ways in which they are replaced. Similarly, more students may join a class than anticipated and there is no option but to divide it, while another class fails to recruit and has to be stopped. A range of such possiblities will occur within any planning cycle. In addition, external factors (salary increases or a rise in heating costs, for example) can exert strong influences on the detail of any forecasting, particularly when real costs in projections are converted into actual expenditures. Again the extent to which the institutions should be freed from obligations that might result from such effects is raised. An autonomous school or college cannot expect complete protection without destroying much of the rationale for independence. In the examples quoted, if salary or heating costs rise disproportionately then those institutions which, perhaps anticipating this possibility, have minimised these expenditures could argue they deserve to benefit. Obviously, the precise effects of these influences are unpredictable, and can be used to argue against any form of systematic planning: conversely within procedures which maximise flexibility such occurrences, if they have sufficient financial impact, can be integrated into planning arrangements, because of the intention that these should function as a continuous system not an annual episode.

To a large extent the main technical problem in assembling an institutional projection of income and expenditure, which can then be used as a framework for academic considerations, revolves about the issue of detail. To utilize the traditional format of 'object of expense' or 'line-object' budgets (Chapter 3),
   NAME OF OBJECT A B C D X Y
and simply add projected expenditures (X and Y) item by item, for the following budget years would be valueless. This particular format is designed to satisfy the control requirements of fiscal accounting: the purposes of a planning exercise are quite

different. Too much detail could inhibit flexibility, by specifying expenditure figures on a particular item two years hence (say cleaning materials) which somehow then becomes fixed, and also militate against comprehensibility. The feature that requires pursuit is the presentation of a global view of resource distribution and commitment yet still with sufficient detail so that the costs of planned activities, the likely needs of any alternative developments, and the affects of changes in circumstances, are projectable. For these purposes the idea is borrowed from PPBS16 of a series of main programmes or categories, five for expenditure and one for income, with each covering a related group of expenditure items. Using this programme structure as a framework, the requirements of the budget year (the first twelve months of the forecast) can then be compared to potential spending patterns over the next two years, both in terms of underlying inflexibilities in the distribution and the commitment to activities which have already begun (Table 6.2).

The main intention of this phase of the exercise being to generate information on what freedoms however small, are likely to become available. The next stage involves consideration of developmental options, including all activities (even those already in existence) over which the institution has an effective choice about continuing. The analogy has to be with zero-base budgeting (of which this is a derivative) in that all situations, where the feasibility of change exists, require attention: although caution has to be exercised to avoid underestimation of availability as an obligation to employ a teacher, for example, does not mean, with staff development policies, an irrevocable commitment to the courses they have been teaching. The second phase, therefore, consists of estimating the costs of each developmental option, a consideration of what alternative means could be available to achieve the objectives of each, and the extent of any new inflexibilities to which the school or college might be committing itself (Table 6.2). Clearly, the two phases have close inter-relations, as any evaluation of developmental options, or indeed what constitutes a choice situation, can significantly effect those activities which, either voluntarily or not, the institution has determined it wishes to continue.

In all of these considerations the focus has been financial. The necessity of a continuous

TABLE 6.2   Projection of spending patterns (School A – Tables 6.3 and 6.4) by programme

	Current expenditure £ (Year 1)	Current expenditure £ (Year 2) (Approximate irrevocable commitments)	Current expenditure £ (Year 3)
Teacher salaries	684,250	620,000[D]	600,000
Teaching support[A] services	78,200	75,000	72,000
Clerical and[B] Administrative	40,250	35,000	34,000
Premises related[C] costs	143,750	140,000	135,000
Debt charges	27,600	28,000	29,000
Gross expenditure	974,050	1,013,000[E]	1,054,000
Less income	25,550	–	–
Net expenditure	948,000	–	–
Potential expenditure flexibility	–	115,000	184,000

A – Including salaries of technicians, auxiliaries, books and equipment.
B – Including stationery, telephone, and clerical salaries.
C – Including caretaking services, heating, lighting, etc.
D – After allowances for likely salary increases, and staff reaching retiring age, concluding short-term contracts, etc.
E – Assuming a 4% increase in gross expenditure in cash terms.

translation into the educational items concerning courses to be organized, staff to be employed, skills to be sought, support materials to be bought, buildings that require modification etc. is obvious. However, the intention is not that one set of parameters should dominate the other. Previously, in education so little attention was given to financial factors that any attempt to achieve a balanced approach risks adverse comment because it has to raise that attention level. Such criticisms, though, are short-sighted: not only because they fail to appreciate the integrative benefits, in any circumstances, of considering educational and resource parameters simultaneously but, with static resourcing, in situations characterized by rigidities, it provides a methodology for maximising distributive flexibility in support of institutional development.

MANAGEMENT CONTROL

Without a profit motive, the direct obligation upon educationists to employ the techniques,and develop the attitudes, appropriate to financial managers does not exist. This is no argument for making schools or colleges profit-based organizations, or allowing them to become less reliant on state support (Chapter 7) but it does help explain why issues associated with management control have received so little attention. Essentially, this function is concerned with the efficient and effective use of resources in the accomplishment of organizational objectives. Of course many (perhaps all) with managerial responsibilities in education would claim that the prosecution of this function is central to their approach. Their school, faculty or whatever, formulates objectives, acquires resources and utilizes them to pursue goals: while the ensurance that resources are deployed to achieve maximum progress constitutes an essential component of the management task. However, even the most strident proponents of such arguments would have to admit that in most institutions (including LEAs) the development of this function has been at best covert,usually unsystematic, and often haphazard.

The dominant requirement for managerial control is information: about objectives and their achievement obviously, but, as important, about the detail of the resource used. Until quite recently interest in the resource side of this relationship was minimal. There had been some cost-studies of tech[17] nical colleges and secondary schools(in Scotland)[18] during the 1960s, and a consideration of the LEA - institutional funding arrangements in three authorities,[19] but the coverage of each was limited and comprehensive follow-up studies were not attempted. What they did reveal, however, particularly for schools (largely confirmed by a more recent study)[20] was the difficulty encountered in eliciting information about the expenditures of individual schools. Not surprisingly, when figures had been discovered, inter-school variations in spending patterns proliferated. As far as information collection is concerned, many LEAs simply do not isolate spending on a school by school basis. Apparently this situation is changing but exists even for spending items such as salaries or heating bills where the individual school, through the LEA, makes a clearly identifiable payment from which it solely benefits. There may be little to be gained through the generation of information in circumstances of shared facilities (the imputed costs of central administration or advisory services, for example) simply to minimize inter-school disputes about relative contributions. However, when spending can be clearly attributed to individual schools its non-availability can only suppress the management control function. Additionally, if the ability of LEAs to monitor expenditure profiles is underdeveloped, a natural concomitant must be the likelihood that variations in spending per school on a range of items can evolve quite unintentionally simply through lack of awareness. In other words the LEA cannot be sure of the distributions being made to individual institutions while, they in turn, do not know the resources they use.

Intentionality of course, implies a policy: and if there is concern for dissimilar expenditure patterns by schools in the same LEA suggests a goal of equal funding. This will not be true for all LEAs, as some pursue schemes of positive discrimination to assist schools in deprived areas, but the conventional allocative mechanism from LEA to school based on resource rationing, assumes this intention. However, when a LEA assembles inter-school expenditure patterns, expressed on a per-pupil (or unit cost) basis, using the programme structure, differences in total costs and expenditures under main sub-headings emerge (Table 6.3). Take the case of school G serving an urban area, with substantial population decline, and therefore NOR shortages exaggerated by parental choice under the Education Act, 1980. It appears the most generously funded

TABLE 6.3

Expenditure per pupil in ten schools of LEA district – £

School	A	B	C	D	E	F	G	H	I	J
Teacher Salaries	595	610	568	536	612	642	782	604	586	674
Teaching support services	68	91	74	62	76	88	101	74	63	79
Clerical and Administrative	35	48	36	29	41	48	72	49	50	55
Premises related costs	125	149	125	104	152	138	188	119	129	138
Debt charges	24	12	38	102	24	44	12	15	38	19
NOR	1,150	1,075	1,090	1,280	980	960	740	1,050	1,225	870
Total expenditure per pupil	847	910	841	833	905	960	1,155	861	1,025	965

with high teacher and building unit costs but these reflect the relatively few pupils and, in the context of any re-organization, the low marginal cost of increasing roll-size. In contrast, school D, with children from a new estate on the edge of the town (housing many families originally living in the catchment area of school G) has lower unit-costs, to some extent because of its large roll. Yet, including the high interest charges, resulting from the new premises for school D, reduces the difference in expenditure per pupil. In other words pupils in D are relatively less disadvantaged financially, and because of their new buildings, educationally. Conversely, those in G are more advantaged by the high average salaries of the older and more experienced teachers in this longer established school.

More generally, knowledge about the expenditure patterns of all schools of the authority (not just those highlighted in this example) is the beginning of a rational debate on allocative methodologies. Other factors - educational, social and political - have to be merged into any consideration of, for example, the relative merits and claims of schools G and D. Does, for instance, the more experienced staff of school G provide better teaching and a more dynamic curriculum? To what extent are pupils in school D disadvantaged by the high PTR? Does this lead to larger classes and less availability of options? How do the average TCRs in the two schools compare? More directly, having discovered variations in school expenditure there still remains the question of what the LEA should, and can, do about them. If an authority establishes an equity objective it has little alternative but to try and bring unit costs in all schools to the same level. However, in doing so, it must overcome the same types of problem encountered by NAB in devising arrangements to fund AFE activities through the 'pool'. Although the intention is a scheme, combining equity and efficiency objectives, in which target student number in conjunction with a national set of unit costs are used to calculate the total allocation to each college (Chapter 3) such arrangements cannot be introduced without preparatory work. There has to be mechanisms to allow for the different subject mixes of colleges. Also, as a range of unit costs across colleges, even in the same activities, exists, the achievement of such targets will prove unattainable for expensive colleges, without some time for readjustment, yet generous to low cost institutions, threatening aspects of the efficiency objective of the exercise. In fact, a LEA seeking a distribution mechanism based upon unit-costs would be faced with the same two problems. First, the range of activities offered by each school (allowances for laboratory or workshop activities, the proportion of older pupils etc.) would have to be entered into the calculation: second, the differences between schools in unit-costs at the start of the exercise would require attention. If, in the example quoted, a target per pupil expenditure were set at the average level then that figure would only be attainable by school G if either it attracted many more pupils (unlikely given the characteristic of its catchment area and leading to fewer children and raised unit-costs elsewhere) or reduced its expenditure, most obviously by losing staff. Conversely, school D would have a legitimate claim for additional resources, but unless it accomplished more objectives as a result would become less efficient.

In their pursuit of both an equity objective (or some derivative influenced by positive discrimination) and an efficiency objective (maximising the accomplishment of goals for minimum expenditure) in distributing resources to institutions, it would seem that a LEA has two choices. It can attempt to standardize unit costs. This would be a lengthy process, necessarily involving cumbersome formulae: more so in authorities with a mixed pattern of schools, colleges and tertiary institutions. In other words, it would be a type of resource rationing directed towards a uniformity of expenditures. Alternatively, it can continue with the original procedure of resource rationing in which the LEA met all fixed expenditures while allowing a small margin of institutional freedom, with limited sums apportioned on a capitation basis. The arrangement prospered on account of its relative simplicity, because it appeared to work (to the extent that the requirements of fiscal accounting were satisfied) and as the non-collection of information prevented consideration of its effects, particularly in relation to inequities. There is, however, a third choice utilizing institutional autonomy, so that individual allocations result from direct negotiation. Once LEAs become informed about the expenditure distributions of individual schools, themselves aware of inter-school comparisons, the framework exists for a LEA school allocative debate. The authority establishes an expenditure limit, the school provides a budget (within which it can vire) and by monitoring actual spending in relation to curricular organization and achievements, a basis is provided for discussion about the next allocation. With this mechanism the LEA pursues whatever inter-school equity intentions it specifies. If the unit-costs of a school prove too high, for example, it can attempt amelioration by raising pupil numbers (reducing entry quotas to other schools) closing part of the buildings, or not replacing staff who leave, and by comparing actual expenditures with budget allowances both assesses success and modifies policy.

As important as equity, institutional autonomy can contribute directly to the accomplishment of efficiency objectives. Most managers would argue that a continuous drive for internal efficiencies is the norm in their institutions, whatever the circumstances and the financing arrangements, with staff free-time (as opposed to non-contact time) staff absences, heating and lighting bills, telephone costs etc., minimised as a matter of course. Coercion and directives from management (both in the LEA and school) may have some influence, but the disadvantage of a resource rationing situation is that no direct motivation exists, other than the personal inconvenience lack of action could produce, for staff to strive for any of the potential reductions mentioned. Indeed, if the authority pays the heating or telephone charges for a group of schools, without individual identification of costs, staff are in total ignorance of the specific effects of their actions although, perhaps certain, that savings made will not translate directly into alternative spendings of which they might approve. Yet, an important element in any search for efficiency must occur at institutional level. Insisting that schools produce their own budgets might help, but not if it involves strict and non-transferable categorization of expenditures. With this, there is a tendency to inflate budget figures to allow for reductions during negotiation, and to avoid the possibility of over-spending through unforeseen circumstances.[21] The only goal for the school is to hold expenditure within the agreed limits: little is to be gained by savings resulting from internal efficiencies if unspent balances cannot be carried into the next year, and monies saved are not usable for the purchase of additional items in other categories. Without autonomy, therefore, the pursuit of the efficiency objective is blunted.

However, with the granting of some measure of autonomy, the LEA is obliged, as a responsibility centre itself, to refine its managerial function, while assisting and pressurising schools in their own developments. It could do this as part of the negotiation process with schools, and by monitoring outcomes in relation to equity and efficiency objectives. In schools, similarly, the acceptance of such responsibilities means additional duties and the evolution of a systematic managerial function. From an expenditure perspective alone, a huge volume of information can be generated, even in one school (Figure 6.1) contrasts a simple calculation of the average cost of each lesson in a secondary school (basically through dividing annual expenditure by the total number of lessons) with a more complex and time-consuming assessment of the real cost of a specific lesson. In the latter, using the programme structure, imputed costs for each main category are estimated, but the methodology adopted raises numerous questions. Teacher costs are estimated by sharing salary among lessons taught, but should allowance be made for the seniority of the teacher (which affects salary) or the administrative support offered by the headteacher, both of which would raise per lesson teaching costs? How should the cost to the lesson of support staff (administrative and technical) be evaluated? An equal apportionment to all lessons would be unfair, and a similar problem arises with the relative demands of laboratory based sessions for equipment. Building costs present fewer problems, because floor area and time occupied as a fractional product of total floor area and working year of the school, can be used to assess the demands of each lesson. However, is the implicit assumption that all space in the school produces equal expenditures on cleaning, maintenance, heating etc. valid? Will there not be differences between class-rooms, laboratories, workshops, games halls etc? Indeed, only when an item is consumed in the lesson (paint, wood or whatever) can there be clear attributional costs.

While such a complex process would give a closer approximation to the true cost of a lesson than a calculation of averages, it also raises the fundamental question of the value of such efforts. Does it improve the managerial function by providing information and insights not already available? Such is the dominance of teacher salaries that schools should be aware of the most expensive lesson

FIGURE 6.1   Expenditure per period (School A - Tables 6.3 and 6.4)

(a)   Average gross expenditure per period

NOR: 1150

By year
1	198
2	202
3	210
4	215
5	224
6	64
7	37

Total number of periods by year (per week)

1	280
2	280
3	320
4	405
5	410
6	195
7	170
	2,060

Gross expenditure £974,050   therefore average expenditure per lesson = £974,050   2,060   40*
= £11.82

* On assumption of 40 weeks in school year.

(b)   Estimate of a Physics period expenditure (£)

Programme   1 7.78^A
(as in   2 1.78^B
Table 6.2)   3 0.46^C
                4   2.61^D
                5   0.50^E

                Total   £13.13

A - 3.4 Physics teachers from 68 staff, offering 110 periods per week (40 weeks in school year).
B - Estimated use of 10% of teaching support services.
C - Estimated use of 5% of clerical services.
D - Estimated use of 8% of premises.
E - As for D.

on a per pupil basis - those with few children: and
on any other assessment (use of other staff equipment, support services or buildings) they are unlikely to be relatively less demanding on resources.
In developing the managerial function there is
always the risk of searching, without a sufficiently
close focus, and producing too much information. In
schools and colleges the most rewarding search concerns the separate expenditures of faculties, departments or main units. In Table 6.2 two examples
(one for a FE college, the other a school) display
departmental and faculty expenditures according to
programme structure. Arbitrary allowances and
apportionments have to be made, but their effects
on the overall inter-unit distribution of expenditure is small. It could be argued that any costs
not directly attributable to the unit (staff salaries, books, equipment etc.) should be ignored
but, in the same way as for LEA - school considerations, this would impinge upon the equity-efficiency intention of the exercise. An important aspect consists of alerting units to their responsibilities for shared services (building, administrative and technical) and while the accounting processes of the institution may not allow direct identification of costs incurred by each unit, some
attempt at separation is essential. Indeed there
can be advantages in charging for shared servcies,
such as photo-copying or the time of administrative
and technical staff.

The issue remains, though, that having produced an expenditure distribution how should the
school or college utilize such information? By
moving units towards responsibility centres it has
contributed to the efficiency objective. With regard to equity, the examples show, as expected, a
non-uniformity in per-pupil or student costs.
There are several explanatory factors - variations
in class-size, space requirements, technical support needs, and consumable equipment, all occur. To
some, but not a precisely definable, extent these
are characteristics of the subject area: but inevitably other differences accrue from sources less explicable by logistical analysis, as in the case of
inter-institutional variations in expenditure. The
problem of reducing such differences, if required,
still remains. If one faculty has high expenditures
through generous staffing, and this is judged to be
inequitable, then it still takes time to achieve
some equalization through staff leaving or being
retrained. In the meanwhile additional non-teaching

FIGURE 6.2 Faculty and Departmental expenditure by programme

(a) Four faculties in fe college

	Faculties (Expenditure £)			
	A	B	C	D
Lecturers salaries	121,400	215,720	62,220	115,370
Lecturer support services	36,820	68,290	10,790	45,290
Clerical and Administrative	18,790	34,420	4,380	39,780
Premises related costs	44,220	78,920	14,760	42,180
Debt charges	5,480	6,210	2,110	8,720
Gross expenditure	226,710	403,560	94,260	251,340
Income	10,780	25,320	1,350	45,750
Net expenditure	215,930	378,240	92,910	205,590
Net expenditure per fte student [1]	2,056	3,002	1,255	3,316
Expenditure per successful completion of course in single year (per fte equivalent) [2]	2,203	9,225	1,366	10,820

1 - Fte's of 105, 126, 74 and 62 for each faculty respectively.

2 - Number of fte students completing in one year, 98, 41, 68, 19 respectively.

FIGURE 6.2 (cont'd.)

(b) Four departments in school (School A)

	Departmental (Expenditure £)			
	1	2	3	4
Teacher salaries	34,200*	61,400	10,580	29,480
Teaching support services	7,800	10,320	2,690	4,820
Clerical and Administrative	2,000	3,400	720	1,850
Premises related costs	11,500	18,750	3,740	10,750
Debt charges	2,200	3,810	760	2,095
Gross expenditure	57,700	97,680	18,490	48,995
Gross expenditure per^A pupil in school	50.17	84.94	16.08	42.60
Gross expenditure per^B pupil period offered in subject	0.60	0.48	0.46	0.64
Gross expenditure per^C 'O' level pass	1,110	1,575	2,054	1,113
Gross expenditure per^D 'A' level pass	11,540	8,140	9,295	9,799

* To nearest £100 (compare detail in Figure 6.1(b))

A - NOR = 1150
B - Estimated number of pupil periods per week: 2,400, 5,000, 1,000, 1,900 respectively.
C - Number of 'O' level passes: 52, 62, 9 and 44.
D - Number of 'A' level passes: 5, 12, 2 and 5.

support may be awarded elsewhere but this is a gradual process. For schools one issue of equity, the distribution of resources by age of pupil, requires particular attention. In the secondary range, during years four and five, and particularly in the sixth form, option availability reduces class sizes and therefore increases, proportionately, per-pupil costs. This effect can be demonstrated with a distribution by year of expenditure across the school, and for one subject (Table 6.3). Allowances for shared costs (some arbitrarily determined) have to be made, but the resultant information constitutes another element in the debate within the school, and the LEA, of the most appropriate distribution of resources as between the sixth-form, say, and the rest of the school. If a school with few older children, decides to organize a wide range of options, not only will these prove expensive on a per-pupil basis but expenditures on younger children will be lowered to compensate. On cost grounds complete equity is not sought. Both DES and LEAs make additional allowances for older pupils,[22] but part of the managerial function consists of determining acceptable differentials. However, when a differential factor of ten in per-pupil expenditure emerges, the requirements of neither equity nor efficiency are being satisfied.

The predominant need, therefore, as institutions develop their management control expertise, is a profile of education and resource related factors. In effect this constitutes a Management Information System (MIS). Clearly the sophistication sought in such an arrangement depends upon institutional size, both in terms of the volume of information which might be generated, and the likelihood of producing a system which is cost-effective in its own right. Quite simply, establishment and organization of MIS uses resources (although not to the extent that might be estimated as many of the tasks involved should be part of the normal duties of education managers) and unless the institution is large (perhaps a minimum of 20-25 professional staff) insufficient complexity exists to guarantee that (leaving aside equity considerations) any efficiency benefits will outweigh the resources committed for their achievement. A formal system in a small primary school would be of little value, but this does not mean that the headteacher, informally, need leave management control elements underdeveloped. In contrast, in many colleges because of size, the need to produce budgets, a

FIGURE 6.3

Estimated Expenditure by Year (School A - Tables 6.3 and 6.4)

(a) For whole school

Year	Total annual expenditure £	Expenditure per pupil £
1	132,384	668.6
2	132,384	655.4
3	151,296	720.5
4	191,484	890.6
5	193,848	865.4
6	92,196	1440.6
7	80,376	2172.3
Total	973,968*	

(b) For one subject (Physics)

Year	Total annual expenditure £	Expenditure per pupil £	Expenditure per pupil studying subject
1	11,029	55.7	55.7
2	11,029	54.6	54.6
3	11,029	52.5	52.5
4	7,870	36.6	131.2
5	8,403	37.5	140.1
6	4,202	65.7	466.9
7	4,202	113.6	600.3
Total	57,764		

Costs are estimated on the basis of the number of lessons offered to each year as a fraction of the total (2,060) lessons per week (see Figure 6.1).

* Rounding error, compare to Table 6.2, and Figure 6.1(a).

Using estimate cost of £13.13 per Physics lesson (Figure 6.1), and actual number of lessons offered per year-group (Years 1-3, 21: Year 4, 15: Year 5, 16, Years 6 and 7, 8 Lessons). 60 pupils take Physics in Years 4 and 5: 9 with 9 and 7 pupils respectively in Years 6 and 7.

complex range of tasks, and a heightened interest over a number of years in resource deployment (to some extent sponsored by DES) the managerial function has been increasingly developed. In some cases the marginal costs of additional students entering a course, or the effects of organizing additional practical classes, for instance, can be accurately projected. Were these developments to be reflected in schools the institutional base for negotiation with LEAs over resource needs and deployment would be greatly strengthened. The onus would then be on LEAs to, similarly, develop their own managerial control function.[23]

'VALUE FOR MONEY' CONSIDERATIONS

The limited interest for the elements (planning and management control) of the two previous sections is easily translated by the critical observer into lack of concern about 'value for money'. Paradoxically, the potential developments in these functions as described failed to deal explicitly with the achievement of organizational objectives. Although the co-ordination of educational and resource planning was directed towards goals, while the equity and efficiency objectives of managerial control were integral in policy intentions, the basic thrust in both cases centred on input parameters. It does not take a critical outsider to realise that the achievement of a particular equity objective, equal per-pupil expenditures in the schools of a LEA, is no more than an intermediate step. The more important issue is whether this new distribution of resources leads to the accomplishment of additional educational, and education-related, goals. Similarly, an efficiency objective is achieved through accomplishing the same goals using fewer resources, which does not necessarily follow the elimination of small classes or reductions in building maintenance costs. Logically, of course, arguments such as these are irrefutable: but the intention pervading the strengthening of these two functions is that development will contribute to the accomplishment of final objectives, and therefore enhance 'value for money'.

The question of whether a school or college does give value implies a tangible and assessable output, but in the absence of overall acceptable measures of output, and with input control so circumscribed, dismissing 'value for money' considerations as irrelevant is an attractive option.

Fundamentally, the case relies on the nature of the education process, but as assessed from an educationist's perspective. Yet education is not dissimilarly placed to several public services. While the perspective may be unique, there are many others. Parents, governors, councillors, ratepayers etc. provide overlapping constituencies well capable of producing individual and group opinions on 'value for money'. The intangibility of output, for example, may be less significant to them than an educationist might suppose, because of the numerous situations in private and public activities, where needs are satisfied without tangible outcomes - a trip to the cinema, national defence etc. In other words, individuals continuously make 'value for money' judgements and a perception about the quality of the education service, as they experience it, and relative to tax levels, is one among many. Clearly, such views must be highly subjective, much dependant on recent events as they have impinged upon individuals, and (often) lacking an appreciation of the subtleties and sophistications in the relationships among education, other services and payment through taxation. As a result they are more certain and definitive than the views of insiders with expert knowledge who, because of their appreciation of the complexities of the situation and doubts about simple measures refuse to consider the 'value for money' issue in crude terms.

However, educationists as experts, convincing themselves about the irrelevance of 'value for money' may be of little consolation to their constituents. Even the collection of detailed resource deployment statistics (as in the CIPFA figures) does not answer potential criticisms. The fact that a particular LEA has a lower PTR, or spends more on teaching materials, than another says nothing about the relative efficiency of the two education services. A concentration on input measures is demanded by fiscal accounting, but they cannot be considered even as vicarious assessments of output. As a result arguments against planned reductions in educational spending are more difficult to sustain because the full range of links between input and output have received inadequate attention. If the actual outcomes resulting from fewer teachers or less buildings could be forecast, resistance to such budgetary proposals might be strengthened. More emphasis on planning and management control activities goes part of the way towards achieving this end, including some measures of faculty or departmental output expressed on a per-pupil expenditure basis (Table 6.2) but the issue of the real impact of lower expenditure, the actual effect on input-output relationships, still merits consideration. A search for precise objectivity would be pointless. The complete output of a school or college cannot be neatly quantified, and if it were attempted the methods selected would stand no chance of universal acceptance. A few indicators of final output (number of graduates, examination passes etc.) are available, but they tend to be isolated. In other cases, such as the APU, standards are monitored but the process of light sampling is insufficiently rigorous to assist either LEAs or schools in their managerial control tasks.

In the absence of comprehensive 'hard' information, observers will establish their own judgements of whether the range of outcomes as specified and assessed by them, is adequate. In such circumstances, possibly the best that can be achieved by output agreements, is to balance opinion, vested interest and prejudice with fact. Undoubtedly, over-concentration on input factors will never be eliminated, perhaps best demonstrated by situations in which a misallocation of resources appears to exist. A comprehensive exposition of spending, as with the CIPFA figures, may not be too revealing because input averages can disguise large differences in per-pupil expenditures, resulting from the basic unit - the LEA - including schools with a wide variety of circumstances. However, if input variations do emerge at whatever level, concern then centres on the equity objective. Without supportive evidence to explain such differences, or the additional outcomes achieved with the extra resources, the achievement of this objective becomes an end in itself. In other words, schools, colleges, LEAs, faculties (all the sub-units) are awarded equal distributions by the main unit unless some form of discrimination is practised, on the assumption that each will achieve the same outcome. Really in the absence of output measures the main unit has no alternative. Yet by doing so neither equity nor efficiency objectives are capable of accomplishment, unless all sub-units are equally effective in converting inputs to outputs. If not, inequality of outcome will occur and some clients must be relatively disadvantaged.

More disadvantages from concentrating on inputs arise with unequal distributions which appear to go uncorrected. It is easy to transmit, through the soft information channels, the impression not only that 'value for money' is not being sought, but also that such a possibility seems a relatively unimportant element in the decision-processes. Small teaching groups provides the clearest example of what would be regarded as a misallocation. The distribution of sixth-form pupils in the schools of a geographically compact area of one LEA (Table 6.4) demonstrate both a small average group size (half the classes with less than six pupils) and situations of only one or two pupils studying a particular subject co-existing with identical arrangements at a neighbouring school. On educational grounds, ignoring adverse influences in the rest of the school, the lack of stimulation from other pupils in such situations can only be balanced by the greater individual attention given to the children. From both efficiency and equity perspectives, however, such arrangements are highly doubtful. Resources (teachers, other staff, buildings and materials) are being utilized by a small number of children when, by co-ordinating the work of schools, the same service could have been offered at a lower per pupil expenditure: while children in other parts of the school are being denied access to teachers or option choices because of this over-commitment. Even were it possible to demonstrate good 'A' level grades through 'overuse' of resources these would need to be off-set against opportunities, such as improved 'O' level results or better job placement rates, foregone elsewhere in the school. Similar conclusions could be drawn about any small group situations in schools and colleges. Management could argue that there were no misallocations, that the pursuit of 'value for money' is maximised, even with one child in a class, but the validity of their case relies upon evidence about outcomes. Significantly, as authorities take more interest in institutional organization, both internal and external staff need convincing that such arrangements do not represent misallocation.

With regard to the most general question in a 'value for money' context, of whether schools and colleges waste money, the answer must be yes, with the important qualification that so do all other institutions. The organization has yet to be developed which could not function using slightly less

TABLE 6.4
Pupils studying at 'A' level (First-year) in ten schools of LEA district

School	A	B	C	D	E	F	G	H	I	J	Total number of pupils	Pupils per teacher period*
Art	10	3	12	4	8	6	4	8	14	4	73	0.91
Biology	12	5	16	6	7	10	3	9	18	5	91	1.14
Chemistry	8	2	9	4	–	12	4	5	12	3	59	0.82
Computing	–	–	–	–	–	8	–	–	12	–	20	1.25
Economics	4	4	10	–	–	9	2	4	16	–	49	0.88
English	16	5	12	4	5	10	8	5	24	4	93	1.16
French	5	1	5	–	2	8	4	4	9	–	38	0.59
Geography	8	5	8	4	7	16	8	5	16	10	87	1.09
German	2	–	4	–	1	6	–	1	4	2	20	0.36
History	8	6	8	4	5	10	6	4	16	4	71	0.89
Home Economics	12	4	5	–	–	6	–	4	10	–	41	0.85
Latin	–	–	–	–	–	–	–	–	4	–	4	0.50
Mathematics	15	4	9	2	4	12	5	6	20	5	82	1.03
Music	4	–	4	–	2	4	–	–	–	–	14	0.44
Needlework	8	–	–	–	–	–	–	4	4	–	16	0.67
Physics	9	2	7	4	2	8	4	6	14	4	60	0.75
R.E.	–	–	8	2	–	4	5	8	10	–	37	0.77
Sociology	10	–	–	–	–	8	–	–	11	–	29	1.21
Spanish	–	–	–	–	–	1	–	–	1	–	2	0.12
Technical Drawing	6	–	–	–	–	–	4	–	6	–	16	0.67

* On assumption of 8 periods per week per subject.

electricity, floor-area or whatever. More contentiously, schools and colleges would still function if staff was paid minimum Burnham allowances (see Chapter 5), but in this case, and the others, the real issue concerns the potential trade-off between lower expenditure and reduced educational outcomes (however assessed). A search for internal efficiencies, by savings and through effective staff deployment, is important, but the consideration centres on 'value for money' not cheapness. A particular challenge for education is to focus its attention, and those of observers, on outcomes, because if this does not occur the provision of the service at minimum cost can easily become a dominant theme.

The previous sections have already developed the theme that the productive route towards efficiency involves awarding staff freedom in resource decisions, using the related procedures to provide appropriate motivation. Staff are more likely to use less electricity if there is some direct return to the institution as a result: they may even willingly accept minimum Burnham allowances if this maximises numbers employed or guarantees job-security. It would be unwise to view wastage as an internal phenomenon - resources which could have been put to more effective use elsewhere in the institution. With allocative competitiveness in a static or declining situation it is unlikely that such a view would prevail beyond the school or college. Increasingly, evidence of resource wastage even if limited to a peripheral activity, and, by implication, inadequate 'value for money' will exaggerate demands for transfer of expenditures and calls for reductions in public spending.

Increased interest in wastage, and a greater thrust towards 'value for money' by economic conditions can paradoxically concentrate attention upon intermediate parameters, such as class-size or SSR. The shortage of objective measures of achievement and the lack of agreement over the appropriateness of those that do exist, appear to give the activities (related to education) of the newly established Exchequer and Audit Department, and Audit Commission, a bias towards input and intermediate measures.[24] This has already been demonstrated by events although consideration of the 'efficiency, economy and effectiveness' of services provides the key phrase in the legislation.[25] Certainly this would appear to direct attention towards output, but it is highly improbable that these bodies can develop the expertise in the short-term to go far beyond staff deployment rates, class-sizes, building and room occupancy figures, use of materials etc. For example, guidelines to local authority auditors when examining the 'efficiency' of FE colleges are dominated by input measures, with some limited interest for intermediate issues, but minimal concern for output.26 If audit attention switches to schools almost certainly the same type of item would be considered: with small groups in the sixth-form highlighted as examples of misuse of resources while low staff contact-ratios and under-used equipment will be identified, but as ends in themselves. There are situations (already described) in which it would seem that there have been gross misallocations, to the extent that outcomes cannot possibly compensate, but the main focus of audit should be the relationships between resources and achievement.

The practical possibilities may be limited. However, by relating input measures to criteria of success which can be made available (course completion figures, examination passes, test scores, etc.) and subjective judgements of achievement in local advisory and HMI reports (for example) audit activities can become a component and a catalyst, in LEA and institutional developments in planning, managerial control and 'value for money' functions. What both LEAs and institutions require from audit is information about their practices compared to others similarly placed, relative to staff deployment, teaching arrangements, and the utilization of other resources, but not restricted to inputs. If the purpose of audit is to achieve a uniformity of input, it becomes an exercise in cheapness for its own sake. The system requires of LEAs the ability to establish a framework, to negotiate with institutions within that framework, and monitor the activities of schools and colleges in relation to the negotiation. These elements are necessary as institutions achieve levels of autonomy which will enable them to fulfil all their obligations. In particular, to facilitate staff awareness of the inter-relationships between the educational and financial components of their work: more specifically to demonstrate, especially to critics, that the intention is to maximise output, as agreed between them and their institutional constituents, per unit of input.

NOTES AND REFERENCES

1. See for example in *Engineering Today*, 4/11/80, pp. 20-24.
2. 'Resource Management in Practice: Inputs and Outcomes as Perspectives of Efficiency', *Coombe Lodge Reports*, Vol.15 No.12 (1983) pp. 515-539.
3. P.A. Pyhrr, *A Zero-Base Budgeting: A Practical Management Tool for Evaluating Expenses*, (Wiley-Interscience, New York, 1973).
4. H. Fayol, *General and Industrial Management*, Pitman, London, 1949).
5. K. A. Knight, *Matrix Management: A Cross-Functional Approach to Organization*, (Gower Press, Farnborough, 1977).
6. E.W.H. Briault, 'Virement and the Alternative Use of Secondary School Resources', *Secondary Education*, Vol. 3, No. 2, (1973) pp. 1-10.
7. ILEA, *Allocation of Resources and the Alternative Use of Resources (AUR) Scheme*, (1982).
8. Cambridgeshire LEA, *Local Financial Management Scheme*, (1982).
9. Solihull LEA, *School Finance Autonomy Scheme*, (1982).
10. CMND 3006, *A Plan for Polytechnics and other Colleges*, (1966).
11. DES Circular 7/73, *Development of Higher Education in the Non-University Sector*, (1973).
12. CMND 5174, *Education: A Framework for Expansion* (1972), paras 13-34.
13. DES Circular 2/73, *Nursery Education*, (1973).
14. DES Circular 10/65, *The Organisation of Secondary Education* (1965), and DES Circular 4/74, *The Organisation of Secondary Education*, (1974).
15. DES Circular 10/65, para 6.
16. D. Novick (ed.), *Current Practice in Programme Budgeting (PPBS)*, (Rand-Heinemann, London, 1973).
17. C. Selby-Smith, *The Costs of Further Education: A British Analysis*, (Pergamon, Oxford, 1970).
18. C.E. Cumming, *Studies in Educational Costs*, (Scottish Academic Press. Edinburgh, 1968.
19. E. M. Byrne, *Planning and Educational Inequality*, (NFER, Slough, 1974).
20. J.R. Hough, *A Study of School Costs*, (NFER, Slough, 1981).
21. A.H. Marshall, *Financial Management in Local Government*, (George Allen & Unwin, London, 1974).
22. For example, in the arrangements for calculating unit-totals in schools, or between 1967 and 1974 when the separate components in the RSG

calculation were publicised (SI 1974/428, <u>The Rate Support Grant Regulations</u>, (1974).
23. V.J. Delany, 'Value for Money in Education', Management Accounting, (January 1983),pp.24-25.
24. CMND 8325, <u>Role of the Comptroller and Auditer General</u>, (1981).
25. <u>Local government finance act</u>, 1982.
26. The Department of the Environment: Audit Inspectorate, <u>Colleges of Further Education: Guide to the measurement of resource efficiency</u>, (HMSO, London, 1983).

Chapter Seven

CONTRACTION, PRIVATIZATION AND OTHER CHOICES

POLITICAL CHOICES

The intention of this book has been to focus on resource management in education. As such two themes have dominated. The first of these concerns not so much the autonomy available when decisions have to be made (although on many occasions more freedom exists than is appreciated) but the many levels at which choices occur. To a large extent this feature results from a decentralized system, and is reflected by the comparatively wide disparity in resource utilization patterns that do emerge. It would be misleading to suggest that the differential outcomes from numerous decision-centres have not received attention. Table 1.1 (Chapter 1) displayed the variable resource profiles for a number of LEAs: and while complementary figures at institutional level are much less readily available, situations that have been researched suggest inter-school and college variations, even within the same authority. Yet such differences are hardly surprising given the number of decision-centres, and the lack of systematic monitoring at point of delivery in the institutions. Indeed, it could be argued that though not sought, they are certainly encouraged by the political dimension in decision-making. Having a number of independent choice centres (government, local authority, LEA, institution and governors) avoids the likelihood of domination by one particular group, and provides an essential safeguard in a democratic society. According to this view, the fact that a choice in one place can be made less effective by a contradictory decision elsewhere is simply the price that has to be paid. A Chief Education Officer advice, for example, that a particular form of tertiary education would on logistical

Contraction, Privatization and other Choices

grounds (lowest costs as against greatest expected outcomes) be the most effective means of organizing that phase of education, may be rejected.[1] The notion of lowest costs might be acceptable to politicians but their interpretation of outcomes could include a wider range of factors, including party political considerations. More generally, resource decision-making, in this context, occurs both within an overt political environment, subject to lobby by parent associations, teacher unions etc. in the local authority, and groups of staff in the institution.

The second theme, highlighting the influence of political forces on resource decision-making, has been the impact of contraction. When resource volumes reduce, priorities need much greater clarification, with groups and individuals finding opportunities for development receding. From the perspective of resource management, a shortage of funds has at least highlighted the impingement of expenditure related issues on every aspect of the work of the institution. Previously, if resource matters did not affect task performance, many staff paid them little overt attention. Now that situation has completely changed. If a neighbouring school appears to have bigger allowances, or has been able to achieve what seems to be a more appropriate resource mix, these can become topics of considerable interest, particularly when they might include (according to the perceptions of participants) some consideration of relative job-security. It would be far too cynical to imply that teacher concerns for resource deployment have been solely catalyzed by job-security or promotional factors, but retrenchment does provide an opportunity to extend the interests and commitment of staff. For example, another factor which reduced previous staff inclinations to become involved in resource decisions was the view that so few flexibilities remain. In other words, the freedom available to the institution restricts itself to a fraction of total expenditure. To a certain extent this is true: capitation allowances, often offering the only freely allocable resource in school, have declined, therefore reducing choices about books and equipment. Yet, what such a fact must be contrasted against is the potential flexibility available in relation to the use of the most expensive resource - the time of staff. Of course, in practical terms, such flexibility can be disputed: to be achievable, considerable personnel and institutional barriers have to be overcome.

Individuals, for example, may well have settled into a particular work pattern, utilizing the resource of their own time in a unique fashion, contributing to institutional arrangements which become difficult to change. Yet, what the differences in LEA and institutional resource deployment figures demonstrate, accompanying the influences of several decision-making centres in a political environment, are the choice possibilities that do exist. Two schools, with identical PTRs, may have very different TCRs and as a result different average class-sizes: two LEAs might have variations in resource mixes, one with a relatively low PTR and limited expenditure on other items, but similar spending per child:while two polytechnics could award different priorities as between teaching support staff and equipment. These examples, and the many others which could be quoted, cannot be used to imply a rigidity in resource deployment patterns.

In the examples quoted, and in most other circumstances, a major change in deployment strategies in the short-term would be impossible. There is no contradiction between this fact, and comments about the availability of flexibility, and the failure of LEAs and institutions to fully realise its potential. Indeed, any contradiction is between perceptions of spending rigidities and the differences in resource deployment that emerge. From a LEA or institutional standpoint, the answer could be that contraction strengthens resistance to change (from individuals, groups and trade unions) while taking away the additional funding that might have facilitated adaptation. Therefore, variations in expenditure patterns reflect greater flexibility during expansion. Yet, there never has been a time when spending strategies could be dramatically altered. All change, in this context, has been gradual: some adjustments may take longer with contraction, but that as a disadvantage must be contrasted with the benefits of clearer priorities and more precise statement of objectives achievable with retrenchment. For when resources are scarce their utilization generates even more attention. However, in any circumstances, resource issues can easily become input dominated: overlooking the purposes of spending. Simultaneously, the institutions become inward looking: ignoring the changing needs of clients. Even were this not to occur with contraction, an opportunity would be missed if no systematic attempt was made to match variations in deployment strategies that have evolved to differential outcomes. Many examples of variable inputs that could be assessed, and their impact in the form of differential educational outcomes, have received surprisingly little consideration - the organization of staff and student time in schools and colleges on learning rates, the effect of differences in teacher contact time per pupil on progress in particular subjects, the impact of contact hours in FE on student achievement, and the relationship between relative expenditures on teaching staff, non-teaching staff, books, equipment etc. and teaching methodologies adopted. In a democracy, where input decisions will always be subject to political forces, information on issues such as these would be beneficial. Without it, a main thrust seems likely towards inter-institutional equity as influenced by political forces, often with little knowledge about its achievement, and less concerning the interaction between resources, institutional factors and environmental constraints in the accomplishment of educational objectives.

COSTS AND BENEFITS OF PRIVATIZATION

While contraction may assist education to focus upon objectives, priorities and achievements, paradoxically, lack of concern for those items, may well have exaggerated the extent of retrenchment in relation to other public sector activities. In broad terms, aggregate educational spending (capital and current) has either been static or in gentle decline since the mid 1970s. There are few indications that the situation will change before the 1990s. Much depends upon growth rates in the economy as a whole, but even were these to be large in historical terms (3% say) the likelihood of sustained educational growth at levels of the 1960s is highly improbable. Therefore, the tensions between resource providers and curriculum suppliers will continue, if not strengthen. However, this represents one component of more general tensions - which have been apparent since the first systematic attempts to constrain public expenditure in the late 1950s - between the Treasury, attempting to control aggregate expenditure, and the main spending Ministries. Even in the Conservative administrations of 1979 and 1983, with a stated policy to reduce the total level of public expenditure,[2] these conflicts still occurred. Ministers and departmental staff, subject to various external spending lobbies, argue for more resources, with explanations for their actions ranging from the increased status and importance that would result, to the extra needs that could be satisfied. Also, before elections, a government committed to lowering expenditure long-term, can perceive electoral benefits in more spending. In both situations, though, the expenditure and control tensions are exaggerated.

Within this framework of comprehensive scrutiny and increasing efforts (not always successful) to reduce spending, the potential solution of government opting out of activities has obvious attractions. In other words, reversing the processes by which over the years public agencies, government departments and local authorities have become responsible for activities which if they did exist were left to private groups, charities or individuals. If a government wishes to reduce involvement, four main strategies seem to present themselves: 1. Less supply by public agencies of goods and services. 2. A lower level of government involvement in the actual delivery of services. 3. The introduction of user charges, where they do not already exist, to increase awareness of the cost implications of providing services. 4. The maximisation of competition between public agencies, whenever feasible.[3]

Of the practical ways in which these might be pursued other than by reduction in total educational expenditure, three have attracted particular attention. A system of loans to replace maintenance grants for students in higher education, essentially utilizes the third strategy, and depending upon the detail of any scheme might reduce aggregate spending by several percentage points (Chapter 1): while the notion of education vouchers can encompass elements of each of the separate strategies. Numerous variations on the basic theme of vouchers exist, but in broad terms parents are supplied with a voucher which can be supplemented, if the parents choose, or cashed, with the funds used to assist in fee payments for private schooling.[4]

Obviously, by enticing clients away from state schooling, the role of government and local authority as providers would be reduced, although not in a direct ratio to the numbers involved, because of the diseconomies that emerge with institutional size reduction, and need to maintain available places if parental preferences change. Simultaneously, a component of user-charges would be introduced, if not for all consumers, then certainly for those choosing to supplement their allowance, and inter-school competition for pupils would

undoubtedly be strengthened. Indeed, without a
voucher system, that competition must grow with fewer pupils, and a greater availability of parental
choice in the Education Act, 1980.[5] This apart,
though, loans and vouchers remain theoretical ideas,
seemingly unlikely to be implemented. In contrast,
the Assisted Places scheme,[6] by which government
pays the fees (according to parental means) of some
pupils selected for independent schools represents a
mix of possibly higher total spending (government
contributions to fees not being compensated by
savings on places unused in LEA schools) with a lower level of public involvement in the actual delivery of education services.

It is no surprise that all three privatization
schemes have been subject to sustained and staunch
criticism. To a large extent these views develop
the idea that any restriction on education spending,
whatever form it takes, is wholly reprehensible, and
stem both from an ideological perspective, favouring
public as opposed to private sponsored activity, and
an adversorial standpoint, in that education must
compete with other public activities for resources
in an environment with changing and debatable criteria. As a result,the case for education spending
must be pursued irrespective of other factors. In
addition the perceived likely impingement of privatization on job-security and career prospects cannot
be excluded from any consideration. Yet, from a
more objective stance, overlooking the ideological
perspective, the critics intend a maximisation of
educational spending, but what the last ten years
have demonstrated, and all reasonable projections
up to 1990 suggest a continuation, is that education cannot attract much, if any, additional resources. Therefore, proponents of extra spending
are presented with a dilemma. They must continue
to lobby, but with little expectation of real success, or they can turn to arrangements in which the
place of publically-provided facilities become less
important. One example of the latter has been the
increasing reliance of some schools on parental contributions towards the purchase of books and equipment, supplementing local authority allowances.
Criticisms of such arrangements are easily developed: that they must lead to inequalities of provision by benefitting children in more affluent
areas, for example. More generally, any privatization scheme in education has inherent defects,
because of the potentially deleterious effects of a
market-place philosophy. A need exists in the

modern world, increasingly dominated by complex technologies, with inherent monopolies of both labour and capital, to protect individuals from the worst aspects of uncontrolled market forces. In education this case is particularly strong, with central and local authorities providing the only feasible protective mechanism. For a market involves competition which can rarely be fair in education: the history of attempts to achieve greater equality of opportunity make that point. Similarly, inter-institutional competition to be effective, assumes a reasonable level of knowledge by all consumers. Clearly, this does not occur in relation to parents choosing schools: some have an excellent knowledge and wish to pursue their preferences, others know very little and may not seem interested in making choices.

More generally, what sort of market forces would education react to and in what ways? Would such forces, for example, provide an innovative system, responding both to individual consumer and, more general, regional and national needs? What one form of privatization in higher education demonstrates (University College, Buckingham) is that the particular and rather limited wants of a small group of clients can be satisfied by concentrating teaching on areas which lead naturally to higher status and better paid occupations. Any successful attempt to extend these arrangements, involving a wider range of activities (especially in science, engineering and technology, where the full costs chargeable to each student will need to be much greater) while attracting a broader clientele from a range of social and economic backgrounds, would be a sounder display of their viability as an alternative to public financing.

Yet, dismissing such schemes, and any other forms of educational privatization as irrelevant, or retrograde, both down-grades the potential advantages of competition, and does nothing to resolve the basic dilemma of those rigidly opposed to any form of privatization who argue for more education services with little chance that their views will be accepted. With regard to competition, a middle ground presents attractions: competition may rarely be fair but to try to eliminate it completely, at inter-institutional levels say, hinders the pursuit of many efficiency objectives. This item, though, relates to the nature of a dilemma. The thrust of education proponents is directed presumably, towards increasing the scope and effectiveness of educational services, and not in search of increased educational spending for its own sake. They may claim that one follows naturally from the other, but they must demonstrate the veracity of such a view.

PRISONERS OF DECISION-MAKING

As well as accepting that little growth in total resources can be expected, LEAs and institutions have to function in an increasingly complex decision-making environment external to themselves, over which they can exert few influences. This fact has been clearly shown by the experiences of individual local authorities as the intentions and methodologies associated with RSG settlements have changed. The arrangements since 1981-82 may, in theory, be a laudable way of achieving needs and resources equalization across authorities, but in practice, the perceptions of authorities are directed towards the extent to which derivatives of the basic procedures can be used to pre-empt choices which previously had been made at local level. Increasingly, the view exists, to be exaggerated by legislation to limit rate rises,7 that an anticipated decision about aggregate expenditure is handed on to each authority by government. Within that total spending, authorities at least have autonomy to 'vire' among services (though were an education block grant to evolve that freedom would disappear) accompanied by local responsibility for determining aggregate spending levels within each major expenditure category. Although an unlikely development it does highlight the extent to which each local education service has become dependant on external decision-making. Yet, these processes in relation to revenue support can be followed. Through the negotiations between central government and the local authority associations, and then the applications of the formulae to distribute the block grant, each local authority can see how the procedures effect the final grant. They may disagree with both the mechanisms and the outcomes, but a certain visibility exists. Not so with permission to make capital expenditure where, although each authority bids, and may well lobby for special consideration, permission to spend might bear little relationship to the individual claims of authorities, and be difficult to reconcile according to perceptions of their own needs, or those of neighbouring authorities relative to their allowances. More directly, the distribution of total allowable capital spending occurs within private government procedures, about which those most affected - the local authorities - have little knowledge.

Although this particular distribution provides perhaps the clearest example of autocratic decision-making its impact on local education is limited by falling rolls reducing the demand for new premises: while restrictions on revenue spending reduce LEA enthusiasm for entering into new commitments. Arrangements, as they have evolved, for AFE expenditure display a similar autocracy, although exercised through the NAB, but as the decisions are aimed at revenue spending they impinge more directly on institutional activity. Essentially, the funding of AFE has ceased to be a local matter. As a result it would have been difficult to consider within the four territories of decision (Chapter 3), and has to be discussed separately. This has always been the case, as arrangements for pooling stemmed from systems of inter-authority payment in FE, and attempts by LEAs to share the costs of facilities provided by a minority of authorities. In NAFE, a recoupment scheme continues (organized by DES) with inter-authority payments, at standard rates, when a student attends at the college of another LEA. In AFE, with the range of courses and the number of students involved, such arrangements become impracticable and the AFE pool was established in 1958: with all authorities paying into the pool, and those supporting AFE courses making claims upon it, dependant upon the proportions of AFE to NAFE activities (assessed through lecturer time commitments) in relation to total FE expenditure. Until 1974-75 the contribution of each LEA to the pool was based equally on non-domestic rateable value (a measure of its industrial and commercial base, and therefore an assumed surrogate for its utilization of AFE facilities) and school population. From that year the previously separate training of teachers pool was subsumed into a larger AFE pool, with the contributory basis directed more towards school population (69%) with an equivalent reduction in the contribution non-domestic rateable value (31%). As such, both arrangements represented a form of national recoupment, which was relatively easy to administer (although slow, as a result of the time after the end of the year when settlement was complete). It was disadvantaged, though, in that individual authority contributions bore no clear relationship to their utilization of the AFE facilities to which they were part contributors. Obviously, the number of students from a LEA studying at AFE level bears some relationship to school population, and to the rateable value of industrial and commercial premises, but no attempt was made to explain why the particular percentages were selected, nor why other factors did not appear in the calculation. When evidence was sought it demonstrated wide differences in LEA pool contributions per FTE student living in their area. In other words receipts, in terms of student support, did not match payments. [8]

However, it was concerns about the college expenditures which the pool supported that produced such drastic changes in pooling arrangements. Up to 1979-80 all AFE spending of authorities was automatically reimbursed, but the Secretary of State, using powers in the Education Act, 1980 (agreed with the local authority associations) has set a limit since 1980-81 on the aggregate expenditure to be met from the pool. More directly, the pool is 'capped', with the total announced each year, accompanied by its distribution among LEAs and major institutions, around the time that RSG figures are published. The total distributed for 1983-84 (the AFE quantum) was £560.5m. The rationale of the new procedures, to limit local autonomy by restricting spending freedoms, is clear. From an expenditure control perspective a pooling system in which authority contributions bear little relationship to utilization and all spending can be recouped, has obvious disadvantages. Few direct incentives exist to pursue efficiency objectives when LEAs share costs with 100, or so, other potential contributors. However, conversion from one funding procedure to another presents difficulties exacerbated on this occasion, by differences in institutional resource utilization patterns and the potential inflexibilities these variations represent. As a result efforts to achieve inter-college spending consistency continue to be inhibited. For example, 1981-82 actual unit-costs by institution, even when allowances were made for mixes of students, ranged from under £2,000 to over £4,000 per student: [9] clearly making any form of 'common funding', (the same payments from the pool for equal student loadings) difficult to implement in the short-term. Undoubtedly though, a system based upon student numbers and target average-costs represents the main distributional intention with the capped pool. As a result, a college's allowance during 1983-84 for common funding purposes, used the product of actual student numbers from November 1981 (converted to FTEs) classified into Group 1, Group 2, and Art and Design Faculties (Chapter 4), and an estimate of costs per student in each of the categories, to assess the distribution of 88% of the pool (85% the previous year as common funding becomes more dominant). The remaining portion of the pool (further funding) required special arrangements, in the main to provide a safety net for institutions with high unit-costs, and was related to actual expenditures within individual colleges.

Even with these special allowances the year on year changes in net allocations between 1982-83 and 1983-84 show considerable inter-institutional variations (Table 7.1): while expectations of gross expenditure reductions in real terms between 1981-82 and 1983-84, reflect the impact of the new arrangements. In addition, up to 1983-84, polytechnics and OMEs (Other Maintained Establishments) had different systems of allowance relative to common funding, while that year was the first occasion on which all OMEs with more than 10% AFE had their allowances separately calculated. In other words the arrangements, as for all policy initiatives, involve elements of gradualism and modification, through refinement. Almost certainly, the next change will attempt a much narrower reclassification of institutional activity to replace the three faculty groupings. Already NAB have introduced 14 programme areas:[10] A. Initial teacher training, B. In-service teacher training and other education, C. Medicine, dentistry, pharmacy and ancillary health subjects, D. Engineering, E. Other technology and manufacture, F. Agriculture, forestry and vetinary studies, G. Science, applied science, H. Mathematics and computer studies, I. Business management, accountacy and law, J. Social and administrative studies, K. Other professional and vocational studies, L. Language and literature, M. Humanities, N. Music, drama and visual arts. A target cost per student (unit of resource) could then be specified for each area, and combined with NABs responsibility for planning student numbers by programme within institutions, would effectively relate projected population figures to expenditure control.[11] During the middle and later 1980s this will almost certainly include efforts to reduce the average unit of resource. Realization of such objectives, though, presents considerable practical difficulties. The need for some form of short-term protection when institutions have established high cost activities has already been mentioned. Perhaps, the explanation may

TABLE 7.1 Allocations from Capped Advanced Further Education Pool to Polytechnics

LEA	Polytechnic	1982-83 Net alloc. £m cash	1983-84 Net alloc. £m cash	Expenditure reduction in real terms 1981-82 to 1983-84
Barking	NELP	18.032	16.485	-10.9%
Barnet	Middlesex	16.223	15.993	-11.6%
Kingston	Kingston	12.152	12.344	-13.0%
Inner London		54.464	54.081	-9.1%
Birmingham	Birmingham	12.759	12.576	-3.8%
Coventry	Lanchester	13.550	13.721	-4.4%
Wolverhampton	Wolverhampton	12.360	12.203	-11.3%
Liverpool	Liverpool	13.709	14.734	-10.1%
Manchester	Manchester	19.451	19.723	-7.1%
Sheffield	Sheffield	18.611	18.805	-4.2%
Kirklees	Huddersfield	10.718	10.572	-8.8%
Leeds	Leeds	14.147	14.005	-3.3%
Newcastle	Newcastle	14.885	15.051	-6.2%
Sunderland	Sunderland	9.933	9.717	-7.1%
Avon	Bristol	13.005	13.299	-7.1%
Cleveland	Teesside	7.038	7.280	-16.6%
Devon	Plymouth	8.916	9.152	-8.4%
East Sussex	Brighton	13.123	12.683	-12.4%
Hampshire	Portsmouth	16.107	15.660	-5.1%
Herts.	Hatfield	10.427	10.408	-5.4%
Lancashire	Preston	9.849	9.486	-9.5%
Leics.	Leicester	14.764	15.253	-6.1%
Notts.	Trent	17.493	17.985	-5.5%
Oxon.	Oxford	8.842	9.541	-7.6%
Staffs.	North Staffs.	10.442	10.577	-13.6%

Source: DES Press Notice 22/12/82, Advanced Further Education Pool Allocations for 1983-84.

include factors, such as expensive premises, over which the institution has little current control. Refinements, if they are to be applied fairly, have to take the whole range of cost effects, as they impinge upon institutional or departmental functioning, into account. It also assumes, that costs per student are the same for all activities within a programme area. Take programme H, in which, almost certainly expenditure per student on computing, because of equipment requirements will need to be higher than that on mathematics: as a result equal funding across the programme will advantage colleges offering mathematics, but without computing courses.

A common level of funding across equivalent courses although a desirable objective (through equalizing input factors across a wide range of institutions) must involve an increasingly complex system of decision-making, to allow for the evolution of new mixes of college activities in a changing environment. In fact, a single quantum distributed by a consistent methodology will remain as an aim for some little while. So vital are the allowances to the functioning of polytechnics, other higher education institutions, and AFE courses elsewhere, that powerful lobbying forces, supported by general and specific pressures, will try to influence the distributive processes. In effect, NAB determines a figure analogous to GRE for each institution, but with powers of enforcement, in excess of the DoE in relation to RSG settlements. A LEA can supplement the pool allowance to its polytechnic, say, but that proves difficult both because of the aggregate restrictions on local authority spending and the possibility that NAB, with its overall control, will lower subsequent allowances. As a result arguments to modify the full effects of a common funding policy seem likely to continue, particularly if the units of resource continue to be eroded. The case for more quanta - one for polytechnics, another for higher education colleges perhaps - because of their different characteristics will be pressed, as will special distributions for some institutions, because of their perceived special circumstances. The most likely outcome for the whole arrangement is a common funding mechanism dominant, but modified by a mix of political and educational judgements. Overall though, because of their inherent resource inflexibilities, the institutions seem certain to become with retrenchment still more prisoners of complex, and often little understood, decision-making.

Contraction, Privatization and other Choices

THE EXPANSION OF EDUCATION

Apart from capital spending allowances the thrust from government in trying to achieve greater control over LEA and institutional expenditure is directed towards more uniformity over inputs. As a policy intention, with regard to the block grant mechanisms in the RSG and capping the AFE pool, it offers many advantages. Its pursuit, though, co-inciding as it has with public expenditure retrenchment - indeed RSG and pool capping have been the main vehicles in achieving greater control over total spending - introduces situations in which local authority and institutions perceive themselves as captives of complex, and irrational, decision-making processes. In other words the search for equity objectives, even when in relative terms some LEAs and institutions are advantaged, has remained invisible within the more general and pressing problem of maintaining aggregate spending within expenditure limits, imposed with what would seem to be increasing arbitrariness. A difficulty exaggerated in education by the high labour costs relative to total expenditure, and the large proportion of the remaining spending which also appears to be fixed. As a result, with government, assisted more or less willingly by local authorities, trying to contain LEA expenditure, easy targets have suffered disproportionately, even to the extent of HMI, paradoxically as representatives of central government, voicing concern over standards of provision.[12]

Yet, in pursuit of greater resource distribution equity it is easy to overlook the fact that resource distribution facilitates the pursuit of certain intentions, it does not represent an end in itself. As RSG arrangements and pool capping become more complex and convoluted it becomes increasingly attractive to ignore this fact, and view equitable distribution among LEAs or colleges, dependant upon their individual characteristics, as the objective of the exercise. An efficiency objective must be, at least, as equally prominent as any equity goal.

It can, of course, be argued that the equity and efficiency objectives relative to distribution are minor issues, compared to the major item of an education service becoming steadily poorer with static or contracting resource levels. In other words, provided there are no gross inequities in distribution, and because resource shortages are reducing the accomplishment of objectives, the main concern should be directed towards obtaining more resources, and nothing else. What such views tend to ignore is the notion that resources come to education on the assumption they will support certain activities and achieve likely outcomes. However, the job of educational managers involves not only organizing these activities and, as a result, maximising outcomes, but also ensuring a public awareness that these processes are in fact occurring. The view must be that educationists collectively have not been particularly effective at transmitting a positive vision about what is being achieved with the resources received or what additional benefits might accrue from any extra support. This judgement can be applied both to times when the service has expanded (during which equity and efficiency goals were, perhaps, down-graded in relation to the actual processes of organizing growth) and the sustained period of contraction, in which coping with the problems that arise (and, on occasion, exaggerating their prominence to argue for less reduction in resources) can easily become more dominant than the maximisation of achievement with the fewer resources available. It is very easy for participants in education, as staff or clients, to concern themselves about a whole variety of factors, adversely affected by shortage of funds. Many of these have been considered. Obviously, these anxieties will become greater, and involve extra personnel, the more sustained the period of contraction. Yet, no matter how justified these concerns they will have minimal impact until personnel in education can convince those directly involved in decision-making processes, of the adverse effects of retrenchment, not so much on education itself, but in relation to the other societal effects which an effective education service should facilitate. In this process of persuasion educationists are disadvantaged, by long time-scales and lack of tangible outputs, but in an environment of competition with other public sector activities, and with public expenditure under challenge, they cannot choose the conditions in which education must compete.

Yet, such an outlook has to be placed in the context of the need for more education in a rapidly changing technological environment. The key question of how this is to be achieved, both in relation to quality and quantity, has to be answered. The fact of growing MSC involvement in comparison to a decline in traditional education activity both demonstrates the ineffectiveness of the current lobby to increase the flow of resources through the territorial hierarchy, and raises queries about the extent to which many MSC programmes represent crisis management. In the main they do not include systematic attempts to raise the general level of skill, knowledge and ability in the population. Yet, if the public sector cannot support a sufficiently high level of funding, if the education service can only provide a dynamic and responsive system through acquiring more resources, and if the privatization of activities on a large scale does not appear viable (for whatever reasons), is there any other alternative? Could, perhaps, firms and organizations be persuaded, through some form of privatization, to supply an adequacy of skills and adaptability in the workforce, and by this facilitate economic growth? Previous experience with the necessity of more public intervention in the 1960s and 1970s would suggest that this is unlikely. Perhaps, the only solution to this huge range of problems lies with a different form of privatization. At the nub of all these inter-related issues is the fact that education has become dominated by an institutional basis, which exaggerates many of its demands for resources and produces the inflexibilities in resource deployment that have dominated much of the book. With a less prominent institutional framework it seems more than likely that a much greater volume of education activity could be generated with the same level of resources. In other words, the privatization centres around the individualization of client needs, and the adoption of the most appropriate means for their satisfaction: but not necessarily within a standard course, nor as part of the programme of a conventional school or college. It is the aggregate of all activities in relation to their purposes, which matter, not where they occur. It would be a slow process of gradual modifications to existing practices, but the technological changes which have created so many of the underlying problems may in time also provide solutions. The development of computer soft-ware packages, and the availability of effective communication modes, being the two most obvious examples. Obviously, any attempt to further reduce the institutional bias of publically provided education would be strongly resisted, but such a transformation provides the only viable route towards the regeneration of the education system, and through that sustained economic expansion in a technologically advanced society.

NOTES AND REFERENCES

1. DES, *Costing educational provision for the 16-19 age group*, (1981)
2. CMND 7746, *The government's expenditure plans 1980-81*, (1979)
3. E.S. Savas, *Privatising the Public Sector: How to Shrink Government*, (Chatham House, Chatham, New Jersey, 1982)
4. A.K. Maynard, *Experiments with choice in education: an analysis of consumer financing to bring more resources into education by vouchers and loans*, (Institute of Economic Affairs, London, 1975)
5. Education Act, 1980, s. 6-9
6. Education Act, 1980, s. 17-18
7. CMND,9008 *Rates - Proposals for rate limitation and the reform of the rating system*, (1983)
8. J. Pratt, T. Travers, and T. Burgess, *Costs and Control in Further Education*, (NFER, Slough, 1978) pp. 113-151
9. DES, *Advanced Further Education Pool Allocations for 1983-84*, (1982)
10. DES, *Pilot Survey of Costs and Statistics in Further Education 1982-83*, (1983)
11. Ultimate responsibility still resides with the Secretary of State, but in practice has been delegated to NAB
12. DES, *Report by Her Majesty's Inspectors on the Effects of Local Authority Expenditure on the Education Service in England - 1981*, (1982).

INDEX

Academic community 34
ACS 134-5, 138-9, 141, 154
academic year 7
accountability 87, 150
adult education 131
AFE 7, 9, 27, 58, 61, 109, 119, 121, 127, 130-2, 138, 144, 162, 179, 186, 211, 231: pooling 61, 121, 129, 133, 162, 258-62
ALH 134-5, 137-9, 143-4, 152
A-levels 129, 135, 160, 184-6, 244
apprenticeships 43
APU 17
ASH 134-5, 137, 139, 143-4
architects 27
Assisted places scheme 255
Audit Commission 246
Audit Inspectors 143
autonomy 193, 219, 224: professional 208
AUR 215-6
average costs 234, 259

balance sheet 208
Bains 90
B.Ed. 179, 184
Black Paper 17
Block grant 77-8, 81, 84-9

books 9, 15, 69, 94, 100, 105, 110, 169-70, 215, 218, 220, 251, 253
Brent 116
BTEC 130, 135, 137, 220
budget 94-5, 98, 104, 168, 223, 233: base 98: day 66: zero-base 211: object of expense 225
building use 2, 110, 112-3, 139, 164-5, 213: closed 166: costs 211: maintenance 2, 211-2, 242: work station 166
Burnham 137, 141, 143, 157, 160, 191

Cambridgeshire 216-7
capital expenditure 6, 9, 14, 65, 68, 102, 105, 222: investment 44
capitation 98, 100, 251
cash limits 23, 67
Chief Executive 90-2
CIPFA 242-3
civil servant 63, 71
class size 111-2, 122, 139, 149, 151-4, 160, 181, 192, 236
cleaning staff 164-6: materials 217, 226
clients 4, 103, 177, 252
CNAA 132, 144, 157
college principal 62-3, 137, 190
computers 32, 54, 168:

267

INDEX

machine tools 169: stock control 38: studies 28
Conservative administration 68, 253
Consultative Council on Local Government Finance 80
Corporate management 90-2, 103
corporatism 18
Council 89, 99
councillor 63, 71
curricular guidelines 147-8, 161: inflation 157: model 161: planning 111: protection 158, 161

defence 25, 68
demographic factors 25
Department of the Environment 62, 64: Secretary of State 80
DES 1, 17-20, 61-9, 71, 75, 86, 89, 115-7, 132, 138, 144-50, 156, 165, 171-2, 178, 184: Teachers Branch 20: Financial Services 20: Secretary of State 138
DES-LEA relationships 69, 71, 83
Department of Industry 169
deskilling 40
development costs 133
Director of Education 89-92
discretionary services 75-6
domestic rate relief 74
drama 155
Durham 169

Economics 111, 122
economic growth 3, 25-6, 30-1, 39, 56, 67: performance 68
Education Act, 1944 129, 145, 147, 196
Education Act, 1980 145, 255, 259
education committee 64, 89, 99-101: Chairman 102
educational needs 125-8, 139, 156-7
education psychologist 14
education research 192
efficiency objectives 232-6, 241, 265
elections 186
employers 27, 138, 146 148: local 128, 141
English language 28, 146, 181
entrepreneurship 2
equalisation needs 73: Resource 73, 84: equity objective 231-4, 241, 264
equipment 9, 15, 69, 94, 100, 105, 110, 113, 139, 169-72, 215, 251, 253
Essex 116
evaluation 24, 25
Exchequer and Audit Department 246

fees 6, 64: income 2
floor-space 2
financial year 7
FE 1, 7-8, 13-27, 102, 104, 106, 114, 129, 145, 152, 154, 157, 160, 165, 179-80, 192, 219
FTE 114, 123, 131-2, 222
full employment 3

Geography 122, 146
German 111, 155
glass manufacture 33, 129
Gloucestershire 168
governors 28, 63, 104, 120, 128, 148, 219: articles 145
graduation 5
Grants working group 79

268

INDEX

grants 10, 70: exchequer 80: specific 80, 150
Great Debate 17, 146
GDP 9, 13-4, 20, 81, 109

headteacher 63, 105, 113, 190
health service 18
heating 2, 100, 105, 125, 229
HMI 20, 84, 170, 263
high technology 32-4, 40: fibre optics 32: instrumentation 32: microprocessors 32: robotics 32: semi-conductors 32
higher education 4, 27
highway engineer 91
human learning 54

ILEA 116-7, 120, 168-9, 215
import controls 39
income tax 72: local 72
Industrial Revolution 32
Industrial Training Boards 45, 58
industry 18: nationalised 18: output 22: plastics 32: television 32
inflation 22, 67
Inner area partnership 91
input measures 126-7, 247
inservice training 87
Japan 34, 36, 40
job-effectiveness 61

Labour authorities 76, 78
labour market 28, 43, 48, 178
labour intensiveness 213
law and order 68
lawyers 27
Layfield Report 72
LEA 2, 10, 18, 57, 62-3, 70-1, 82-7, 93-106, 110, 115-6, 120, 125, 129, 135, 141, 145-65, 171-2, 178-84, 208, 211, 214, 218, 222, 222, 224, 229, 232-3, 239, 247, 259, 263
Leeds 169
lecturer grades 135
lighting 2, 100, 105
loans, students 254
local authorities 4, 6, 7: associations 150: reorganisation 93
local autonomy 81, 88
Local Government Act, 1974 74: Finance Act, 1982 78: Planning and Land Act, 1980 74, 77, 82, 102

managerial effectiveness 207
Managing agent 48
market forces 131, 255; survey 17
matrix management 214
Maud committee 90
Metalwork 155
MIS 239
MSC 7, 15, 19, 45, 47, 57, 104, 137, 141, 150, 264-5

NAB 109, 119-20, 138, 144, 157, 163, 231, 258-62
NAFE 8-9, 19, 27, 65, 69-70, 75, 87, 129-32, 141, 258
NATFHE 135
National Extension College 55
needlework 155
NTI 47

'O' levels 29, 129, 135, 220, 244
Oil-price 23
Open Tech 55
Open University 55
options 155
OME 260
output 127, 243, 246

INDEX

parents 125, 146, 148, 256
penalties 85
performance resources 212
PESC 23, 66, 79, 86, 178, 196, 221
PGCE 179, 184
Physics 170
planners 27, 91
Plowden 21, 66
pluralism 18
Policy and Resources 64, 99-102, 104
polytechnics 7, 14, 112, 115, 119-20, 124, 133, 180, 215, 262
post-industrial society 32
PPBS 226
professional associations 27
profit motive 228
programme structure 229-30
public expenditure 3, 7, 9, 20-2, 24, 67

rates 10, 61, 72-3, 85, 99, 257
ratepayers 85
rate-poundages 82
RSG
recession
Research Councils
resource dependancy 81, 148, 150-1: rationing 214
responsibility centre 236
retiring age 39
Roads and transport 68
Robbins 21-2
Royal Commission & Local Government 72

schools, all-age 22; comprehensive 4, 134: grammar 4: leavers 47: low-attainers 53: meals and milk 103: middle 196: minimum leaving age 13: primary 8, 17, 28-9, 70, 87, 114, 151, 153, 178-80, 196, 216: private 254: sixth-form 122-3, 196, 244: regulations 70: reorganisation 71, 222 secondary 6, 8, 17,22, 29, 70, 87, 114, 120, 153, 178, 196: secondary modern 4: special 8, 14, 87
science 196, 163: laboratories: Nuffield 170
Scotland 278
selection procedures 185
SEO 85
small firms 44
social services 25, 81, 103
social wage 21
social workers 27
sociology 155
Solihull 216-7, 219
Somerset 116
South Korea 39
South Tyneside 73
staff age profile 111: appraisal 207: aspiration levels 16: compulsory redundancy 143: contractual obligations 120, 135: defining needs 158-9: development 189-90, 208, 219: non-teaching experience 188: over-teaching 132: performance 2, 113: professionality 61: salaries 209-10: teaching loads 123, 132, 135, 141, 153, 193: temporary 212: travel 217
statutory obligations 16
students part-time 124, 130-2, Sandwich 130, 132
support staff 169
Sutton 73
Taiwan 39
target expenditures 78-9,

INDEX

86
tapering multipliers
  77, 79, 86
tax-base 84, 87: payer
  85
TCR 149, 151-3, 155,
  158, 171, 182, 252
teacher attitudes 127:
  day 192-3: job sat-
  isfaction 181-188:
  job-security 127,
  163, 191, 251: moti-
  vation 189: payment
  levels 188: proact-
  ivity 195: proba-
  tionary service 191:
  promoted posts 105-6,
  151, 196: require-
  ments 179, 186: salar-
  ies 94, 109: shortage
  154, 180, 183-4: staff
  establishment 110:
  training 178, 187:
  quality 185: unemploy-
  ment 179: unions 252
teaching hours 120
team teaching 183
technical consultancy 34
technicians 164, 224
technological develop-
  ment 31-2, 36, 39, 53,
  55, 57
tertiary education 250
thresholds 77, 79, 86
timetabling 1, 182
training 43-6, 48, 52,
  57
Treasury 62, 64, 86,
  156, 171, 253
TSD 45, 46-8
TVEI 18, 50, 57, 150

unemployment 21, 47, 50,
  56: youth 27, 47-8
unit costs 109-110, 231-
  2, 239
units of command 214
university 7, 9
University College,
  Buckingham 256
UGC 7

USA 36
unspent balances 233
VAT 72
virement 94, 102, 217
vocational preparation
  49
vouchers 254

Waltham Forest 169
West Germany 36, 40
woodwork 155
word processors 36

YOP 48
youth service 9
YTS 17-8, 47-8, 50, 53,
  57

271